ACCESS and ALTERNATIVE FUTURES

for higher education

Edited by
Gareth Parry • Clive Wake

Hodder & Stoughton
LONDON SYDNEY AUCKLAND TORONTO

British Library Cataloguing in Publication Data
Access and alternative futures for higher education
1 Great Britain. Higher education. Access
I. Parry, Gareth II. Wake, Clive
378.41

ISBN 0 340 51919 3

First published 1990

Typeset by Wearside Tradespools, Fulwell, Sunderland.
Printed in Great Britain for the educational publishing division of Hodder and Stoughton Ltd, Mill Road, Dunton Green, Sevenoaks, Kent by Page Bros (Norwich) Ltd.

Contents

List of contributors

Michael Duffy is Headmaster of the King Edward VI School in Morpeth, Northumberland, and a former President of the Secondary Heads Association.

Sinclair Goodlad is Head of the Department of Humanities at Imperial College, and Editor of *Studies in Higher Education*.

Gordon Higginson is Vice-Chancellor of the University of Southampton.

Geoffrey Melling is Director of the Further Education Staff College, Coombe Lodge, in Bristol.

Gareth Parry is Lecturer in Continuing Education at City University, and founder Editor of the *Journal of Access Studies*.

Naomi Sargant is Acting Chief Executive of the Open Polytechnic and was formerly Senior Commissioning Editor for Channel Four Television.

Peter Scott is Editor of *The Times Higher Education Supplement*.

Geoff Stanton is Chief Officer of the Further Education Unit.

George Tolley was formerly Director of Sheffield City Polytechnic and was Chief Officer for the joint Department of Education and Science and Department of Employment Review of Vocational Qualifications which reported in 1986.

Peter Toyne is Rector of Liverpool Polytechnic and joint chairman of the Access Courses Recognition Group (ACRG).

Alan Tuckett is Director of the National Institute of Adult Continuing Education.

Leslie Wagner is Director of the Polytechnic of North London and was previously Deputy Secretary of the National Advisory Body.

Clive Wake is Emeritus Professor and Chairman of the School of European and Modern Language Studies at the University of Kent. He was previously Secretary of the Standing Conference on University Entrance.

Introduction

Gareth Parry and Clive Wake

The eighties were much concerned with the issue of widening access to higher education in the United Kingdom. But, while this was a decade in which the pressure to widen access gathered considerable momentum and some steps towards change were taken, it was not the decade of its achievement. This book brings together much of the thinking on wider access to higher education that characterised the debate in the eighties, but seeks to carry it forward into a decade of decisive action and achievement.

The urge to change higher education admissions and curriculum practices in the quest for wider access comes to some extent from within higher education itself, where there have always been those who, even before Robbins, accepted the principle that education at any level should be available to all those who can benefit from it. It has seemed to them to be a simple, incontrovertible question of social justice. But even now, although their numbers have grown during the eighties, not least of all among the heads of higher education institutions, the influence of these people on their reluctant colleagues is not likely to be strong enough on its own to effect actual change.

Pressure has however built up outside higher education, in further education, in the schools and sixth-form colleges, in industry and in government, to a degree that is certain to have a more compelling impact. In particular, government has profoundly unsettled higher education by the financial cuts of the early eighties and, although this has caused a certain amount of seemingly unnecessary damage from which higher education will only recover with great difficulty, it has forced higher education to take a closer look at its market and thereby contributed to weakening the power of the old academic conservatism with regard to admissions. Through policies developed in White Papers like *Higher Education: Meeting the Challenge* (DES 1987), government has also given explicit official support to the principle of wider access by urging higher education to accept vocational qualifications and access courses as equal to the traditional academic qualifications. However, while government has considerable power to influence the development of higher education through its funding policies, both by giving (as in the sixties) and by taking away (as in the eighties), exhortation on its own has little real effect apart from contributing to the general climate of changing attitudes; government policy as regards widening access does not at present go much beyond exhortation (Wagner 1989).

Many organisations (and individuals within them) have contributed to the changing of attitudes within higher education, ranging from the Royal Society, the Foundation for Science and Technology, The Royal Society of Arts (through its Industry Matters initiative), the Council for Industry and Higher Education and The Engineering Council, to government bodies such as the Training Agency (formerly the Manpower Services Commission), an interest group such as the Forum for Access Studies, and higher education itself through the Council for National Academic Awards, the National Advisory Body, the Committee of Vice-Chancellors and Principals, the Standing Conference on University Entrance, the National Association of Teachers in Further and Higher Education and the Association of University Teachers, all of which have separately or in collaboration held public meetings, seminars and conferences, and published research and reports aimed at telling higher education what the world around it feels about the question of wider access. It is clear however to those who work in higher education institutions that the extent to which this message has actually penetrated higher education and effectively changed attitudes, especially in the universities, is still too limited, and recent research has shown that the engineering professional bodies, for instance, which share responsibility for the engineering curriculum, have been largely unaware of the efforts being made to widen access to higher education (Parry and Davies 1990).

Bread-and-butter factors are more likely to effect real change, as the reduction in the public funding of higher education in the United Kingdom has shown. Pressure from commerce and industry as we approach 1992 could therefore be decisive as far as widening access is concerned. Much has been made of the impact on all aspects of life of the serious decline in the number of 18-year-olds, which is expected to reach its lowest point in the mid-1990s. All the evidence shows however that this demographic decline will have little direct effect on higher education since it will not touch the social classes that traditionally enter higher education to nearly the same extent as it will other parts of the community. But this disguises the fact that the need of commerce and industry for graduates is not standing still but is on the contrary growing faster all the time. While it is clear that the pool of A level applicants to higher education can be increased by the simple expedient of making more places available, this is unlikely on its own to produce enough additional students to ensure that the numbers entering higher education will increase to the extent they must if commerce and industry are to satisfy their growing professional and management requirements. There is a further complicating factor, one which it is for the employers to sort out, although it affects recruitment to higher education in the first instance. The shortages in some key professions, such as engineering and teaching, have much to do with the way they are perceived by young people, who are reluctant to enter professions which not only do not pay as well as others but which also do not bring with them the social status that can be achieved in other forms of employment.

At its simplest, the overriding need is for more qualified people and therefore for an increased intake into higher education (Pearson, Pike, Gordon and Weyman 1989). This goal can only be partially reached by making more places available to entrants from the traditional A level route; it will also need the facilitation of access to higher education for two groups whose presence there is traditionally small, particularly in the universities: on the one hand, students from the vocational side of secondary and further education whose studies are not deemed to be a sufficiently theoretical preparation for higher education courses, even in the vocational areas; and on the other hand, mature students, especially those from disadvantaged sections of the community who do not have the educational opportunities available to others or those returning to education after a period spent earning their living or bringing up families. These two groups overlap to a large extent with the social classes which, as Gordon Higginson shows in this volume, higher education, and the universities in particular, have failed to attract in significant numbers.

The United Kingdom has of course two sectors of higher education, the polytechnics and colleges on the one hand (formerly known as the 'public sector') and the universities. In his closely argued contribution to this book, Peter Scott discusses the importance for wider access of the profound changes that are taking place now in the binary structure of higher education. Attitudes to widening access have been very different in the two sectors and it is very difficult to consider them together in any discussion of the development of wider access in higher education. The perceived superiority of the universities has enabled them to cream off the most highly qualified applicants and to fill most of their places with the products of the GCE A level system which forms the educational foundation of the vast majority of schools and to a lesser extent of the sixth-form colleges in this country. As a result the universities have never felt the need to admit many applicants with other qualifications, and without the pressure of self-interest to do so the social justice argument has had little force and less effect.

The polytechnics and colleges on the other hand have had to look to a wider market to fill their places and, although many polytechnic admissions officers would prefer to offer places to larger numbers of A level applicants with the highest grades in order to enhance their status in relation to the universities, they admit far more mature applicants and far more applicants with qualifications other than A levels than do the universities. As a result they have a greater understanding of the needs of such students and have acquired considerable expertise in devising the kinds of curricula that can enable them to benefit most effectively from a higher education course. The experience and practice of the polytechnics is often fragmentary and ill-organised, according to Her Majesty's Inspectorate (HMI 1989a). The essential point is however that the polytechnics, because they have had to struggle to achieve their viability in terms of numbers, have learnt the hard way that the admission of students from a wide variety of academic and non-academic backgrounds can be managed by institutions and that the kinds of students rejected or ignored by the universities can often be very successful. As Peter Toyne shows, their experience has also encouraged the polytechnics to play an active role in developing ways of improving opportunities for non-traditional applicants through such new ventures as access courses, credit accumulation and transfer and the recognition of experiential learning. This they have done by creating links with further education where the universities have concentrated in the main on their relationship with the schools and sixth-form colleges.

Selective entry to higher education, particularly to the universities, has been a major barrier to widening access. This practice is a feature of higher education in this country (whereas on the continent higher education is open to all who achieve the minimum qualification) and it has been maintained largely for financial reasons, as a way of keeping the cost of student support at a level acceptable to the Treasury. It also has the effect of ensuring that entry to higher education is competitive, not only for the applicants but also for the institutions: with more applicants than places, institutions can admit those with the highest examination grades, but since institutions themselves are placed in a hierarchy of excellence by applicants, or rather by their schools and parents, some can demand higher grades than others for entry to the same subject. The majority of students admitted to universities are selected not on the basis of ability to benefit from higher education, but of having done better than others in the one qualifying examination, A levels, still regarded in practice, if no longer in principle, as the standard route of entry by most university admissions tutors. Of course, those who are accepted by this method can be deemed as 'able to benefit' from higher education, but the practice excludes many others also able to benefit because the preference for the A level route effectively excludes even-handed consideration of applicants from other routes. This situation has created a concept of excellence and of standards associated with A levels and with academic achievement at the point of entry to higher education that militates very strongly against widening access, and the simplicity of using A level points scores as the normal criterion for entry reinforces this approach.

Standards are an issue because of the belief that the quality of an institution is reflected in the quality of its students at entry. It is often a principle of admissions policy in institutions that it is only possible to attract the best students if applicants are required to achieve high A level grades: and it works, because this perception of excellence permeates our educational system. A consequence of this approach is that institutions come to see themselves, and come to be seen by others, in terms of the A level points scores of the students they admit, and it is noticeable that both within institutions and outside much less is made of the quality of the degree achieved at the end of the course, except as part of the perennial argument about whether or not A level scores are good predictors of final degree results. There is a reluctance to admit students who do not measure up to these demonstrable levels of prior attainment because, it is argued, this will affect both the external perception of the institution and its academic standards.

Higher education must have the courage to shift the focus of its conception of standards from the periphery to the centre of its enterprise. Standards are determined and maintained not by the average points scores achieved by its entrants, but by the quality of the teaching, research and scholarship of the academic staff. There is no reason why this should not be the case whether they teach bright students selected from a single source, bright students selected from a variety of educational or experiential backgrounds, or students of varying ability selected from a variety of backgrounds. All the students have to measure themselves against the same standards. It will simply mean recognition of the fact that at one end of the spectrum the weaker students will show their ability to benefit even if they only obtain a third class degree and at the other end mature students without formal qualifications will have the opportunity to demonstrate that they can reach the greatest heights of academic success, as many do (Bourner with Hamed 1987).

Widening access also means increasing the participation rate for higher education in the United Kingdom. There is much argument about whether or not this country has as good a record in this respect as others, and there is much disagreement about the validity or otherwise of the statistics used. Although this form of the argument is relevant in the context of the United Kingdom's industrial competitiveness in the modern world, it is not relevant if the issue is considered from the point of view of social justice. The people are there, so why should they not have the opportunities for study and self-improvement they deserve? Adequate funding is a crucial factor in increasing participation. If more places are to be made available in higher education, including more places for mature students, as the government has itself said there should be, the problem of how they should be funded cannot be avoided; it is significant that most of the authors in this book refer to it. The question is examined in detail by Leslie Wagner, who suggests how it should be answered. Social pressures have to be very considerable indeed for issues of social justice to prevail on government spending, and experience has shown that higher education does not fit into this category. A means will nevertheless have to be found to persuade government to expand the present state-financed system of grants for the payment of fees and student support, whether it continues to be by the state alone or, as seems more likely now, by a mixture of state, industrial and personal contributions, and to provide adequate funding for mature students preparing for entry to higher education. Considerable care will need to be taken to ensure that any new system does not penalise those least able to afford to support themselves, otherwise those already socially and economically disadvantaged will remain non-participants in higher education.

While widening access is largely to do with winning parity of access for mature applicants, there are problems for 16 to 18-year-olds as well. The question of parity of treatment for qualifications other than GCE A levels is only part of the story; as Michael Duffy argues, embedded within the A level route there are concerns of fundamental importance affecting access which arise from the role and character of the examination itself. The universities have for long effectively ensured that the secondary curriculum should meet their needs before any others because the GCE examining boards with one exception all derive from them. Nowhere is this more clearly exemplified than in the case of the Joint Matriculation Board, which acts both as a GCE examining board and as the body that determines the entrance requirements for five of the country's major universities.

The universities have tended to prefer their applicants to have specialised before entry, especially in the sciences, and this has produced a secondary examination system intended to meet this need. Whether they plan to enter university or not, most sixth-formers take three of more A levels in essentially the same restricted range of science or arts subjects. Future university students are required to put all their eggs into one basket and make up their minds whether they wish to study science or arts at the early age of sixteen. In recent years there has been a movement away from the rigidity of this approach on the part of the students themselves, with the growth in the numbers taking mixed A levels (Smithers and Robinson 1986). The Department of Education and Science recently introduced the controversial Advanced Supplementary (AS level) examination which has the value of half an A level and at least in theory is intended to enable sixth-formers to study at least one subject outside their specialism. The universities have acknowledged the change in mood and have accepted this limited broadening of the sixth-form curriculum by agreeing to recognise AS levels for entrance requirement purposes. Many departments have expressed the hope that applicants will take the opportunity to study contrasting subjects (Standing Conference on University Entrance 1984; Wake 1989).

But AS levels, albeit a step in the right direction, are a wholly inadequate response to the need for a broader sixth-form curriculum. The arguments for a more radical broadening of the sixth-form curriculum are very powerful both on purely educational grounds and in terms of what commerce, industry and the professions need if this country is to meet the challenges that lie ahead. These arguments were made very forcefully in the eighties, culminating in the recommendations of the committee set up in 1987 by the Secretaries of State for Education and Science and for Wales, under the chairmanship of Dr Gordon Higginson, vice-chancellor of the University of Southampton, to review A levels (DES 1988b). The government lost the best opportunity for change that has occurred so far by immediately rejecting the crucial recommendations that would have led to a more fundamental broadening of the sixth-form curriculum, in favour of proceeding on the basis of AS levels.

A broader sixth-form curriculum is however also vitally important for widening access. The A level system, with its highly specialised curriculum and examinations, excludes from the sixth form and therefore from the opportunity of gaining access to higher education, at least at eighteen, those students for whom specialisation at such an early stage is, for one reason or another, not attractive. Most of these will leave school at sixteen and some – not as many as might have done so given the chance in the first place – will seek a 'second chance' later as mature students, with all the financial and personal difficulties that this entails. Many more might be retained for higher education if entry to the sixth form were widened by a broader sixth-form curriculum.

A crucial step in achieving a broader sixth-form curriculum which has not yet been widely appreciated will be for the GCE examining boards to end their constitutional links with the universities and, acting entirely independently of the universities, to give priority to producing syllabuses that meet the broader needs of sixth-formers, not mainly those of intending applicants to higher education. We shall then move away from an educational system which has a built-in tendency to narrow access as it moves upwards because it is determined largely by the needs of the universities as perceived by themselves and implemented through their association with the examining boards. Effectively responsible more directly to secondary education, the latter will be better able to respond to the student-centred approach in secondary education that has been gathering momentum in recent years and which has been reinforced by the introduction of the GCSE. The universities themselves will be in a healthier relationship to a secondary education system they no longer dominate by their own requirements and have instead to meet on its own terms. The polytechnics, which have contributed so much to our understanding of students' wider potential, will no longer be part of a higher education system which ignores their existence in determining the qualifying education of a large proportion of their entrants.

Parity of access for young adults with vocational qualifications and for older adults returning to study will involve higher education in new and enhanced relationships: with employers as sponsors, suppliers and recruiters of students; with further and adult education as providers of vocational, liberal and access education; and with advisory and guidance services as sources of information, counselling and advocacy for and on behalf of adults. Unlike current relationships with schools, mediated by the A level system and managed by the GCE examining boards, the participation of higher education in these environments is likely to be more direct and less protected. These are areas where higher education is just one provider – competitor as well as partner – in the continuing education and training of adults, and certainly not the dominant and determinant interest as has been the case in most sixth-form education.

In the case of employers, the twin pressures of demography and skill shortages may tempt them to offer higher salaries and better training opportunities to attract school-leavers who might otherwise go on to higher education (Mortimore and Mortimore 1989). Although many employers will continue to look to graduates to expand their managerial and professional positions, some of these same employers and others will need to give more attention to recruitment at technician (especially higher technician) level where the shortfall in some sectors is already acute. At the same time, for some young people the decision by the government to phase out maintenance grants in favour of loans may serve to increase further the appeal of direct entry to employment at sixteen or eighteen. These and other influences may indeed lead to fewer school-leavers entering higher education in some subject areas, although a number may continue to take advantage of sandwich arrangements and sponsorship schemes where links with employers are established at an early stage.

It would be a mistake of course to assume that those entering employment or training straight from school are somehow lost or beyond the reach of higher education. Whether through in-company or government-sponsored training schemes, the establishment of a common framework for vocational qualifications as proposed by the National Council for Vocational Qualifications (NCVQ) should enable more young people to build on vocational studies at school and to acquire credit for structured learning at work, with clear routes of progression into further and higher education. The formation of a credit accumulation and transfer scheme based on the National Vocational Qualification (NVQ) will parallel and complement that envisaged for other areas of post-school education and for higher education itself, although progress in the non-vocational sphere is likely to be uneven and uncertain (NCVQ 1987; NAB/UGC Continuing Education Standing Committee 1987). At present, the separate development of these credit-based systems has tended to respect rather than connect the vocational and academic sides of post-school education and training. However, the concepts of competence and capability have emerged as key elements in curriculum design and development on both sides of this conventional divide, and it may be through the elaboration of these notions, along the lines outlined by George Tolley, that more integration and transferability of learning can be achieved. Some higher education institutions have already begun to extend their accreditation to in-company training so that work-based learning can be assessed for credit and counted towards academic qualifications.

Arrangements of this kind at national and local level, together with the provision of courses customised to the needs of employers and employees, suggest an extension and diversification of the vocational routes into higher education: no longer tied to initial entry (or even advanced standing) but permitting access at a number of points, by a variety of means, to a variety of levels, and for a range of purposes. What is anticipated here is not simply a movement to more part-time, modular and unit-based programmes across higher education; it also presupposes new ways of working with employers and their increased involvement in the planning and evaluation of academic courses. At present, most customised courses operate outside the mainstream academic curriculum and without reference to a framework for recognition and progression. Rather than rely on more Business and Technician Education Council (BTEC) initial entrants at one end of the system and more post-experience short course students at the other, higher education will need to reach into the world of employment to create more opportunities for those in work to take advantage of vocational and academic studies on a flexible and cumulative basis. Both employers and higher education institutions may feel threatened by such arrangements yet the increasing pressures on the former to improve the quality of the workforce and on the latter to engage with a wider clientele should make for closer collaboration and more experiment.

If these new partnerships with employers have yet to establish themselves, those with further education rest on firmer foundations and have grown apace in recent years. The strategic importance of colleges of further education and tertiary establishments in facilitating and broadening access to higher education has been recognised in a number of ways. Unlike the school and adult education sectors, further education is associated with each of the three major pathways identified by government to raise participation rates in higher education into the 1990s and beyond (DES 1987).

The opportunity to study for traditional sixth-form qualifications outside the schools system, part-time as well as full-time, has offered a 'second chance' for many to qualify for higher education in the conventional way. Until quite recently, most adults intending to apply for undergraduate entry have had to undertake part-time intensive A level courses, studying one or more specialised subjects through a syllabus designed for another age group altogether. Younger students have also used further education in this way, often on a full-time basis and often in order to demonstrate abilities not recognised or realised in schools. Even some of those who have been most successful in their schooling have opted at sixteen for the more adult environment of a college in preference to the sixth form. Whether as adult returners, school refusers or late developers, those completing their academic studies in further education are an increasing proportion of A level candidates and they will continue to be an important source of recruitment to higher education.

Within the array of qualifications to be reformed and rationalised by the NCVQ, those provided by BTEC in particular have offered young people and adults the possibility of staged access into higher education in the fields of science, technology and business studies. Because some further education establishments provided courses at both non-advanced and advanced levels it was sometimes possible to progress to higher education studies without the need to transfer to another institution. That other institution has usually been a local polytechnic or college of higher education (rather than a university), where transfer and bridging arrangements have been made easier by two features: the opportunity to study for certificate and diploma as well as degree qualifications and the opportunity to attend on a part-time as well as a full-time basis. The strength of this link will be tested by the Education Reform Act of 1988 (HM Government 1988) which removed local authorities from higher education, both at the national planning and policy level and at the institutional level, and which gave more financial independence to the colleges of further education. Hitherto the universities have kept their distance from vocational further education, preferring to recruit from the A level pool and in some cases electing to leave places empty rather than admit increasing numbers of BTEC or other 'non-standard' candidates (Fulton and Ellwood 1989). More competitive funding policies and more informed student choice are likely to modify these practices and operate to the advantage of those institutions with good working relationships with further education in their locality or region.

Perhaps the strongest expression of cooperation between these two sectors has been the recent and rapid growth of access courses, and their promotion within open college networks and access consortia. Unlike other forms of preparation for higher education, access courses usually involve some form of on-going collaboration between those in further and adult education who provide such courses and those in linked higher education institutions who maintain places for those who successfully complete their access studies. With some notable exceptions, the early negotiation of these arrangements involved further education making and taking the access argument to higher education or, rather, to those parts of higher education most likely to identify with these proposals: the polytechnics rather than the universities, and the humanities and social sciences rather than the sciences and technologies. This early reluctance to consider alternative entry for adults has since given way to more active attempts by higher education, including the universities, to open up a wider range of subjects to new types of student.

The accessibility of further and adult education establishments and their experience in attracting a wide range of students has made them an obvious location not just for access programmes but for franchise arrangements which take higher education outside of the academy. Some higher education institutions have however developed their own access, foundation and conversion courses in addition to linked schemes with further education, and in the case of engineering some of these have been brought within the scope of mandatory awards following approval for extended degree courses in this key shortage subject (Parry 1990).

In the absence of opportunities elsewhere in higher education for departments to increase the length of their degree courses, access and preparatory courses have sometimes been expected to substitute as knowledge-based foundation courses and to align their curricula to the specific rather than the general requirements of matched subjects and disciplines. This pattern of specialist preparation for specialist provision has been most evident in relation to the more linear and cumulative subjects, particularly in the sciences and technologies, where rapid growth in the knowledge base has contributed to inflated A level syllabuses and overloaded access curricula. This in turn has served to deter entry and to delay curriculum change in these disciplines. Where higher education courses have been reviewed and revised, remedial or equalising studies in first-year courses have been the preferred response rather than the more radical and imaginative restructuring of mathematics-based and science-based degree courses suggested by Sinclair Goodlad in this volume.

Again in the case of engineering higher education, where retention as much as recruitment has been a pressing concern (HMI 1989b), the development of more general integrated degree programmes as proposed by The Engineering Council may persuade higher education and the professional bodies to relocate more specialist elements at postgraduate or post-experience levels, and thereby increase the attractiveness and effectiveness of conventional as well as alternative routes for intending students. The experience of the Open University in requiring course teams in all disciplines to design their degree programmes on the basis of open entry should be an important point of reference for access and higher education providers in this respect, more particularly in regard to mathematics, science and technology, where the use of open and independent forms of study can enhance the efficiency of learning, and more generally in relation to educational broadcasting – the subject of the essay by Naomi Sargant – where new technologies have the potential to mobilise new audiences and formats for continuing and higher education.

One of the positive outcomes of the active involvement of higher education in the design and delivery of access programmes has been the need to make explicit the knowledge and skills to be demonstrated as a basis for participation in undergraduate studies. This can be a difficult and complex task, but it is an essential one if ability to benefit is to be applied in a rigorous and responsible way to the increasing numbers of adults likely to present themselves for initial entry, advanced standing or credit recognition. At present, many adult applicants continue to fall foul of admissions systems which privilege norm-referenced qualifications over criterion-referenced assessments and which are not equipped or inclined to consider candidates with uncertificated prior learning. Rather than be pushed or prompted by those outside who have particular relationships with selected higher education departments, institutions themselves will need to take responsibility for identifying and analysing the learning outcomes to be achieved on all of their courses and for deriving and describing the competencies and qualities expected for someone to complete these studies successfully. As Geoffrey Melling and Geoff Stanton suggest in their discussion of the further education phase, this exercise would enable higher education to communicate its own interests as well as provide clearer targets for students to aim at or to connect with.

Closer working relationships with further and adult education have also brought higher education into contact with the variety of agencies involved in providing guidance for adults returning to education and training. The need for higher education to make comprehensive provision for guidance has become more important as institutions encourage adults to approach them directly as potential students and as arrangements for access and progression have become more diverse and difficult to comprehend. Moreover, such guidance and support will need to be continuous throughout their higher education careers to help adults adjust to the demands of academic study and where necessary to deal with a range of financial, domestic and personal problems which may interfere with their learning. At the same time, the participation of higher education staff at an early stage in recruitment for access schemes and the opportunity for intending students to experience teaching and learning in higher education institutions can make for more discernment and less dissonance in the transition to chosen courses.

Where agencies operate as local and independent sources of educational guidance, advice and counselling for adults, collaboration with them enables higher education institutions to extend the range and to assess the appropriateness of their own services and practices in a number of ways: as networks for information and referral; as partners in outreach and marketing initiatives; as contributors to staff development programmes; and as evaluators of access arrangements. Where they operate within the workplace, the collaborative role of higher education is likely to be rather different. Here, higher education institutions would have the opportunity to accredit prior learning for the National Vocational Qualification and to assess the academic credit to be allowed for work-based learning; they would be involved in providing access to assessment independent of entry to the institution and in contributing directly to guidance and counselling activities available to those in work.

New kinds of association and alignment with employers, with further and adult education, and with advisory and guidance services, together with the impact of increased recruitment of mature and non-traditional students, have encouraged higher education in general to become more aware of the needs and demands of a wider range of clients for their academic and professional services. While much of this activity has continued to be located on the edge of the system, the early emphasis on inputs in arguments for wider access to higher education – building alternative routes and changing admissions procedures – has given way to more critical consideration of processes and outcomes; redesigning teaching and learning and redefining curriculum goals.

This shift in perspective has been inspired in part by the prospect of an increase in the participation rate to somewhere between a quarter and a third of the 18-year-old age group by the beginning of the century and by the possibility of a breakthrough to a mass system of higher education modelled on American rather than European lines (Baker 1989a). Although the present structure of the educational system and current financial constraints create considerable hurdles, these major policy goals have commanded broad support as well as a general acceptance that more will mean different (Ball 1989a; 1990). Just how different is open to question and will largely depend on the priority given to efficiency, expediency and equity in the pursuit of access objectives.

The question of whether adults or school-leavers (and recent school-leavers) should be the principal object of access and institutional strategy into the 1990s has emerged as a key source of tension (and confusion) in recent debates. For those like Alan Tuckett, who advance the interests of older learners, and for those who pursue the goal of an alternative lifelong system of higher education, there would need to be significant changes in the internal structures and processes of institutions as well as expansion and diversification of the system: more open entry and client-focused curricula based on increased use of local provision, part-time and flexible study, mixed face-to-face and distance learning, broad accreditation and credit transfer, problem-based and interest-related inquiry, and multi-form and multi-purpose assessment (Tight 1989). For those who uphold the claims of 16 to 18-year-olds and who prefer to strengthen the existing end-on system of higher education, more specific changes – external as well as internal to higher education – would need to be secured: a common secondary curriculum integrating the academic and the vocational, and financial support for those who continue in education and training after the age of sixteen, alongside the training of admissions tutors and the reform of degree examinations to enable higher education institutions to respond appropriately (Smithers and Robinson 1989).

In each of these designs, as well as in more mixed economy versions aimed at both older and younger learners, a strategy operated to 'increase' participation may be claimed to 'widen' access for under-represented or excluded groups. Yet the experience of open access and mass systems of higher education would seem to suggest that expanded entry and increased flexibility are not sufficient on their own to attract and involve those who have benefited least from existing arrangements, and that positive action in respect of disadvantaged and disenfranchised groups must remain an essential element in access policy and practice. The nearest British higher education has come to affirmative action in these terms has been the development of access and similar courses targeted at women, working class, and black and other minority ethnic groups, and predicated upon guaranteed or enhanced progression to linked courses in higher education. Their initial designation as 'special' preparatory courses and their subsequent separation for particular policy treatment signify something of the unease and awkwardness which such arrangements have posed for an élite and rationed system of higher education (Parry 1989b).

Positive action as a principle of fairness will need to be extended into other areas of education and training if increased and wider access are to be combined into a common strategy. Some of the collaborative models pioneered in relation to colleges and adults may indeed by transferable to schools and school students where negotiated opportunities for progression to local higher education institutions may help to raise aspirations and improve performance, particularly if low participation rates have been long-standing and are taken for granted. Furthermore, where compact arrangements between schools and employers (according to which an employer guarantees employment for those students who meet specified performance and attendance targets) have already been established, the addition of further and higher education as a third party may serve to stimulate new ways of supporting education and training for those entering employment direct from school, especially in sectors where access to paid educational leave or work-based learning is least available.

The principles of targeting, collaboration and progression underpinning access programmes in further education and access compacts in secondary education are likely to figure large in the transition to a more open and plural system of higher education, but the persistence of severe skills shortages may see these principles increasingly deployed in programmes to meet manpower requirements rather than equal opportunity objectives. However, if government and the funding bodies in higher education have to return to selective initiatives to promote recruitment or development in particular fields there may be another opportunity to recommend that targets for under-represented groups as well as for subject areas be built into contractual agreements with higher education institutions (NAB 1988).

It will be clear that for the authors of this introduction widening access to higher education is taken as meaning providing equal opportunity to enter higher education to all those able to benefit from it, without any distinction for this purpose between them. Of course there is a special intellectual stimulus for the teacher in being able to teach uniformly bright students whose academic background is the same as his or her own. Of course there is more work involved in selecting and teaching students of varying ability and from a variety of social, cultural and educational backgrounds. Social justice, however, requires that higher education accept this additional responsibility.

We must be realistic about the implications of widening access for higher education itself, especially for the universities which still have a much greater distance to travel than the polytechnics. A new partnership with secondary and further education will have to be developed by higher education institutions. New ways of assessing student potential at entry will have to be found, so that the emphasis on achievement comes at the end, not at the start, of the course of study. The measurement of the educational and intellectual standards of institutions will have to be separated from the measurement of the ability of individual applicants in terms of their entry qualifications. There will have to be fundamental changes in the structure and style of higher education programmes, not only to take account of the varied educational and experiential backgrounds of students but also of the actual demands of the workplace they will enter on graduating. In particular, teaching and learning methods will have to undergo a radical change, with more emphasis on student-centred and independent learning and on the use of the media.

The result will be a fundamental change in the culture of higher education and when it is completed the intellectual and human complexion of the institutions, especially the universities, will be very different from what it is now. It will be accomplished most effectively if the institutions themselves take the initiative.

References

Full details are provided at the end of the book. Government departments and organisations that are referred to in references in the text by their initials only are given there in full.

1 Post-binary access and learning

Peter Scott

The focus of this chapter is on the structure of higher education in Britain: its binary separation into two great sectors, the universities on the one hand and on the other the polytechnics and colleges; and the equally significant divergences within these sectors. But structure is the focus not for its own sake but because it concretely reflects the values that are embodied in our present system of higher education. These values are both social: who is higher education for?; political and economic: what is higher education for?; and academic: what is higher education? Together they determine the place of higher education in late twentieth-century Britain. So structure and purpose, vision even, are linked. The taxonomy of the system is related to its social and intellectual possibilities. The relationship, of course, is two-way. The present pattern of institutions and their arrangement in a binary hierarchy may encourage, or inhibit, wider access, new approaches to learning and broader definitions of knowledge. In a similar way the presence of new types of student, new teaching techniques and the onward rush of science and scholarship may lead to changes in the structure of higher education. This complex relationship is what this chapter will attempt to discuss.

At the beginning of the 1990s British higher education still has a binary structure. The most prominent feature of the system remains its division into two sectors, the universities and the polytechnics and colleges. But although retained by the Education Reform Act of 1988, the binary structure is in the process of rapid evolution. The rigidity of the old binary policy between 1965 and 1989 has been succeeded by a post-binary fluidity. Since the replacement of the University Grants Committee (UGC) by the Universities Funding Council (UFC) universities no longer enjoy, even notionally, a privileged relationship with the state. The polytechnics and colleges of higher education meanwhile have ceased to be maintained by local education authorities and have become, like universities, independent corporations. The blurring of the once sharp dichotomy between the two sectors is likely to redirect attention to the distinctions between institutions within these sectors. These distinctions have always been significant but to some degree they have been concealed by the binary overlay. In the post-binary 1990s these distinctions will perhaps be given a new emphasis.

Among the universities four main types can be discerned: (1) the great 'civics' with their often rigid departmental structures, which nevertheless remain the heartland of the university system; (2) the so-called 'red-bricks', similar to the 'civics' in many ways but generally smaller and still perhaps more collegiate in ethos; (3) the new universities founded in the 1960s – the opposite pole perhaps to the 'civics' among these university types, they still retain that blended Oxbridge-transatlantic flavour of the days of their early hope as they approach middle age; (4) the technological universities, once at an academic disadvantage but now perhaps coming into their own in the enterprise-oriented 1990s. But this typology excludes Oxford, Cambridge and London, Britain's most eminent but least typical universities, and also Scotland and Wales, where universities still enjoy a subtly different relationship with their nations' societies and cultures.[1]

The university sector has never been monolithic. The historical origins of universities were diverse. They were created to serve different constituencies: metropolitan élites, the professional/business service class, provincial establishments, the rising generations of 'scholarship boys' and so on. From the creation of the University Grants Committee in 1919 until the 1950s university development was marked by a process of convergence as institutions commonly funded and similarly governed, increasingly by academics rather than lay people, came to serve similar constituencies and have common missions.[2] This process was interrupted in the 1960s by a return to divergence as the new universities were established and the colleges of advanced technology were promoted to university status, divergence that was frustrated by the imposition of the binary policy and the creation of the polytechnics. In the 1970s the pattern of convergence in university development was resumed as all universities were caught up in a common cycle of austerity. But in recent years divergence has again reasserted itself, partly because the UGC (and now the UFC) and the Department of Education and Science have exercised increasing discrimination in allocating funds to universities and partly because universities have responded in different ways to the trials and challenges of the 1980s. So the experience of the universities is not of a cohesive bloc of broadly similar institutions, indistinguishable in terms of their underlying values and current practices. There are many more differences than the levelling rhetoric of national policy-making allows. These differences are likely to become more prominent in the 1990s.

In the polytechnic and college sector there is equal, or greater, diversity. The two main components, of course, are the 29 polytechnics in England (and one in Wales) and the 54 colleges of higher education in England. The former make up a comparatively coherent group, although they vary considerably in size. Manchester Polytechnic has almost 11,000 full-time and sandwich students while the City Polytechnic has fewer than 3,000 (although it has a large number of part-time students). But among the colleges there is great variation.[3] Some, like Humberside, are scaled-down polytechnics, comprehensive multi-faculty institutions with substantial numbers of students. Others are essentially monotechnics: either 'stable' monotechnics like the free-standing colleges of art or music, or 'unstable' monotechnics, teacher training colleges that have weakly diversified into adjacent fields of liberal arts or applied social science.

If differences of ethos are considered, further variation emerges. Even within polytechnics, faculties and departments continue to reproduce the different traditions of the colleges of technology, commerce, education and art and design which were amalgamated in the 1960s and 1970s to form these new institutions. The contrast between local authority and voluntary (ie church) colleges has persisted into the age of corporate independence for both. Here there is often a fundamental divergence of values, more profound than any found among polytechnic faculties. The former reflect an open tradition of further education that emphasises individual qualifications and particular courses rather than a rounded education. Their students are often commuters. The latter reflect a more closed tradition that emphasises a holistic, even hermetic, ethos of education. Their students are generally, and necessarily, resident. These differences have been softened in the past twenty years as the polytechnic and college sector, like the universities, has undergone a process of convergence. But they have not disappeared entirely. Also in Wales and more especially Scotland the non-university sector moves to different rhythms in its organisation and its ethos. The development of the Scottish central institutions reflects a tradition of tight central control by the Scottish Education Department and a commitment to a more circumscribed utilitarianism, while the Welsh polytechnic and colleges have retained, accidentally and perhaps anachronistically, their links with the wider world of local authority education.

This description is wholly confined to higher education in a narrow British sense. It excludes further education, more than 700 colleges with 1.3 million students. Many of these are over the age of 18 and a substantial minority is studying on advanced courses.[4] The separation between polytechnics and colleges of higher education and the broader system of local authority further education, which was a principal objective of the 1988 Act, has still not produced a clean break between advanced and non-advanced courses. Many of the former, particularly part-time courses aimed at post-experience students, continue to be provided by further education colleges. The description also excludes adult education: almost 4,500 evening institutes covering 2.2 million students.[5] Although the bulk of these courses is low-level and recreational rather than academic or vocational, the growth of continuing education has tended to invalidate these old distinctions. Post-binaryism is likely to embrace not just higher education in a narrow sense but the whole system of post-secondary education.

The rest of this chapter is divided into two sections. The first will consider issues of structure. The most important is the movement from a binary system to post-binaryism, but bound up in this are other significant issues, the balance between national and regional or local priorities in the development of mass higher education, the tension between public-service and 'market' models in terms both of underlying values and of detailed practices, and the continuing validity of the traditional arrangement of our post-secondary system into higher, further and adult education segments. The second will consider the intellectual environment of a post-binary system. The most obvious and pressing aspect is the potential conflict between (academic) quality and (social) access. But there are other significant issues here: the tension between intellectual coherence and vocational relevance, which is closely linked to the choice between liberal education and vocationalism and between a knowledge-led and skills-based approach to higher education. Indeed this grand encounter between coherence and pluralism is almost as important as the more familiar dispute between quality and access in determining the prospects for post-binaryism. The two, of course, are intimately linked. Structural and academic issues cannot be kept apart.

Structure and access

The most obvious of the structural changes in higher education in Britain is the movement from a binary system towards post-binaryism, a set of relationships between institutions that is still undefined. It is only possible to begin to define post-binaryism when the binary system itself has been properly defined. This is not as self-evident as it seems. First, an important distinction must be made between the binary *system* and the binary *policy*. The former represents the pattern of different institutions – universities, polytechnics and colleges – with their diverse roles; the latter the construction placed on these differences by politicians, civil servants and involved public opinion. The binary policy cannot be discussed in any detail in this chapter.[6] But a brief outline is necessary. Until the early 1960s advanced further education and teacher training were regarded as a residual element (or, in the case of teacher training, a subordinate element) within a higher education system comprehensively dominated by the universities. The creation of the colleges of advanced technology in 1956 was perhaps the first flicker of an alternative view, of a complementary sector alongside the universities, but it failed to burst into political flame and was extinguished by the Robbins report.[7] Then in the later 1960s and 1970s the success of the new polytechnics, the creation of which had given coherence to the whole non-university sector, encouraged a radically new view of British higher education, as Anthony Crosland and his advisers had intended. This was of a twin-track system with the once dominant university sector now shadowed by a vigorous alternative. Finally in the 1980s the decay of traditional university culture, as a result of cuts in funding and ideological assaults, and the continuing development of the polytechnics culminating in their release from local education authority control, have produced a relationship between the two sectors that is more like one of rivals than of partners. So the evolution of the binary policy has been marked by a steady shift in how the non-university sector has been perceived – first as residual, then as complementary, later as alternative and now as rival. This trajectory does not suggest that the immediate next step is likely to be a peaceful *rapprochement* between the two sectors and solidarity among their institutions. The rhetoric that has grown up around the binary policy makes such an outcome unlikely.

However, consideration of the binary system may lead to a different conclusion. Even in its heyday, between Anthony Crosland's Woolwich speech in 1965 and the end of local authority control twenty-four years later, the binary system was never as clear-cut as the binary policy implied. The very important variations within the two main sectors have already been discussed in the first part of this chapter. Neither was ever as homogeneous as the political rhetoric suggested. In an important sense the dichotomy encouraged by the binary policy obscured the diversity inherent in the binary system. That system was the outcome of an accumulation of historical accidents. Institutions with similar origins, values and practices were allocated to different sectors by the anomalies of their own development and the vagaries of higher education policy. Surrey became a university because in the 1950s Battersea College was chosen as one of the new colleges of advanced technology, which in the 1960s were upgraded into universities. Hatfield is a polytechnic because it was decided in 1964–65 to establish no more universities. But, despite being on different sides of the so-called binary line, Surrey and Hatfield have far more in common with each other than they have with many institutions in their own sectors.

The binary system, therefore, is based on the segregation of institutions according to bureaucratic rules, and only loosely related to their educational missions. The formal differences between universities on the one hand and polytechnics and colleges on the other concern their government and administration; their methods (and amounts) of funding; and their freedom to award degrees. Universities have always been independent corporations while polytechnics and colleges only became so in 1989 with the ending of local authority control (the five inner-London polytechnics and the voluntary colleges were always corporate bodies and so exceptions). Universities receive state grants through the UFC, which replaced the UGC in 1989. Polytechnics and colleges receive the bulk of their income through a separate but parallel body, the Polytechnics and Colleges Funding Council (PCFC). Before the break with local government their budgets were fixed by the National Advisory Body for Public Sector Higher Education (NAB), although individual local authorities were free to provide additional income. Finally universities are free to award their own degrees and to regulate their own teaching, while polytechnics and colleges must be accredited to award degrees or have their courses validated by the Council for National Academic Awards (CNAA), and their teaching is scrutinised by Her Majesty's Inspectors.

These differences, on which the binary system is based, should not be exaggerated but neither should they by ignored. On the one hand it can be argued that the autonomy of the universities and, before 1989, the subordination of the polytechnics and colleges were both more apparent than real. They suggest a powerful status distinction that is not really there. The universities depend for the bulk of their income on the UFC, which in turn is closely supervised by the DES. The polytechnics and colleges had largely escaped from the control of local education authorities, except at the level of petty bureaucratic routine, long before 1989. In practice they were funded, and so directed, by the NAB and now the PCFC. On the other hand it can as easily be argued that two separate funding councils have been established by the government, which will have the effect of perpetuating the different administrative traditions of the two sectors. Already the UFC and PCFC have begun to adopt different, and not easily compatible, approaches to funding their respective institutions.[8] Also the two sectors have tended to drift apart since 1989 in terms of institutional government. Despite the Jarratt-inspired efficiency reforms of the mid-1980s, universities have maintained the traditional pattern of bicameral government, within which lay councils are disposed to defer to academic senates.[9] Under local authority rule polytechnics and colleges had tended to move towards this university pattern with their large and diffuse governing bodies steadily losing influence to academic boards. Now that trend has been sharply reversed. The influence of academic boards has been curbed and effective power given to small tightly-knit lay-dominated boards of governors. The ethos of polytechnics and colleges as a result has become more managerial (possibly a reversion to the authoritarian style inherited from further education), while that of the universities, for all the talk of vice-chancellors as chief executives, has remained collegial. This is a very important difference between the two sectors, and clearly a powerful obstacle to closer integration in the post-binary future.

Only in the third area, the award of degrees and regulation of teaching, has there been a straightforward dismantling of the old differences between the sectors. All polytechnics and several colleges are now accredited by the CNAA and no longer have to submit to course-by-course validation. Provided they can maintain respectable internal procedures for the admission, teaching and examination of students and for the approval and revision of courses, they are in effect free to award their own degrees, as free as most American universities. On the other side of the binary line, universities have become increasingly sensitive about their alleged lack of accountability in academic matters. During the 1980s the Committee of Vice-Chancellors and Principals twice established inquiries into academic standards; the first under Professor Philip Reynolds, former vice-chancellor of Lancaster University, recommended the tightening-up of external examining[10]; the second under Professor Stewart Sutherland, vice-chancellor-elect of London University, went much further and recommended that universities establish an independent system of external academic audit.[11] In practice the balance between freedom and constraint is likely to be similar in 'accredited' polytechnics and 'audited' universities. Then the only significant difference remaining between the two sectors in the area of academic control would be Her Majesty's Inspectors' continuing access to polytechnics and colleges and exclusion from universities (except for education departments and on invitation). Although the inspectors are likely to press hard for access to universities in the short term, in the long term they are more likely to see their present role in polytechnics and colleges atrophy.

Perhaps it is not an accident that the dismantling of the old binary structure has proceeded more rapidly in the academic sphere and more slowly in the administrative. For the binary system was and is largely a bureaucratic construction. Certainly the differences between the universities and other higher education institutions do not correspond to any coherent stratification of the system into 'first cycle' and 'second cycle' higher education because no such distinction has ever been known in Britain although it is common in the rest of Europe. Indeed the separation between the two sectors has made any such arrangement impossible. Institutions have never been assigned clear academic missions that oblige them to concentrate on particular subjects or students or to confine themselves to offering courses up to specified levels only, as is the case in California.[12] As a result, with a few exceptions (medicine has remained a university monopoly while most art and design courses are offered in polytechnics and colleges), all subjects are taught in both sectors and there is no restriction on non-university institutions offering courses leading to higher degrees, up to and including PhD.

Therefore any academic differences between the two sectors are ones of implied emphasis rather than specified role. For example, it may still be assumed that universities have a national mission while that of polytechnics and colleges is more regional or local, although patterns of student recruitment hardly support this conclusion. But with obvious exceptions like Oxford and Cambridge, British universities were established as regional institutions (an origin still celebrated in the title 'civic') and in recent years they have placed increasing emphasis on closer links with their local economies and communities. This is demonstrated by the proliferation of science and technology parks. Conversely polytechnics and colleges, while not necessarily neglecting their local roots, have developed much more pronounced national roles over the past two decades. As a result some polytechnics are now more 'national' in their ethos and catchment than some universities. A second common assumption is that universities are more academic in their approach to higher education and polytechnics and colleges more vocational. But this assumption too is misleading. First, no satisfactory demarcation can be made between academic and vocational subjects at a time of rapidly shifting disciplinary boundaries. And, if a 'heavy metal' definition of vocationalism must be adopted, the technological universities and the voluntary colleges are clearly in the wrong sectors. Secondly, more science and engineering graduates are produced by the universities than the polytechnics and colleges, while the most rapid increase in the number of students in the latter during the 1980s has been in arts and social science (although mainly in applied subjects like business studies). Thirdly, there are no significant differences in employment patterns between graduates from the two sectors, other than those that can be explained by subject choice and institutional prestige.[13]

Of course the binary system has an academic dimension that cannot be made to disappear entirely. There remain important differences between universities and other institutions which have significant implications for the style and quality of higher education they provide and so are relevant in any discussion of post-binaryism. First, polytechnic and college students are more diverse. On average they are less well qualified, at any rate as measured by academic achievement in secondary education. On average they are older, many returning to regular education after a gap in their studies. On both counts they are likely to be less well prepared for higher education than university students, which clearly has important consequences for the style of teaching polytechnics and colleges need to adopt. Secondly, polytechnics and colleges offer a much wider variety of courses than universities. One in four of their students is studying part-time; in universities, with the exception of the Open University, part-time study is rare. Many of their courses lead to diplomas or professional qualifications, often pejoratively described as 'sub-degree', rather than to degrees. And the structure of polytechnic degrees is more likely to be modular, allowing greater breadth of study and increased student choice, although perhaps at the cost of the academic coherence achieved by more focused university degrees. Polytechnics and colleges are also more heavily engaged in continuing education, particularly post-experience vocational courses.

The most significant difference between the two sectors however remains the universities' much greater stake in research, which absorbs between 30 and 40 per cent of their budget. The polytechnics' and colleges' commitment to research is substantial and rapidly increasing but not (yet) on the same scale. In their orientation universities remain research-led institutions, a quality reinforced by the UGC's and UFC's successive exercises in research selectivity when all university departments were graded on a five-point scale. In their orientation polytechnics and colleges remain teaching-led institutions. Their experience during the 1980s has been dominated by efforts to increase access by enrolling extra students without matching resources. But even here it is misleading to draw too sharp a contrast, for two reasons. The first is that each sector contains a spectrum of institutions, not a single type. Among the universities, for example, some receive more than half of their UFC allocation for research while others receive less than a fifth for this purpose. The second is that universities too are likely to place greater emphasis on effective teaching as competition for good students increases in the 1990s, while in the polytechnics and colleges a stronger research culture will become established. Overall the prospect is for convergence not divergence in academic matters between the two halves of the binary system.

As a result this system will depend more than ever on the bureaucratic differences that separate the two sectors, and which have been maintained despite the incorporation of the polytechnics and colleges and the creation of two parallel funding councils. These differences were and are clear; the supposed academic distinctions between the sectors have always been merely suggestive extrapolations. Before 1989 it was carelessly assumed that because polytechnics and colleges were locally owned they must have a local mission. Now it is assumed, as carelessly, that because they are responsible to a separate funding council they must have a distinctive mission. The PCFC indeed has tried to reinforce the distinctiveness of its sector by attempting to describe how it differs from the university sector. However the new binary policy embodied in the division of responsibility between the UFC and the PCFC is weaker than the old policy that rested on an apparently clear-cut distinction between an 'autonomous sector' composed of the universities and a 'public sector' composed of polytechnics and colleges which formed a province of the much larger empire of local authority education. Clearly the new arrangements provide a less effective *cordon sanitaire*. Despite the PCFC's efforts in its aims and objectives to assert the distinctiveness of its sector, it will become more difficult to derive distinctive educational missions from the different bureaucratic regimes that prevail on opposite sides of the binary line. Or, more precisely, it will become more difficult to allow the latter to serve as proxies for the former. Local authority control of the polytechnics and colleges had an educational message, even if that message was only dimly recollected by the 1980s; the UFC-PCFC condominium has no such message.

Two outcomes, and so two interpretations of post-binaryism, are possible. The first, to which the majority unthinkingly subscribes, is that the two sectors will grow into one and the residual anomalies inherited from the old binary system will wither into insignificance. The second is that the scaling-down of the binary bureaucracy will stimulate the search for new ways to maintain the diversity of higher education. Because bureaucratic differences will no longer be available to serve as proxies for distinctive academic missions, a more deliberate and direct attempt will have to be made to formulate these distinctive missions.

Both outcomes are possible. A unitary system, to which it is generally agreed post-binaryism will tend, can emphasise either uniformity or diversity. Under the conditions that were thought to prevail in the 1960s and 1970s it was feared a unitary system, such as had been envisaged by the Robbins committee, would lead to greater uniformity. 'Academic drift' was the phrase that summed up the basis for this concern and the experience of the technological universities seemed to confirm it. This was why the binary system was reinforced in the later 1960s and a binary policy aggressively articulated, to protect and enhance the pluralism of higher education. It is still a matter of controversy whether these measures were appropriate or effective. But that question cannot be debated here. In any case it is to a large extent moot. The binary policy was implemented. However the conditions likely to prevail in the 1990s will be different. Wider access, more part-time courses, an increasing number of mature students, more flexible patterns of learning: these and other widely predicted phenomena of higher education's next decade will encourage diversity. At the same time the forces that have traditionally encouraged uniformity – selective entry, a strong research culture, a preponderance of full-time courses for young adults – are likely to weaken. So it is far from a foregone conclusion that a unitary system in the 1990s would fall prey to 'academic drift' as many feared would have happened to such a system had it been allowed to develop in the 1960s.

Perhaps unitary is the wrong adjective to describe the form of a post-binary system. Plural may be better. Three specifically structural factors are likely to encourage greater diversity in higher education in the next decade (academic factors will be considered in the concluding section of this chapter). First, the system will become less national. It will become less national because the international context will become more significant. If the 1980s were the decade of the full-cost fee paying overseas student, the 1990s are likely to be a decade that sees a rapid increase in the exchange of students within the European Community under ERASMUS (the European Action Scheme for the Mobility of University Students) and other programmes. The system will become less national because part-time and mature students, of whom there will be a growing number, are much less mobile than full-time ones. The substitution of loans for grants as the principal means of student support will also tend to discourage nationwide mobility, even among full-time students.[14] The metropolitan attraction of London with its powerful nationalising influence too will be reduced. Finally the growth of continuing education will inevitably strengthen higher education's local commitment. The system will also become less 'national' in ethos. As access is widened higher education will cease to cater so overwhelmingly for future national élites that are mobile both socially and culturally as well as geographically. As regional diversity grows, the system's capacity to set national standards will be diminished. Higher education will become a more rooted enterprise.

Secondly, the growing popularity of free-market ideas will erode the traditional concept of higher education as a public service.[15] It can be argued that this latter concept, which was reinforced by the system's increasing dependence on public expenditure between 1945 and 1979, tends to emphasise common standards of national provision and so, arguably, encourages uniformity. The former ideas, which have been vigorously promoted although ineffectively implemented since 1979, emphasise variable standards determined by market demand and so may encourage diversity. Of course the contrast cannot be as clear-cut as this simple description suggests. The market tends to normalise as well as to fragment. It too can lead to uniform standards and common costs. That is the frequent outcome of competition. Nor is a properly free market in education possible. A large volume of public expenditure will always be devoted to higher education, whether in the form of grants to institutions, scholarships to students or research contracts. There must be rules to regulate this expenditure which will constrain the operation of any supposed market.

It is far too simple to align free-market ideas with diversity and a public-service ethos with uniformity. The binary policy articulated during the 1960s by Anthony Crosland and others is an example of planned diversity. Yet the growing emphasis on market ideas is likely to reduce the power of central planners in the DES, UFC, PCFC and other agencies and to push more decisions down to institutions. If this happens the potential, at any rate, for greater diversity will be enhanced. At the very least the system will become more fluid and less predictable. The growing power of institutional managers within higher education, another phenomenon of the 1980s unlikely seriously to be reversed in the 1990s, may also tend to have the same effect. This *corps d'élite* of chief executives will be less influenced by the unifying loyalties so strongly felt within the academic *collegia* that came to dominate universities in particular in the middle years of the century.

Thirdly, the very category of higher education is likely to be dissolved as all post-secondary institutions come to be seen as part of a wider system. The old demarcations between higher and further, initial and continuing, academic and vocational and recreational, full-time and part-time education will make less and less sense in such a system. The inwardness of the universities, to which the polytechnics and colleges have also been powerfully attracted in the last twenty-five years, may be modified by a resurgence of the open-access tradition once regarded as more typical of further education colleges. Indeed within the post-binary post-secondary system of the 1990s the emphasis could switch from higher to further education. According to a recent study Britain produces almost as many graduates as its European neighbours (the scale and context of American higher education are quite different). Where Britain under-performs is in the production of those with intermediate skills, especially technicians.[16] The best, it seems, have been the enemy of the good: not for the first time in the history and culture of our nation. But, whatever the balance struck in a wider system of post-secondary education, this system is certain to be much more diverse. It will be committed to pluralism to an extent unknown even in the expanded system of higher education that has developed in the past decades in the shadow of the binary policy. Post-binaryism will be pluralism, its structure and form determined by a deepening diversity.

Quality and access, coherence and pluralism

The changes that have just been described in the likely structure and balance of the system and in the roles of institutions within it have profound implications for the academic values bound up in higher education, which in turn are reflected in styles of teaching and patterns of research. Post-binaryism will be an intellectual as much as a political phenomenon. The aim of this concluding section is to explore the academic issues likely to be raised by the move towards a more open and diverse system of post-secondary education. Such issues, of course, cannot be regarded as separate from the structural issues just discussed. In higher education the political and the intellectual inevitably are joined. For example, the proposal made in 1988 by the Advisory Board for the Research Councils that all institutions should be classified (and funded) as R (research), X (some research) or T (teaching) was both: a political plan for the stratification of the system based on academic assumptions about the nature and needs of research.[17] Efforts to create a credit transfer system that would bind together different courses in different institutions in order to encourage student mobility fall into the same intermediate category.

However, the concern here is not with such detailed proposals but with the broader intellectual issues raised by the development of a post-binary system. These issues can be reduced for the sake of simplicity to five presumed contrasts: between quality and access: coherence and pluralism; knowledge and skills; liberal education and vocationalism; and personal and social goals. Only the first two of these will be discussed at any length in this chapter. But, before the start of this discussion, two warnings are necessary. First, these are not straightforward contrasts. They are not always opposites. Indeed one of the preconditions of post-binaryism is that there need be no conflict between quality and access. And the personal and the social goals of higher education are generally regarded as mutually supportive. Secondly, it is inaccurate to align the first set of attributes (quality, coherence and so on) with more élite forms of higher education, binary or even pre-binary forms, and the second set (access, pluralism and so forth) with more popular forms, the post-binaryism that is the subject of this book. At best such alignments are very ragged; at worst they are wrong.

The contrast between quality and access is regarded by many as the most fundamental and the simplest to describe. In the 1950s and the early 1960s the conservative cry of the anti-Robbins brigade was 'more will mean worse'. Even the liberal majority that rejected their objections to expansion did not reject entirely their underlying metaphor. That majority's favourite image was of 'a pool of talent', much deeper of course than conservatives imagined but not inexhaustible. That imagery has remained with us through the years of expansion since the early 1960s. It has survived intact as more and more students have been admitted without any measurable decline in entry standards in most subjects. It is still there deep inside the system's collective consciousness doing its silent work on the brink of post-binaryism. The resilience of this image in the face of apparent refutation can be explained by the fact that this impression of scarce or, at any rate, limited talent arises not from pragmatic investigation of increasing staying-on rates in school, the rising tide of A levels or the academic success of non-standard students. The image is not about academic quality at all in a specific sense, although it is fed by grumbles about less literate students. Rather the 'pool of talent' is a cultural construction that reflects a still narrow view of the possibilities of higher education, perhaps also a fear about the consequences for the present arrangement of society if the opposite were proved to be true. And it is this cultural construction that must be dismantled if the underdevelopment of British higher education is to be successfully overcome.

Of course, higher education remains restricted in a quantitative sense. Access is still sharply rationed, although in the late 1980s indirectly by the uneven pattern of pupil expectations in schools rather than directly by higher education's own admissions policies. Only 15 per cent of young people go on to university, polytechnic or college and that proportion is only expected to rise to 23 per cent by 1995 according to the government's latest projections of student demand. But higher education is rationed in a qualitative sense too. Even in its most liberal and extended compass – the pioneering work of the Open University, the impressive achievements of the new universities, the spectacular growth of the polytechnics – it remains a deliberately restricted enterprise. It is only designed for those who have the ability, motivation and, in many subjects, the prior education to benefit. Its business remains the advanced intellect not mass education. It is 'higher' in relation to the rest of education not simply in a sequential but in a hierarchical sense. Of course, this restricted view of higher education is confused, contaminated even, by considerations of social class. For the professional middle class higher education has become a standard expectation, almost a universal experience, as a result of the Robbins/Crosland expansion. For the working class, even its most prosperous members, it remains an exceptional experience. And for the new under-class that is such a disturbing social phenomenon in modern Britain opportunities for higher education are insufferably remote. Statistics of the social origins of students, even in non-élite institutions, bear this out.

Britain remains an exceptionally determined society, in a cultural even more than material sense. Higher education is both a producer and a product of that determination; accomplice and victim. It is bound up in, and bound by, the tangled web of social expectations and cultural habits that have grown out of Britain's historical experience. That experience has not always been as recalled by sentimental memory or benign reinterpretation. Our national élite has never been as open as we like to imagine. Even today, much expanded in our age of democracy and mass culture, it has retained some deep-grained habits from the past: to define by exclusion rather than inclusion, to divide society into 'them' and 'us' according to deeply felt but shallowly reasoned criteria, to promote by co-option rather than competition. Higher education is inescapably part of this wider cultural pattern, most directly in the striking of the balance between quality and access.

So the rhetoric of access is crucial. It lays down limits as well as providing directions. Successive formulations of who is eligible for higher education, recalibrations of the balance between quality and access, amount to powerful mission statements for the entire system. The most famous, of course, remains the Robbins principle: 'we have assumed as an axiom that courses of higher education should be available for all those who are qualified by ability and attainment to pursue them and who wish to do so'.[18] As an operational statement the Robbins principle was never much good. Although the balance between subjects and institutions and the demand for student places were treated in detail in the report's appendices, there was no link to the principle itself. Yet this does not detract from its importance, indeed its fame. The Robbins principle remains the founding text of our modern system of higher education, not perhaps in terms of operational details but in the context of underlying values and fundamental aspirations. Today Robbins is a quarter of a century old, and so thought of as out of date. A better way to evaluate the report is as coming two decades after the 1944 Education Act which established for the first time free secondary education for all. The Robbins principle itself can only be understood properly in this grand succession of educational and social reform. The Forster Act of 1870 led inexorably to the Butler Act of 1944 which led quickly to the Robbins report of 1963. Elementary, secondary, higher: here was a rising tide of educational hopes, a powerful thrust to social and cultural freedom that marked British society in the nineteenth and twentieth centuries. That is really what the Robbins principle was all about. It exactly applied the tenets of this aristocratic liberalism, honourable but limited, to postwar higher education.

But the Butler Act has been superseded by the Baker Act: the Education Reform Act of 1988, based on contrary principles, more populist surely but also anti-liberal. Does this invalidate the Robbins principle? Over the past decade two processes have been at work here, a reformulation of the principle and a repudiation of it. For the first half of the 1980s the emphasis was on the first of these; in the second half on the latter. Since the 1988 Act these processes have tended to coalesce. In 1985 the former UGC and NAB, both of course abolished by the Education Reform Act, suggested a rewriting of the Robbins principle in a joint statement on higher education and the needs of society.[19] They proposed that the reference to ability and attainment be replaced by the simpler formula that 'courses of higher education should be available for all those who are able to benefit from them and who wish to do so'. The UGC and NAB also proposed that a fifth aim of higher education should be added to the four identified by Robbins. This was 'the provision of continuing education in order to facilitate adjustment to technological, economic and social change and to meet individual needs for personal development' (NAB 1984: 5).

In one perspective this suggested rewriting amounted to an extension of the principle in order to take account of the development of the binary system since 1965. The emphasis on ability to benefit was a signal to institutions to worry less about A level grades and an encouragement to them to develop access courses and other strategies to attract non-standard students who had failed to pass through the all too narrow sixth-form bottleneck. The emphasis on continuing education too encouraged institutions to look beyond standard young adults and to address the higher education needs of the whole, or a much wider, community. But within this rewriting of the Robbins principle lurked the seeds of its repudiation. Higher education had become a less liberal enterprise by 1985, less intimately related to individual improvement and more tightly linked to economic outcomes (as much in the minds of students as of policy makers). This was reflected in the rewritten principle: technology was placed first, personal development last. This shift was also reflected in the terms in which the government in its 1985 Green Paper (DES 1985a) endorsed the rewritten principle. Rather perversely ministers interpreted 'ability to benefit', surely intended by the UGC and NAB as a measure of individual potential, as a reference to some form of cost-benefit analysis, a measure of socio-economic affordability: a very different, even antithetical, idea.

In the last two years an anti-Robbins principle has become more explicit. In 1988 Lord Chilver, the chairman of the UFC, suggested in a newspaper interview that a student's willingness to contribute his or her own resources to obtaining a higher education should supersede or, at any rate, supplement the criteria laid down by Robbins.[20] In the same year in a private paper to fellow ministers, Mr Robert Jackson, Parliamentary Under Secretary at the DES, proposed that institutions charge students 'top-up' tuition fees, over and above the fees reimbursed by local education authorities, to help them overcome their chronic funding difficulties and, along the lines argued by Lord Chilver, to sharpen the motivation of students.[21] In 1989 the Committee of Vice-Chancellors and Principals agreed to explore the option of charging all students full-cost fees (hoping that most would receive state scholarships to cover much of the cost). In the same year the government introduced legislation to replace grants by loans as the principal means of student support, so reversing the generous policy introduced following the report of the Anderson committee the year before Robbins.

Taken together these initiatives demonstrate how far we have drifted from the assumptions about access that prevailed during the four postwar decades and which were summarised in the famous Robbins principle. Then higher education was seen as something to be deserved, to be aspired to; now it is increasingly regarded as something to be purchased by the prudent or fortunate. There is now a powerful movement away from the idea of higher education as a public service. It is no longer to be seen as a cultural, even moral, enterprise in which the notion of intellectual authority plays a key role, but as an economic enterprise in which customers, whether students or others, are enabled to buy services. This shift of view may help to reduce the obstacles to wider access, however reluctant liberals may be to admit it. For if higher education is stripped of its deeper cultural significance and is regarded in more commonplace terms, there is less need to restrict access to the system. The cohesion of the nation's élite, high academic standards, western civilisation – such grand issues are no longer at stake.

If this rewriting of the Robbins principle during the 1980s tended to use the language of market enablement rather than liberal entitlement, it simply borrowed the political vocabulary of the Thatcher decade. If politics had been different, the rewriting of Robbins would have taken a different form. But it would still have been necessary. A precondition of a mass system is the deconsecration of higher education. For the present system is running up against its own limits, the inhibitions inherent in its social, logistical, academic and, above all, conceptual construction. A post-Robbins post-binary system (to be preferred to the anti-Robbins system being developed in embryo by Conservative ministers and their unreflective allies) would not be restricted in these ways. It would not have to rely on the ever more intensive exploitation of existing student constituencies, the logic that lurks behind much of the detailed work on projected student numbers in the 1990s and which, of course, would also be the effect of a market system driven by the ability of students to pay. The fact that higher education draws its students disproportionately from social classes I and II is the disease not the cure. Instead a post-binary system would need to work towards a repositioning of higher education so that it could cultivate new constituencies. A precondition of this is an entirely new view of who higher education is for – and so of what higher education is – not the relaxation of existing tests of eligibility within a basically unchanged view of its extent and purpose.

There are signs that this is beginning to be realised. Until very recently higher education's approach to wider access was rather like that of St Augustine to chastity. Or, because that parallel may be unfair or inexact, it was in favour of wider access but on its own terms. The UGC's priority was to protect existing unit costs which it suspected were already too low to sustain a satisfactory research base in many universities. In a similar spirit, discussions within the NAB were dominated by arguments about the unit of resource, which fell rapidly during the 1980s because of under-funded polytechnic and college expansion. These arguments revolved around the belief, often unspoken, that, for the polytechnics and colleges to secure their place in higher education's promised land, they needed an appropriate level of funding which had to be determined, at any rate initially, in relation to university standards. Behind both the UGC's devotion to unit costs and the NAB's preoccupation with the unit of resource, lurked a surprisingly traditional set of values about the character and purpose of higher education: academically selective, intellectually intensive, knowledge-led, socially exclusive, pastorally committed. Foreign observers of British higher education see such values in their true, and perhaps embarrassing, light as a stubborn defence of a standard of higher education which they unquestioningly label élite.

That élite tradition and the practices that sustain it have been very much weakened during the 1980s. At any rate the practices have been eroded and finally the tradition has succumbed. The universities have been unable to defend their unit of resource. Even in the funding crisis of 1981 the UGC conceded that some erosion was inevitable. Broadly half the burden of the cuts was borne by a reduction in student numbers; half by a reduction in the unit of resource. In the polytechnic and college sector it was the 20 per cent decline in unit costs that gave the debates in the NAB their urgency. Important reasons for this decline in the élite tradition were lack of resources, the key factor in the early 1980s, and political bullying, more prominent in the second half of the decade. But perhaps the most important reason was the sea-change within higher education. The ice of the old élite orthodoxies has at long last begun to break up. It is now more likely to be accepted that in the past too much emphasis was put on protecting traditional measures of academic quality (not necessarily the same as quality itself) and too little on maintaining and expanding access to higher education. Today the system seems much readier to accept a diversity of standards rather than a single gold standard: *qualities* rather than *quality*. The polytechnics are no longer mesmerised by university models. And in the universities the process of divergence that was interrupted by the imposition of the binary policy in the mid-1960s has begun to reassert itself. Perhaps the experience of the last decade has made higher education less afraid of pluralism; or perhaps the same experience has simply battered the system out of its old élite ways. But a more substantial explanation may be that this erosion of the élite tradition was an inevitable after-shock of the expansion and diversification of higher education undertaken a generation ago, a belated recognition of its long-range implications. According to this interpretation higher education did not so much change course in the 1980s; it discovered the course already set.

Whatever the reason the outcome is plain. There has been a decisive tilt towards wider access and away from academic excellence narrowly conceived. Britain has come off the gold standard. Of course there is a risk with such categorical language. It makes this shift in academic attitudes and political opinions sound far too deliberate. What has happened is the convergence of different trends and opinions, ranging from detailed changes in Treasury rules governing public expenditure to the self-interest of a system that fears it may be on the brink of a demography-induced decline, that together have created the impression of concerted movement. Rather higher education is blundering, and being bundled, blindly or only with half-sight, towards a mass future. The implications of this movement have yet to be properly explored or, in some cases, even identified. Near-open access, lower unit costs, a plurality of standards – all will disturb the equilibrium of higher education in unforeseen but profound ways.

So far debate has been largely confined to a few optimistic allusions to the experience of the United States, without taking any proper account of the very different political and intellectual cultures out of which the much admired American system has grown. On the other hand the experience of mainland Europe, with which Britain in the 1990s will inevitably have a deepening relationship, has been dismissed.[22] Yet it can be argued that European higher education has been more successful in avoiding the degeneration of academic standards suffered by some mass institutions in the United States. Academically the European road to extended higher education looks less risky and, therefore, more attractive than the American road to a mass system. To follow this European road is likely to be gentler on the academic sensibilities of British higher education. Similarities between secondary-school systems and social values reinforce this identification with the European experience.

The balance between coherence and pluralism, the second grand dichotomy encountered in this attempt to describe the intellectual environment of post-binaryism, is becoming more and more difficult to strike as higher education moves from being an élite to become a mass system. Yet it, perhaps more than the balance between quality and access, is the key to the future character of the academic system. It confronts a dilemma of fundamental cultural consequence. As such it tends to subsume those other contrasts listed at the start of this section between liberal education and vocationalism, knowledge and skills, personal and social objectives. These subsidiary issues are swept up in the larger question of the balance between intellectual coherence and cultural pluralism, a question that brings together the epistemology and sociology of modern higher education. For it reflects a crucial divergence about the future role of higher education. On the one hand, on the side of pluralism, there is the belief that by overemphasising academic excellence universities and, to a lesser degree, polytechnics and colleges risk becoming marginal institutions in our developing democracy or, at any rate, institutions that are unable, by design, to reach out to touch the whole people. On the other hand, on the side of coherence, there is the strongly held belief that by abandoning intellectual rigour for an ill-judged relevance higher education risks selling out the ultimate values with which it has so long been associated. The university in particular, it is argued, is bound up with notions of intellectual hierarchy, cultural discrimination and professional excellence that must always sit uneasily with the rougher values of mass culture.

Of course, the dichotomy just sketched is far too simple. It cannot be a question of 'one or the other'. Higher education, pre-binary, binary or post-binary, cannot make an exclusive choice between the populist and academic roads. It cannot be entirely open or closed. In the real world it must strike a balance. And this balance has been struck in different ages and by different nations in different ways. Many other European countries have adopted versions of the British binary policy, under which universities have been allocated an élite mission and other institutions (polytechnics in Britain, *instituts universitaires de technologie* in France, *fachhochschulen* in West Germany) have been established to undertake a more popular role. This approach has also been adopted by many individual states within the United States, which have divided their public higher education systems into two or three levels of institution. Sometimes the relative position of the universities has been reversed. In France the *grandes écoles* and in the Soviet Union the many institutes of the Academy of Sciences enjoy greater prestige.

The balance between élitism and populism, quality and access, coherence and pluralism is also struck within institutions. Undergraduate courses may reflect the second set of broad characteristics, while graduate schools emphasise the first. This may be a particularly significant strategy in mass systems like the American today and the British in the next century, although this stretching-out of higher education has serious implications for resources. And, of course, the balance is struck within academic disciplines. All combine private knowledge with public values. History, for example, is a deeply scholarly pursuit, a rigorous science. Historians comb archives; they use computers; they play with complex social theories. But as Hugh Trevor-Roper argued more than thirty years ago in his inaugural lecture as regius professor of modern history at Oxford, 'history that is not useful, that has not some lay appeal, is mere antiquarianism'. Finally the same balance must be struck, and constantly restruck, in the lives of both teachers and students. A sentence in one of Henry James's prefaces sums up this diurnal struggle.

> There are degrees of feeling – the muffled, the faint, the just sufficient, as we may say: and the acute, the intense, the complete, in a word – the power to be finely aware and richly responsible.[23]

In the past the striking of this balance between coherence and pluralism was largely a private matter. It was contained within the routines of the academic system. In a post-binary system this will be much harder. The right balance will increasingly be seen as a question for public policy. There is a growing demand for higher education to re-emphasise rigour and excellence, whether in terms of basic skills, so-called cultural literacy or the reaffirmed values of western civilisation. But there is an equally insistent demand that higher education offer courses that are relevant to students' future employment and which reflect the cultural diversity of the modern world. In other words higher education is being asked to deliver excellence under conditions of accelerating pluralism; it is expected to offer coherence in an increasingly incoherent world.

The pressure for excellence and coherence is especially strong in the United States, evidence of the intense conflicts generated within a mass system. Allan Bloom's *The Closing of the American Mind*,[24] former Education Secretary William Bennett's war on the liberal academic establishment, the controversy about Stanford University's reform of its core course in western civilisation in order to embrace other traditions: the American evidence is plentiful. But this is not just a transatlantic phenomenon. In Britain the Open University has been criticised for serving up ill-digested social science courses to impressionable and credulous students. In France too there have been demands for a return to Cartesian rigour in the guise of a reinforcement of Republican virtue. Everywhere there are complaints that students are no longer literate, even in élite universities. Clearly here is a deep-rooted and global phenomenon.

But it is also a complex one. At least four different strands have come together to produce it. The first is the sense of disarray that grips modern culture, the feeling that despite our material success, despite our great achievements in science (or perhaps because of them), our civilisation has slipped its mooring and is adrift on a sea of uncertainties. There are many ways to describe this unease. More than a century ago Matthew Arnold wrote in 'Dover Beach' of a 'melancholy, long, withdrawing roar'.[25] He had in mind the ebbing of organised religion but wider applications are possible in our secular age. George Steiner in his impressive book *Real Pretences* has written of the dislocation between the word and the world, the deconstruction of an older moral order that is like a fracture running through the high bourgeois civilisation of the west.[26] The implication is plain. Far from preserving these essential integrities higher education has conspired in their destruction. This is the most serious charge against the academic system, not that it has admitted too many sub-literate students. It is difficult to mistake, after Auschwitz and Hiroshima, the recessional strain in modern culture. The best, we instinctively imagine, is behind us.

The second strand is more precisely aligned with what is often called neo-conservatism in the United States and in Britain 'Thatcherism'. There are those like Allan Bloom who have argued that universities have deserted their posts by surrendering to vociferous special interests demanding courses in black or women's studies, which they believe are not academically valid, and by promoting the amoral deconstructive theories deplored by Steiner, which undermine all sense of intellectual authority. As a result, in Bloom's phrase, 'the foundations of the university have become extremely doubtful to the highest intelligences' (Bloom 1988: 144). The answer, according to such critics, is to turn our backs on pluralism, because pluralism implies relativism, which in turn denies the good, the true and the beautiful. Such views are more vociferously expressed on the right than on the left. But a similar unease is sometimes felt by liberals. Their unease about pluralism generally takes the form of the determination that first-generation students should not be fobbed off with a second-best higher education or the fear that, under the guise of relevance, 'minority' students will be denied proper access to 'majority' culture. In Britain the teaching of English has been a principal battleground on which right and left have become hopelessly confused.

The third strand is often summed up in the call 'Back to Basics', although it can be expressed more positively by emphasising the need for all students to be taught effective cognitive, affective and rhetorical skills. But either way it reflects a worry that today's students cannot write, read, argue and analyse as well as their predecessors. However, this unease about standards seems to be tied up with two different things. First, traditional western culture is a culture of the book but clearly the late twentieth century is not an age of the book (even if more are published than ever before!). So even the whisper of declining literacy is perceived as a wider threat to our bookish civilisation. It touches a raw cultural nerve. But this unease may arise from a misperception of the true nature of the modern world. Ours is no longer a traditional humanistic culture rooted in literary and philosophical values. Rather it is a scientific and technical civilisation, speaking the language of social science, governed by managerial practice and deeply dependent on expert skills. Higher education's difficulty here is obvious enough: it has a foot in both camps, as a powerful guardian of traditional culture and a source of modern technology.

Secondly, students urgently need to learn skills that are portable, ones that can be transferred from job to job (because the nature and content of jobs will change at an ever-increasing rate) and also applied to their personal and social lives as well as to their employment (because as leisure expands in a post-industrial society work will cease to dominate life). This need suggests that the emphasis will have to switch from particular skills to more general ones, from knowledge that is specific to more open-minded forms of knowledge. There is likely to be a renewed demand, not so much for literacy in an old-fashioned sense, but for fluency, articulacy and other communication skills. So these two different currents, the first running back to a perhaps anachronistic view of culture as essentially a literary enterprise and the second running forward to the skill demands of a post-industrial society, have come together to support the complex call for 'Back to Basics'.

The fourth strand appears at first sight to stand in opposition to the third. But despite what has just been said about the growing need for transferable skills, the modern world is inexorably a place for experts. Police officers need to know more and more about the law. Once nurses did just that, nurse; today they play a crucial role in medical intervention. The examples of professionalisation and credentialisation can be expanded almost at will. Many of them are intimately linked to the postwar expansion of higher education. There is little reason to suppose that this embrace will not become even closer as higher education moves towards a mass future. Universities, polytechnics and colleges will be expected to set more and more standards – initial entry, post-registration, post-experience and so on – for more and more professions. Clearly the inexorable growth of the professional society is an important component of the demands for quality and coherence.

However, the contrary pressures on higher education to become more open, more relevant, in short to assert the claims of pluralism, are as powerful and insistent as those for quality and coherence. If a post-binary system cannot reconcile these competing forces, it risks being torn apart by them. The drive to pluralism has three main components: the political, the economic and the cultural. The first is best summed up in the phrase 'equal opportunities', a political programme that has been marginalised in our present élite system and in Britain's semi-closed society but is centre-stage in America with its mass system and wide-open society. In any democracy an élite system of higher education is inherently difficult to justify; and that difficulty is compounded if, as in Britain, the competition to enter such a system is contaminated by issues of class, race and gender. On the brink of the twenty-first century there is an instinctive reluctance to accept the existence of, in Eric Ashby's phrase, 'a thin clear stream of excellence' (Ashby 1971: 101). Today, for reasons discussed in the previous section, that stream is seen as less clear but also as less exiguous. The very notion of excellence has become pluralistic.

The civic quality of modern higher education is as important as its academic character in the context of equal opportunities. Today access to higher education can no longer reasonably be regarded as a privilege. Instead it has become an entitlement or, in the language of the free market, an enablement, in either case a right. In most advanced countries higher education is woven into the expectations of the middle classes in their broadest sense, which, many argue, makes it even more important to safeguard and expand access opportunities for less privileged groups if an alarming fissure is not to open up between academic 'haves' and 'have-nots', another of those damaging disequilibria of affluence. Clearly it is desirable that the student body in higher education should be reasonably accurately aligned with the balance of the overall population in terms of race, class and gender, because higher education confers advanced socio-economic status. Only on this basis can continued academic selection be permitted without violating democratic principles. So there are vital issues of civil rights and public policy bound up with the drive to pluralism.

The economic component of this drive can be described more briefly because the arguments are familiar. First, the growth of expert society, referred to earlier, requires the upgrading of the skills of all citizens. In an important sense we all need better skills just to stand still. Secondly, the development of post-industrial society in the terms described by Daniel Bell and others will tend to make knowledge itself a primary commodity.[27] So higher education will become a primary producer, not in a symbolic but material sense. This, of course, will place even greater emphasis on the links between the academic and economic systems. The possession of a highly developed scientific infrastructure in terms of R and D capacity and of skilled labour will become a crucial resource for cities, regions and nations. Thirdly, to realise this potential human talents must be fully developed. Everyone must be educated up to the highest level of which they are capable, which will have a particular impact on the size and scope of the higher education system. All these economic arguments support the case for the most extensive possible systems, systems that are pluralistic and no longer restricted by outmoded notions of suitability and eligibility.

But the cultural component of the drive to pluralism is perhaps the most significant. Ours is a centrifugal culture in two senses. First, the explosion of knowledge and the ever finer divisions of academic labour that have been its consequence have made it impossible for a single person to appreciate, let alone encompass, its totality or a decent fraction of it, even in a lifetime's study. The polymath is now the dilettante. Secondly, modern culture thrives on difference. It seeks out divergence. It ceaselessly deconstructs. One reason for this anti-organicist quality is that it is how science makes progress, by deliberately subverting established orthodoxies and substituting better ones (which in turn are subverted). Another reason is that the old certainties have faded; first religious faith and now the secular values of the west. Ours is a multi-cultural society and a polycentric world. Other perspectives and traditions are now recognised and respected. For example, our consciousness has been expanded and enriched by feminism in its broadest sense, a movement towards which the academic system has notably contributed. And the European-North American world has seemed to shrink in a properly global context. Also modern material civilisation is technical rather than literary, governed by experts not by gentlemen. In short our world is an uncanonical place. It is more and more difficult to discern a common stream, a main current of what it is important to know to be properly educated, to be fully alive in the late twentieth century. Or, at any rate, it is more and more difficult to lay down an authoritative canon. In this sense the incoherence of the modern world makes the pluralism of modern higher education inevitable.

How to reconcile these conflicting pressures for coherence and for pluralism, both of which are valid and neither of which can be denied, is perhaps the most difficult task facing a post-binary system of higher education. It is many times more significant than the questions of structure, government, administration and funding that preoccupy policy makers. For higher education has come close to losing its way. Often it has failed to confront the powerful pressures towards fragmentation, whether for a return to more traditional values or for a renewed dedication to pluralism. Its response has been structural rather than intellectual. As a result higher education risks losing its resilience and integrity in the face of these competing demands. Its contribution, so powerful in its parts, has become obscure in its whole. What is the unique role of higher education at the end of the twentieth century? The answer is not always clear. Advanced laboratories sited as readily in industry as in higher education can take care of high-technology research. High-level training can be provided by other agencies, public and private. Even if higher education maintains and expands its stake in post-industrial society, which is a likely outcome, it may be as a bureaucratic structure comprehensible and so justifiable only in managerial terms, from which its own authentic values have drained away. In these circumstances it is not enough to fall back on a strategy of philosophical incantation, anti-fragmentary rhetoric which even those who utter it do not fully believe.

There are three ways in which a post-binary system can respond more positively to these pressures. The first is through interdisciplinary, disciplined connectedness not disorganised choice, pluralism with coherence. The German sociologist Wolf Lepenies has described this as 'a new intellectual ecology'.[28] This is a resonant phrase. Traditional categories, both academic and professional, have to be constantly reviewed, pushed and pulled into more modern shapes. Of course this happens as the result of routine disciplinary development, but privately and without regard for its wider cultural reverberations. Nor are such developments followed through to the curriculum quickly enough. Or, if they are, the impulse is to add new courses or include new material rather than to re-evaluate the whole.

The second way is linked to the first. This is to foster the growth of new subjects, in particular those with synoptic and summative ambitions and especially forward-looking, science-based disciplines. Too often such ambitions are associated with backward-looking arts disciplines. Science and technology, apart from rare Nobel Prize winning enterprises, is regarded as reductionist, utilitarian and therefore myopic. Yet it can be argued that new subjects like informatics, which draws on logical, applied mathematics, computer science, artificial intelligence and other fields of inquiry, is potentially as synoptic in the circumstances of the late twentieth century as classics was in the nineteenth century.

A third way for higher education to meet the post-binary challenge is to subject its own history, values, practices, policies and institutions to sustained intellectual interrogation. More historical studies of the development of academic values and of the scientific tradition are needed, and also investigations of the conflict within modern higher education systems between contradictory values and competing demands. Higher education, it sometimes seems, is good at investigating and criticising everyone and everything but itself. In its ceaseless scrutiny of science, culture, society only feeble attempts are made to 'place' higher education itself within these crucial debates. Its collective mentality goes unexplored. At a more practical level traditional practice, whether in governance, administration and funding or research and teaching, needs to be constantly reviewed.

Modern higher education systems must renew themselves intellectually through interdisciplinarity – Wolf Lepenies' 'new intellectual ecology' – and new subjects, particularly in advanced technology and social science. They must also renew themselves culturally by exposing their own values and practices to sustained inquiry. The severest challenge likely to be encountered in the building of a post-binary system is the urgent need to sustain coherence; not, of course, in terms of traditional academic quality and narrow cultural hegemonies but in terms of a broader vision about the direction of the academic enterprise. In a mass system the capacity to sustain that broader vision is undermined in two ways. First, the fluidity and divergence of roles that are inevitable under post-binary conditions will make it more difficult for institutions to say in touch with each other, or even to recognise that they are parts of a common enterprise. Secondly, the fragmentation of knowledge into more and more disciplines and sub-disciplines, many employing reductionist techniques or organised around vocational preoccupations, will intensify so making it more difficult to recall wider intellectual and cultural impulses. Yet, it can be argued, a post-binary system needs greater not less coherence than the more restricted higher education systems of the past. They shared silent values, although in the 1980s that silence has made it more difficult for higher education to confront its contemporary situation. But a post-binary system, precisely because its commitment to pluralism must be absolute, must have an explicit shape. Post-binaryism must be seen as an intellectual as well as a political question. At the heart of its proper definition is its cultural shape not its institutional structure.

Notes

1 The most illuminating, but polemical, accounts of the different cultural assumptions underlying Scottish higher education remain Davie, G. (1961) *The Democratic Intellect* and (1986) *The Crisis of the Democratic Intellect.*

2 Shinn, C. (1985) *Paying the Piper: The Development of the University Grants Committee 1919–1946* covers the rise of the UGC; Carswell, J. (1986) *Government and the Universities in Britain: Programme and Performance 1960–1980* its golden age. Berdahl, R. (1959) *British Universities and the State* offers a still valuable American perspective on the UGC system, and Stewart, W. A. C. (1989) *Higher Education in Postwar Britain* is a general summary of developments since 1945.

3 Locke, M., Pratt, J. and Burgess, T. (1985) *The Colleges of Higher Education 1972 to 1982* is one of the few accounts of the non-polytechnic part of public sector higher education.

4 Department of Education and Science (1988d) *Education Statistics for the United Kingdom: 1988 Edition,* tables 24 and 26, pp. 30–31.

5 Department of Education and Science (1988a) *Survey of Adult Education Centres in England 1985–86: Enrolments, Courses, Hours of Tuition and Subjects of Study.*

6 The literature of the binary policy and the growth of the polytechnics is less extensive than their importance would suggest. Pride of place must still go to Robinson, E. (1968) *The New Polytechnics.* Other useful books are Burgess, T. and Pratt, J. (1974) *Polytechnics: A Report* and Donaldson, L. (1975) *Policy and the Polytechnics.*

7 Ministry of Education (1956) *Technical Education* was the White Paper that led to the creation of the colleges of advanced technology.

8 The UFC has decided to make universities bid for their entire allocation of students against prices set by the Council. The PCFC, more cautiously, is to allocate grants to polytechnics and colleges according to student numbers, although they will be expected to compete for a modest five per cent of the Council's total budget.

9 Committee of Vice-Chancellors and Principals (1985) *Report of the Steering Committee for Efficiency Studies in Universities* is better known as the Jarratt Report after its chairman Sir Alex Jarratt.

10 Committee of Vice-Chancellors and Principals (1987) *Academic Standards in Universities.*

11 Committee of Vice-Chancellors and Principals (1989) *The Teaching Function. Quality Assurance. Detailed proposal for a CVCP academic audit unit to monitor universities' own quality assurance mechanisms.*

12 Under California's master plan, written in 1960 but frequently revised, higher education in the state is divided into three tiers: the University of California with nine campuses; California State University with 19 campuses; and 106 community colleges.

13 Association of Graduate Careers Advisory Services (1989) *What do Graduates do?* provides the basic information. Also useful is Brennan, J. and McGeevor, P. (1988) *Graduates at Work: Degree Courses and the Labour Market.*

14 Department of Education and Science (1988e) *Top-up Loans for Students* described the principles, although not the details, of the government's plans to replace grants with loans as the main means of student support.

15 At a meeting in Leeds in September 1989, the vice-chancellors reluctantly agreed to explore the idea that all students should be charged full-cost fees for their university courses. They also agreed to explore other options like a graduate tax.

16 Smithers, A. and Robinson, P. (1989) *Increasing Participation in Higher Education* was commissioned by British Petroleum.

17 Advisory Board for the Research Councils (1987) *A Strategy for the Science Base.*

18 Committee on Higher Education (1963) *Higher Education: Report of the committee appointed by the Prime Minister under the chairmanship of Lord Robbins*, p. 8.

19 University Grants Committee (1984b) *A Strategy for Higher Education into the 1990s* and National Advisory Body (1984b) *A Strategy for Higher Education in the Late 1990s and Beyond* contained a common chapter drafted by NAB officials entitled 'Higher education and the needs of society'.

20 'The Chilver principle', interview in *The Times Higher Education Supplement*, 19 October 1988.

21 Jackson, R. (1988a) 'The Funding of Higher Education', a Chevening discussion paper, 25 July.

22 Baker, K. (1989a) 'Higher Education – 25 Years On', speech delivered at Lancaster University, 5 January.

23 Bloom, A. (1988) *The Closing of the American Mind.*

24 James, H. (1986) *Princess Casamassima*: preface to the New York edition (1909), p. 35.

25 Arnold, M. (1985) 'Dover Beach', line 25.

26 Steiner, G. (1989) *Real Presences.*

27 Bell, D. (1973) *The Coming of Post-Industrial Society.*

28 Lepenies, W. (1989) 'A Home of Lost Causes and Impossible Loyalties', in *Universiteit en Hogeschool*, p. 62.

2 The economics of wider participation

Leslie Wagner

Introduction

Higher education is expensive. Governments want wider participation but do not like increased public expenditure. Can this circle be squared? Does wider participation necessarily involve increased costs, and if it does, how might this be justified economically? These are the questions addressed in this chapter.

The cost of higher education

In 1989–90 the Department of Education and Science[1] planned to spend in excess of £3 billion on higher education. Not all of this will go on the teaching of students, for the contribution to the universities includes an element to cover basic research costs. The Universities Funding Council is planning to separate this research element in the funding but to date only a vague estimate has been given of the value, usually in excess of £500 million. It seems safe to conclude therefore that at least £2.5 billion is being spent on the teaching of students.

This expenditure provides for 520,000 full-time students and 342,000 part-time students including the Open University, making 640,000 full-time equivalents in all. The result is an annual average cost per undergraduate of close to £4,000. In comparison the average annual cost of a primary school pupil is just over £1,000 and of a secondary pupil under £2,000. While higher education might be expected to cost more than schooling there does not seem to be any fundamental educational or economic principle which determines that it should be four times the cost of primary education and twice the cost of secondary education.

The reason for the difference is not hard to find. The higher education lecturer teaches fewer students and is more highly paid than her counterpart in schools. Moreover higher education involves a much higher ratio of non-teaching staff support than occurs in schools. This difference may narrow as schools take on more of their own administration and management under schemes of local management but is still likely to be significant.

In addition to teaching costs, higher education also, of course, involves the cost of student maintenance for full-time students. Despite the increasing level of parental contribution the public expenditure cost is in the region of £500 million. While the introduction of student loans will increase the private financial contribution, studies to date show that this will have minimal impact on reducing the public expenditure contribution until much before the end of the 1990s.

The costs of wider participation

Most entrants to full-time higher education come direct from school and are in the 18–20 age group. A great deal of attention has been focused on the effect of the demographic downturn in this age group on the demand for higher education. About the only point of agreement is the starting point, a decline of about 33 per cent in the population of 18 to 20-year-olds.

In the 1987 White Paper (DES 1987) the government produced two projections. The *pessimistic* projection was for a maximum fall in numbers in higher education of about 12 per cent. This assumed that improvements in schooling would increase the percentage of school-leavers with higher education entry qualifications, thus partly offsetting the effects of the demographic downturn. The more *optimistic* projection assumed that an even higher proportion of school pupils would qualify for higher education as a result of the success of the government's policies. The effect would be at first a rise in numbers followed by a fall during the first half of the 1990s to about the 1985 level.

The case for the more optimistic scenario is boosted by another argument which has nothing to do with the success of the government's policies. This is the observation that the falling birth rate in the late 1960s and early 1970s was concentrated in those social groups which traditionally did not send their children into higher education. In the social groups from which higher education draws its clientele there was a much smaller and largely insignificant fall.

The evidence to date supports the more optimistic projections whatever the underlying cause. Higher education numbers have continued to grow in the latter years of the 1980s. Moreover an increasing number of students are staying on at school or going to college to study A levels. The latest figures show an increase of 8 per cent in 1988/89 over the previous year. These trends are recognised in the government's expenditure plans for the period 1991/92 published at the beginning of 1989 (HM Treasury 1989) which revise upwards the optimistic projection. However, this simply creates a higher base line from which any fall in the 1990s is expected to occur. The government's view would seem to be therefore that even in a revised optimistic projection the increase in the age participation rate will result at best in no decline in numbers from the levels of the late 1980s.

The scale of the achievement required to maintain steady state numbers throughout the 1990s needs to be appreciated. Between 1983 and 1987 the percentage of those qualified to go into higher education who did so rose from 81 to 89 per cent (HM Treasury 1989). There is now very little of a reserve pool of those qualified for higher education who choose not to go. The increase in the age participation rate necessary to maintain numbers will have to come almost exclusively from increasing the proportion of the age group with the necessary qualifications. The recent increase in staying-on rates at school is therefore encouraging. However, there is still a long way to go.

Between 1983 and 1987 the age participation index[2] rose from 13.2 to 14.6 per cent. It will need to rise to 18.6 per cent by the late 1990s to enable steady state numbers to be maintained. In other words the rate of increase shown between 1983 and 1987 will have more or less to continue and to rely almost entirely on increases in the numbers qualifying rather than in persuading those qualifying to take up higher education. Moreover according to the projections this steady state target can only be reached if the number of mature students and those without traditional A level qualifications also increases significantly. Some polytechnics in particular have large numbers of students in these categories and other institutions are beginning to look to them as a source of student supply. If the optimistic projections on the 18–20 age group are fulfilled then any gap in numbers might realistically be filled by increased mature student recruitment. However if the more pessimistic scenario was to be experienced it would require a gigantic growth in the number of mature and non-traditionally qualified entrants to maintain steady state numbers overall.

It would seem therefore that even if the most optimistic official assumptions about the success of attempts to achieve wider participation were to be fulfilled, the result will be at best no increase in the numbers actually studying in higher education. In broad terms therefore wider participation need involve no extra costs. The present £3 billion plus expenditure will, in real terms, cover all the wider participation which is likely to be achieved during the 1990s. Moreover, with a static level of spending, as the economy grows expenditure on higher education as a percentage of the gross domestic product (GDP) will fall.

Indeed the expected growth of the economy would allow increased higher education numbers without any increase in higher education's share of GDP. For example, if the economy grew by an average of 2.5 per cent per annum during the 1990s (a moderate enough target) and even assuming unit costs do not fall, the numbers enrolling could increase by about 15 per cent by 1995 and by over 30 per cent by the end of the decade without higher education expenditure increasing as a proportion of GDP. It might justifiably be asked what all the fuss about financial constraints is about.

One answer is that static unit costs are not good enough. Leaving aside any political determination to reduce the proportion of GDP spent on public services there are other, more pressing, demands than higher education for any given level of public expenditure. An ageing population for example makes greater demands on the health and social services budget, not to mention the impact of a less economically active population on taxation revenue. For sound demographic reasons which have little to do with ideology it may not be possible to sustain higher education's share of public expenditure or GDP. Economies must be found.

Indeed during the 1980s they were found. Between 1980 and 1986 unit costs fell by 16 per cent in the polytechnics and by 5 per cent in the universities. As a result an increase in full-time numbers of about 15 per cent was achieved with an increase in real terms expenditure of only about 3 per cent.

However, this reduction in unit costs was achieved during a period of expansion. It is always easier to achieve such economies at a time of growth when an output increase need not be matched by an expenditure increase. This is, in effect, what happened during the 1980s. The polytechnics were responsible for virtually the whole of the increase in full-time student numbers and their productivity increase was three times that of the universities.

This form of productivity increase is relatively easy to achieve both educationally and politically. It involves taking additional students onto existing courses, making course sizes larger, but not increasing costs pro rata. It may require staff to work harder but no reduction in staff numbers is required. These options are not available with static student numbers. Here unit costs can only be reduced through reductions in staffing. The evidence from industry and from other sectors of education is that reducing unit costs with static or declining output is much less easy to achieve.

Moreover it can plausibly be argued that wider participation involves extra costs beyond those associated with the traditional clientele for higher education. With school and college leavers the recruitment process in higher education is pretty well standardised. A prospectus is produced and widely distributed. Increasingly a video is also made available. Students can obtain prospectuses at their school or college or by writing for them, or by attending one of the Sixth Form Fairs which are held locally or regionally. A standard form is then completed. The university or polytechnic will then generally provide open days for prospective students. For the most popular courses individual selection interviews will not be held. The offer will be related to O level results, head teacher's report and expected A level performance. The latter will be based on past experience of the department of the points (or price) at which they can expect to obtain sufficient students to fill the course.

It is an extremely cost-effective method of selection. The potential students are easily found in their schools and colleges and in undertaking A level study they are already being conditioned to continue into higher education. Almost all the other elements of the selection process are mass produced (prospectuses and videos) or involve group behaviour to enable the maximum number to be covered by the minimum input. Insofar as the more expensive individual attention is provided it is concentrated in the post-A level clearing period when it will be most cost effective, resulting in actual enrolments.

The higher costs of mature student participation

The recruitment of mature students is much more difficult. First of all they have to be found. They will generally not be in convenient places like schools and colleges to which a prospectus can be sent to start the ball rolling. Here general advertising and linking with community networks is required. The latter is time-consuming and needs human resources. When the students have been found they need to be persuaded. Unlike sixth-formers they are not on an educational escalator leading inexorably to higher education. And when they have been persuaded they need more careful selection for there will be much greater variation in their ability to benefit from higher education. This will usually require personal interview, another costly resource. Increasingly access courses are being used as the alternative entry route to higher education for mature students. Data provided by the CNAA database project at Bedford College of Higher Education indicated that in November 1987 there were 334 access courses in 189 institutions. By 1989 the figure had risen to nearly 600 courses (ECCTIS 1989).

This is not the place to discuss the educational effectiveness of access courses but in economic terms they do not reduce the costs of selection for higher education institutions. Most successful access courses are collaboratively designed and delivered as a partnership between the college of further education and one or more higher education institutions. From the latter's point of view it is investing staff resources for which the return in terms of student enrolment is uncertain. This applies even to access courses which guarantee successful students a place in a named course at a particular institution. For the guarantee is to the student not to the institution. The student is free to seek entry to a different university or polytechnic from the one which invested in his or her access course.

The development of a national system of recognition for access courses, which was introduced in 1989 under the joint aegis of CNAA and the CVCP, will increase the dilemma facing higher education institutions. An intended and laudable objective of the scheme is to widen the opportunities for non-standard entrants by granting their access course nationally recognised status. This should increase the possibility of such students being accepted by a wider range of institutions.

One effect will be to reduce the incentive to any individual polytechnic or university to invest in the development of an individual access course. Far better, it will be argued, to let someone else invest these resources and put all your efforts into persuading the students to come to your institution when they've successfully finished. In so far as institutions will invest in access courses it is more likely to be through becoming a recognised validation agency. For it may be thought that access students will prefer to go to the institution which has provided the imprimatur for their access course.

By whichever route mature students enter higher education, it is likely to involve the institution seeking to recruit such students in higher costs than those incurred in recruiting school and college leavers. No systematic study of such costs has yet been published but there is no doubt in the minds of those involved with this work that the costs exist. This is an area where some immediate research would be helpful.

The higher costs of mature students, particularly those with non-traditional entry qualifications, do not stop at the recruitment process but are also reflected during their time inside higher education. A major study by the CNAA has indicated that *an average* student with non-traditional entry qualification performs as well if not better than those with A level entry qualifications (Bourner with Hamed 1987). But as might be expected the variation around the mean is much greater. The good are very good but there is a greater proportion who are academically at risk. The more detailed individual selection process which is applied to mature non-traditionally qualified students attempts to reduce the risk but cannot eliminate it. Inevitably and quite properly providing wider opportunities must increase the risk of failure, and so long as admissions policies are not irresponsible in the interests of both the student and the institution a greater risk of failure must be accepted. A safety first policy is not an access policy. Deciding to lower the A level points requirement from 10 to 9 is no great radical move towards encouraging greater participation. Deciding to accept more students with very low A level points or without A levels is, and has consequences for costs.

In part these increased costs arise from the need to provide greater academic support for mature students who have been absent from the educational experience for a number of years. However, access courses are specifically designed to provide both the subject knowledge and more importantly the study skills which such students lack. Moreover there is increasing evidence that 18-year-olds straight from school or college are equally lacking in such skills. In so far as increased attention and resources have to be given to language and learning skills in the first year it may no longer be easy to differentiate between the needs of 18-year-olds and those of more mature students.

However, there are other forms of support which are also required and the general experience seems to be that mature non-traditional students make greater demands on tutors, counsellors and advisers. One reason is that their lack of recent educational experience leaves them unsure of what is expected or required. An unfamiliar environment leads to a lack of confidence and much time needs to be given in the early stages to providing reassurance. The most difficult thing perhaps for the returning student to understand is that criticism is an inherent part of the academic and learning process. Tutors also need to learn that criticism needs to be balanced by praise and encouragement.

Mature non-traditional students are not only at greater risk academically and psychologically but also financially and socially. Some will have made great financial sacrifices which in the end they cannot sustain. Others will have family commitments which hinder their ability to study or do not allow the flexibility they require. In general mature students bring into higher education a much larger and more complex baggage of commitments and external constraints than their 18-year-old colleagues. And when these are combined with the psychological demands of academic study they produce, for some, intolerable stress which tutors, counsellors and advisers try to relieve.

As with the extra costs of admissions, while there is much anecdotal evidence of these extra demands and costs, no systematic study of their size or comprehensiveness has been undertaken. Indeed there is a curious ambivalence within higher education and among those concerned with these issues about recognising that they exist at all. The wish to 'normalise' the mature student experience stems in large part from an underlying lack of confidence that there is genuine and longer-term government support for wider participation in higher education.

The government's present position through White Papers and ministerial speeches is that it wishes to encourage such wider mature student participation, but that unit costs must fall and the pressure on the public purse must ease. Enthusiasts for access seem to have breathed a collective sigh of relief that they have at least attracted this level of commitment from government and they are reluctant to point out that the two objectives may be incompatible. So, while their internal debates and conversations relate to the increased resource demands which non-traditional students impose, their external pronouncements hardly mention the issue for fear that the government will take fright and renege on its basic commitment. So the evidence remains anecdotal and therefore can be easily dismissed.

If the commitment to wider access is based simply on the need to fill the demographic gap this may not matter in the long run. For as that gap is increasingly filled by greater participation of 18-year-olds, as the most recent evidence seems to indicate might happen, so the enthusiasm for mature students will fade away. They will remain the outsiders of the higher education system having to satisfy themselves with whatever crumbs remain after the 18-year-olds have had their fill. Those few institutions that remain committed to greater mature student participation will be in no position to argue the case for more resources.

However, if that commitment is more widely based, and exists irrespective of the demographic position, then the increased resource demands of mature students will have to be recognised. To do otherwise will be to increase their risk of failure to unacceptable levels and/or to devalue the quality of the educational experience they are offered. Either outcome would bring the higher education system into disrepute and enshrine for all time the perception of mature student higher education as second class.

But there is no need for defensiveness on the matter of the additional costs of wider participation and the enrolment of more students with non-standard qualifications. For such costs are more than matched by the educational benefits as measured by 'value-added'. At its simplest an institution which has enrolled a student with non-standard qualifications who emerges with first class honours has added more to that student's educational competence and qualifications than another institution which achieved a similar final result with a student who entered with three A grades at A level. The first institution might be expected to require additional resources to achieve this result. The reality is that it is usually the second institution which receives more resources under our present system!

The 'value-added' approach attracts much criticism, particularly from those who suffer in the comparison. Most of these criticisms are specious. Thus it is argued that the value may not be added by the institution but by the students themselves through their own efforts. Apart from the fact that the institution and its staff may have played a crucial part in motivating those efforts this factor does not seem to inhibit existing notions of prestige. This is firmly based on student academic performance which may also be due as much to inherent ability and effort as to a specific institutional contribution. What do Oxford, Cambridge and the major universities add to the educational ability and competence of their 14- and 15-point A level entrants?

A second criticism is that the example given earlier is the extreme and it is more difficult to identify differences in 'value-added' in the broad range of higher education. This point has some validity because it clearly is not easy to indicate whether a student with 8 points at A level who ends up with an upper second class honours degree has had more 'value-added' than one who entered with, say, three points at A level and ends up with a lower second class honours degree. Yet admissions tutors still seem firmly of the opinion that a particular level of A level points makes a candidate suitable for entry while one point lower does not. If it is possible to make such fine distinctions in relation to entry it is possible, at least conceptually, to make them in relation to 'value-added'.

The difficulty with the 'value-added' concept is that most of the arguments of both proponents and opponents are seen as self-serving. It is more profitable therefore to look at the other forms of benefit which might result from wider participation.

The benefits of wider participation

It is easier to describe the benefits of wider participation than to measure them. They can be categorised as economic, social and personal and distinguished between private and public.

Economic

The benefits to the economy of wider participation are easily understood. With the loss of Empire and the access it provided to cheap raw materials and guaranteed markets, the British economy has had increasingly to rely on its own resources which are essentially human resources. A more highly skilled workforce at all levels is necessary for economic success. At the higher levels it is the technological and analytical skills which higher education can provide. In recent years increased emphasis has been placed on transferable personal skills, enterprise skills and capability skills as necessary to provide the initiative, leadership, teamwork, information processing and inter-personal qualities required in complex advanced economies. Higher education claims it is capable of providing all these skills and therefore the greater the number with higher education qualifications the more the economy will benefit.

In general these claims have been accepted by government and employers although not without rumblings of discontent about the quality and relevance of the higher education experience. Whatever their reservations, however, employers still seek to recruit graduates in increasing numbers and there is evidence that they will continue to do so as an increasing proportion of their workforce in the 1990s. When this increasing demand is put alongside the likely reduction in supply brought about by demographic change the enthusiasm for wider participation in higher education from both government and employers is easily understood.

Economists have attempted to measure the benefits to the economy from larger graduate numbers by measuring the differential salaries of graduates over non-graduates over their lifetimes. From one perspective this makes sense. If graduates are more worthwhile to a firm than non-graduates they will pay them more. Concerned as they are with making profits, firms are unlikely to provide higher salaries for graduates if they could achieve the same results from non-graduates. As firms both seek to recruit graduates and pay them higher salaries there must be a benefit.

Indeed the earnings data of graduates has been related to cost to provide a formal measure of the return to higher education as an investment both from the point of view of the individual and of society. As higher education is largely provided free of tuition costs to the individual, such costs being provided by the taxpayer, it is not surprising that the private returns to higher education are greater than the social returns. While the private returns can be in double figures (and in some occupations well into double figures) the social return can be as low as 5 per cent. As a result of the existing financing system higher education is a more profitable investment for the individual than for society. It is these sort of results that provide some of the intellectual justification, in some people's eyes, for shifting a greater proportion of the costs of education, including maintenance, onto the student.

Of course matters are not as simple as that. Firstly, the data itself is not particularly reliable. The differential income figures of graduates are based on the current income for people who graduated over the past 35 to 45 years. Whether they provide a reliable guide to the differential income of today's graduates over the next 35 to 45 years is very much open to question. Moreover, translating higher incomes into higher benefit is much easier when applied to the individual than to society. A graduate who goes into the City and five years after graduation is earning £40,000 may be earning four times as much as a colleague who went into one of the public services. For the individual the economic benefit is four times as great. But can it sensibly be argued that society is also gaining four times the economic benefit from the daily work of a stockbroker or accountant as it does from the daily work of a teacher or social worker? Only if it is assumed that salary differentials exactly reflect society's economic benefit and that can only be the case if there are perfectly competitive labour markets, which there are not. Economic returns to individuals do not necessarily reflect the economic benefits to society and salary differentials therefore are not a reliable measure of social economic benefit. The rate-of-return concept which attempts to evaluate investment in human resources by the same methodology as the evaluation of investment in capital resources is flawed. It may offer some guidance to individuals but requires too many unrealistic assumptions to be useful as a guide to social investment.

The rate-of-return approach is particularly damaging to the case for investment in mature student higher education. Leaving aside the argument for higher costs set out earlier, the economic benefits of being a graduate are obviously received over fewer years by the mature student, reducing both the private and social return. A mature graduate may have, say ten fewer years over which to achieve a return on the investment.

Clearly if an individual has the option to undertake higher education in the late teens it makes better economic sense to do so. Financial commitments are smaller and the higher salary from being a graduate starts being earned earlier. But that option is rarely available. Few individuals consciously choose to forego higher education earlier and deliberately decide to wait until they are in their mid-twenties. So the appropriate economic question for a mature student is whether, at whatever age they choose to come into higher education, they will be better off economically by sacrificing, say, three years income now to obtain a higher income for the rest of their working lives. The answer for most mature students is undoubtedly in the affirmative even if the return they receive will not be as high as it would have been if they had come into higher education in their late teens. 'Better late than never' is correct advice.

The same applies to investment from society's point of view. The rate-of-return approach will always favour the largest possible period for benefits to be received. If there is a choice between an investment in 18-year-olds or in 30-year-olds clearly the former will be preferred. But that is not the decision option relevant to the 1990s. Society faces the same question as the individual. Would it be better economically for a 30-year-old to receive higher education than to remain a non-graduate? The answer almost certainly is in the affirmative. Graduates in their thirties might not provide society with as much economic benefit over their working lives as those in their early twenties but it will be a higher benefit and a positive one in relation to cost than if they remained non-graduates.

Personal and social

The economic benefits to be derived from increased participation are the strongest ones and undoubtedly they explain both the government's and employers' support for greater student numbers. But there are other less measurable benefits as well. The economic benefits to the individual have already been covered but higher education confers other, what might be termed psychic, benefits on students and graduates. These arise from personal development, increased self-confidence, self-knowledge and self-respect and the sense of achievement that higher education provides. The experience itself moreover widens horizons, expands cultural boundaries and creates long-lasting friendships. Higher education apart from its economic benefits is a good thing, it is argued, because it leads to a better life. Socially too wider participation in higher education provides benefits. Exposure to a broader section of society should remove prejudice, break down barriers, and create a greater sensitivity to differences in culture, belief and behaviour. It can be argued that a more cultured society is a more civilised society although the antidote to such a view is the behaviour of Germany under the Nazis. The civility of a society is determined by its behaviour rather than its culture and it is argued the relationship between behaviour and culture is not easily established.

The Robbins Report, as on so many other higher education issues, made this point over twenty-five years ago:

> education ministers intimately to ultimate ends, in developing man's capacity to understand, to contemplate and to create. And it is a characteristic of the aspirations of this age to feel that, where there is capacity to pursue such activities, then that capacity should be fostered. The good society desires equality of opportunity for its citizens to become not merely good producers but also good men and women (Committee on Higher Education 1963: 8).

It would be nice to finish at this Olympian level of discourse, to believe that wider participation is accepted as a good in its own right to which appropriate levels of finance will be allocated. The reality is somewhat different. Wider participation is supported at present largely because of the country's economic need for more highly qualified manpower. Yet even that need is not pressing enough for more resources to be promised to help achieve it. Wider participation, whether it results in static numbers or expansion, will require reduced unit costs through the 1990s. It is necessary to confront that reality and consider the option for reducing unit costs while providing wider participation.

Reducing costs

The first question is to continue with the policies of the 1980s of squeezing unit costs and seeing what happens. As was indicated earlier the major reductions in unit costs have taken place in the polytechnics. This has occurred despite the attempts by the Committee of Directors of Polytechnics (CDP) to hold the line. A regular feature of the mid-1980s was CDP members on the planning body (NAB) arguing for numbers to be kept in line with the increases in funding to maintain unit costs, protesting loudly when NAB decided to reduce unit costs by setting higher student number targets and then finding that their colleagues had reduced them even further by enrolling above even the increased targets offered by NAB. The reduction in unit costs in the polytechnics was partly officially driven but by far the greater influence was the institutions themselves enrolling students in numbers well in excess of those being financed by the planning body. In the universities the collective will of both the planning body (UGC) and the universities themselves to hold the line on unit costs was greater.

The polytechnics' action during the 1980s can be interpreted as a laudable commitment to access at all costs or a further example of the sector's immaturity, inability to act collectively and self-destructive instinct. There is no evidence that the sector's commitment to access or its inability to act collectively is likely to change in the 1990s. Moreover the incentive to take extra students at below average costs has been increased by the funding policies of the newly created Polytechnics and Colleges Funding Council (PCFC) and the government's decision on fees.

As a result polytechnics will face three factors which will give them an incentive to take increased students at reduced unit costs. The first is that the PCFC will allocate a proportion of its funds each year to institutions on the basis of competitive bids. Any economics A level student should be able to explain that the effect of many suppliers and one customer is a reduction in price. This holds true even if the PCFC does not allocate the funds to the cheapest bidder. Overall the process will lead to reduced unit costs by placing students in those institutions which can best afford to take them at low marginal cost or, at least in the early years, those that have miscalculated and put in too low a bid!

The second factor is the penalty system the PCFC is introducing where, if target student numbers are not reached, funds already allocated will be clawed back. Given the vagaries of the admissions system and the difficulty of hitting targets precisely institutions will be forced to ensure they do not under-recruit. The result will be that they will overshoot and take more students than they have been funded for.

This will be encouraged by the third factor which is the increased fee levels proposed for the 1990s. A greater proportion of the average cost of higher education (more than a half, depending on subject) will be covered in the fee and a lesser proportion in the grant from the funding body. The financial penalty for recruiting in excess of funding body targets will be reduced and many institutions may judge that the fee covers at least their marginal costs.

Similar mechanisms are being introduced in the university sector and will provide the greatest test yet of the vice-chancellors' collective determination to maintain unit costs. The key for both sectors will lie on the demand rather than the supply side. Suppose that the optimistic projections on demand are fulfilled so that into the 1990s there are both 18-year-olds and mature students anxious to enter higher education whom the government through the funding bodies will not fund at constant unit costs. The pressures on institutions, even the universities, to meet this buoyant demand and to accept them on a fees-only basis, or at a lower bidding price, will be too strong to resist. As indicated earlier, during a period of expansion it is easier to facilitate increases in productivity.

But what if the demand begins to fall off and can only be sustained through major marketing efforts? Institutions may be increasingly reluctant to bid to the funding body for students who may not materialise without great marketing efforts, when failure to recruit to target will result in penalties. In a declining and more difficult market a government committed to access should be looking to incentives for institutions and students rather than penalties.

In the end the desperate need for funding may drive institutions to take students at marginal cost. For even marginal funding is better than no funding. The extra funds may keep one more member of staff in post even if as a result staff–student ratios increase.

That is the great unknown about continuing reductions in unit cost. At what point does the system break? Or to put it more formally, at what point does the deterioration in quality become unacceptable? Like the car which is never serviced, there is no answer until it breaks down, by which time it is too late. The universities have been clear to date that *their* quality cannot be allowed to deteriorate further under the pressure of declining unit costs. Will they sustain that into the 1990s? The polytechnics with their validating bodies have cried wolf throughout the 1980s to the extent that future cries may be largely ignored. Moreover, Her Majesty's Inspectorate, who could blow the whistle, have not yet done so. The whistle has been taken out of the pocket. It has occasionally been put to the mouth but it has not yet been blown.

The government and the funding bodies seem ready to call the institutions' bluff, to squeeze unit costs and see what happens. It is a dangerous business and foolhardy particularly when more sensible alternatives to achieving wider access and reduced unit costs are available. It is now appropriate to examine some of these.

Switch to lower-cost institutions

Costs vary within and between sectors of higher education. Often these reflect different subject mixes and different functions. The universities for example are funded through their basic grant for research while the polytechnics are not. This is now in the process of change as a result of greater selectivity in research allocations. However, even allowing for this research element, and standardising for an equivalent humanities student, a DES study in 1985 showed that universities on average spent £500 per student more than polytechnics and colleges (DES 1985b). Given the trends since then the gap is likely to have widened.

It could be argued therefore that a simple way of funding access at reduced unit cost would be to switch students to the lower-cost institutions. In essence that is what happened during the 1980s, planned or unplanned. It is unlikely to be as simple in the 1990s. There was very little increase in physical capacity in polytechnics in the 1980s and the expansion took place by using up what spare capacity existed. Moreover the reduction in unit costs resulted in minimal expenditure on maintenance and repair. PCFC surveys have testified to the poor state of the fabric of buildings in the sector. The sharp reduction in unit costs may not have reduced unduly the quality of the learning experience or the educational outcome. It did impact on the quality of life and the physical environment within which students were educated.

As a result the polytechnics start the 1990s with severe deficiencies in the quality and quantity of their buildings. Their capacity to accommodate substantially increased student numbers is very limited. The universities find themselves in very much the opposite position. Their student numbers have not expanded during the 1980s. Moreover one effect of the increasing selectivity of research funding which is taking place is that some institutions will have available both physical and human resources which were previously devoted to research. The universities in the 1990s will have the greater capacity to reduce unit costs in the 1990s by expansion of their numbers than the polytechnics. And here is the paradox. The universities will have the means but have they the will? The polytechnics have the will but will they be given the means?

Switch to lower-cost subjects

It costs about twice as much a year to educate an engineering student compared to a humanities student. Engineering and science also tend to take up more space and require more equipment. An expansion concentrated on the lower-cost subjects (which include business studies) would seem to make sense. Indeed if accompanied by a *switch* from high-cost to low-cost courses it might be accomplished without any increase in expenditure overall.

What is being considered here is a switch in emphasis, not the wholesale closure of science and engineering. In simple terms a reduction of 10 per cent in the numbers studying science and engineering (say) over a five-year period would enable a 20 per cent increase in the numbers studying humanities and other subjects to be financed. This would produce a 10 per cent increase in overall numbers at no extra cost. Moreover while the demand for engineering and science is slack (and will remain so because of the problems in science and mathematics education in the schools) that for humanities, social studies, business studies and other low-cost areas is booming. In addition an increasing number of graduate jobs now do not specify a subject and the first destination unemployment figures are not significantly different overall. Switching funds to the subjects which are in greater demand and which are significantly cheaper would seem to be a natural policy for a government committed to the power of market forces and to reducing unit costs.

Switch to lower-cost modes

Part-time students are less costly to teach than their full-time colleagues. However, the reasons for this lower cost need to be explored. Tuition costs are cheaper in part because part-time students are costed as marginal additions to an infrastructure which already exists for full-time students. Where these infrastructure costs are allocated more fairly to part-time students the costs differential is narrowed, as the experience of Birkbeck College in recent years shows. Moreover as part-time students generally take longer than full-time students to achieve their qualification any differences in annual costs may disappear when the total costs of the period of the course are calculated. The two elements of cost where part-time students do look attractive to government are fees and living costs. Most part-time students pay their own fees or are otherwise privately financed. So a proportion of the overall cost of tuition does not fall on public expenditure. Even more important for government, part-time students do not receive maintenance grants. With a loans system hardly reducing the public expenditure burden for some years, this factor alone makes part-time students financially attractive for governments. Indeed part-time students have been the focus of the 1980s expansion. Between 1983 and 1988 their numbers grew by almost 20 per cent while full-time numbers grew by less than 8 per cent. A continuation of this growth ratio into the 1990s is one more way of financing wider participation without any significant increase in costs.

Changes in technology

Higher education is essentially a craft process whose technology has hardly changed throughout the century. Clearly audio-visual technology is now in greater evidence but for the most part it is used as a supplement to and not a substitute for lectures, seminars and practicals. Information technology is perhaps used more as a substitute for traditional approaches but still with a negligible impact on costs. As a result the increase in staff–student ratios which has occurred in the 1980s, particularly in the polytechnics, has come about through enrolling more students per class and/or staff taking more classes and/or students receiving less tuition. The process and methodology of tuition have hardly changed.

Dramatic changes in unit cost are unlikely to be achieved with the existing technology. For there is a limit to the extent to which the methods outlined in the previous paragraph can continue to be used without an unacceptable deterioration in quality. Indeed from an industrial perspective the improvements which were achieved in the 1980s while retaining the traditional labour-intensive craft approach are remarkable. The Open University has shown how technology substituting capital for labour through distance learning can have a dramatic impact on costs. With a large throughput of students a mixed media combination of distance-learning and face-to-face tuition makes both economic and educational sense.

However, such an approach is unlikely to be adopted as a means of increasing access without increasing costs. It would require academics to change their working habits in a way they have been singularly disinclined to do in the past. Worse, it would require them to relinquish part of their autonomy over curriculum design, content and delivery. Distance learning used as a supplement does not require this. The lecturer is still in control. Distance learning used as a substitute does. It is not accidental that the Open

University had to be created as a new institution, separate from existing universities. The alternative approach of a sufficient number of universities and polytechnics combining their courses and jointly offering a mixed media package of distance learning and face-to-face tuition was too radical to contemplate then and remains so now.

Without that commitment government is unlikely to provide the substantial investment funds required to establish a soundly-based distance-learning technology for conventional higher education. For the difficulty lies neither with the technology nor with the financing but with the conservatism and defensiveness of the higher education world. As long as 'individual institutions and academic autonomy rule OK', changes in technology will not be introduced and the circle of increasing access and reducing cost simultaneously will not be squared.

Public and private funding

The present government's approach to the problem of providing wider access while reducing public expenditure is clear. It is on the one hand to continue squeezing unit costs while on the other hand seeking to reduce the proportion of costs covered by public funds. To date the latter approach has mainly taken the form of rhetoric and kite-flying by education ministers. Even the controversial student loans scheme will not make an impact on public expenditure until the mid-1990s. By then, particularly if a Conservative government is returned, a full-scale voucher system may be in place with the provision for institutions to top it up through private fees. In such a system the government would set a level of fees which they would be prepared to cover through the mandatory award system and institutions would be free to set whatever fee level they liked. The mandatory award sum would in effect be the minimum fee for higher education tuition. To ensure that unit costs covered by public funds fell the government would simply set the mandatory award at a level which required institutions to secure private funding through fees.

While such a system would undoubtedly increase public expenditure it is difficult to see how it would increase access. No doubt some members of those groups who presently participate in higher education will be prepared, with no doubt a great deal of complaining, to contribute a proportion of the costs of their tuition and to take out a loan to cover their living costs. But the access objective is designed to widen participation to those groups presently under-represented in higher education and less attracted to it. No convincing argument has yet been put forward to explain why people who find higher education unattractive now will find it more attractive when the financial costs of participation are raised. Low financial barriers are not a sufficient factor in themselves to encourage participation but they are a necessary factor. The road to wider participation is not through raising the costs to those you are seeking to attract.

Conclusion

What emerges from this analysis is a relatively optimistic conclusion about the economic and financial impact of wider participation. It is clear that the government's own targets for a higher participation rate can be achieved without any increase in public expenditure in real terms. Indeed, an overall increase in numbers in higher education of 25 per cent could be achieved without a reduction in unit costs or an increase in higher education's share of GDP.

However, governments are likely to want to achieve increased participation and reductions in unit costs simultaneously. This difficult target can be met painfully by a switch from low demand/high cost subjects to high demand/low cost subjects and by increased support for part-time provision. In the longer term changes in the technology of instruction will need to be implemented. The least obviously successful approach is that presently being pursued, namely a switch to greater private finance. This reduces the public expenditure burden but it is difficult to see how it will widen access.

In truth, those who argue for greater private funding only use the potential financial difficulties of wider access as a pretext. For their argument is rooted in ideology not in the practical problems of managing higher education. Whatever the level of participation, they would wish to reduce the public expenditure burden. The reality is, as has been shown, that wider participation need not increase levels of public expenditure on higher education and, indeed, by switches in subject and mode, can reduce it. Resources are always constrained but the degree of constraint is a political not an economic factor.

Notes

1 The peculiar nature of British government means that statistics are rarely produced on a common basis. The figures in this paragraph came from the annual publication of government expenditure plans where the education chapter relates to the Department of Education and Science. This covers England and Wales and Scotland for the universities! The figures provided are of course an underestimate as they omit public sector higher education in Scotland and all higher education in Northern Ireland. However they provide the most consistent and most easily accessible series of data and for that reason are used.

2 The Age Participation Index measures the number of home initial entrants to full-time higher education as a percentage of the relevant age groups, ie half the total number of 18- and 19-year-olds in the population.

3 Achieving wider access

Peter Toyne

The ivory towers of academe have been taking a storm-force battering. Hurricane-force winds of change have swept through the sleepy groves of academe forcing the colleges, polytechnics and universities to wake up to the charge that they are too remote, too élitist, too eccentric and too expensive . . .

Cliché-ridden stereotyping it may be, but who would deny the essential truth behind such a report if it were to appear in the popular press? Rather more to the point, however, who in academe would be pleased to encourage such a report? The plain fact of the matter is that there has indeed been a remarkable amount of fundamental change in higher education in recent years but much of it, as yet, has gone largely unreported in the popular press and largely unnoticed by the vast majority of the population. Yet much of what has been going on has been aimed at widening the appeal of higher education to more people and, for that very reason alone, this message of change really should have been reaching the parts that other messages about higher education have never reached!

Few would deny the point that higher education in the United Kingdom has traditionally been targeted at a very small, perhaps even élite, proportion of the population. Despite the considerable expansion of the system in the 1960s and early 1970s in the wake of the Robbins Report, higher education has remained as a kind of 'add-on' to mainstream education for which relatively few people have opted. That is not to say that there is not a noble tradition of attempting to broaden its scope or appeal; far from it, in fact, as the long-established 'extra-mural' departments, and more recently the Open University and, in part, the polytechnics bear witness. But it is only in the last decade, and in the last few years in particular, that interest in trying to open up the system to more and more people of different kinds has gathered momentum. Various organisations have been at the forefront of this development and, in particular, the Association for Recurrent Education, the National Institute of Adult Continuing Education, the Unit for the Development of Adult Continuing Education and the Polytechnic Association for Continuing Education have all played a significant role in making sure that attention has been drawn to the need to widen access generally.

There have also been several other visionary initiatives aimed at loosening the constraints of the traditional system, foremost among which must be counted the Department of Education and Science's own feasibility study begun in 1978 in response to a call by the then Minister (Gordon Oakes) into Educational Credit Transfer, and the Council for National Academic Awards' decision in 1985 in response to the vision of its then Chief Officer, Edwin Kerr, to establish its CATS (Credit Accumulation and Transfer Scheme) service. The catalytic effect of these two initiatives in widening access to higher education cannot be overstated, as will be seen below.

In 1984, however, two major reports were produced that were to have an especially profound effect (NAB 1984a; UGC 1984a). The National Advisory Body for Public Sector Higher Education and the University Grants Committee established separate working groups (though with cross-membership of the respective chairmen) to carry out investigations into continuing education. Their terms of reference were broadly similar. The NAB group was asked:

> to consider and advise on the appropriate role and extent of continuing education provision . . . and the policies and practices by which this provision might be fostered (NAB 1984a: 12)

while the UGC group was to consider the development of continuing education of all kinds in the universities and the financial arrangements necessary for its development. When the reports appeared they gave a strong signal that the higher education system really did need to change, for both groups came to roughly the same conclusions, as Fleetwood-Walker and Toyne (1985) pointed out:

> perhaps the most striking thing about them is their extraordinary similarity. It might, after all, have been thought that the difference between the two sectors in terms of their courses, aspirations, historical backgrounds, ways of working, academic emphases and funding would have led to largely differing conclusions but, in fact, what emerges is a remarkable consistency between the two. And not only are the detailed conclusions and recommendations broadly similar, but both reports identify the need for a truly transbinary initiative if continuing education is to be developed actively in the years ahead. Above all, the common conclusion is that continuing education must be given a far greater priority not just in the universities, polytechnics, colleges and institutes of higher education but centrally within the educational establishment (DES, UGC, NAB and validating bodies) and in the world of industry, commerce and the professions. In order to achieve that higher priority, both working groups recognise that a fundamental change of attitude on the part of all concerned would be necessary and, in that sense, the reports are nothing less than revolutionary (Fleetwood-Walker and Toyne 1985: 104).

And revolutionary they have indeed been in influencing not just the thinking of their successor bodies (PCFC and UFC) but also the thinking and actions of the institutions they cover and, even more importantly, the thinking and action of the Department of Education and Science itself. Who, ten years ago, would have believed that by now we would be on the edge of revolutionising higher education with government policy overtly proclaiming the need to widen access and, thereby, to move (albeit gingerly) away from the 'add-on' view of higher education to a system designed to be more in line with a vision of 'access for all', or at least for more people than has hitherto been regarded as necessary?

This emerging 'vision' of wider access to the higher education system, or of a revolution in the way in which it is targeted and operated, perhaps owes less, however, to the efforts of great luminaries and organisations (or even national reports) based on educational principle, vision or altruism, than it does to sheer pragmatism. It is the declining birth rate, above all, that has caused the oft-cherished notions of traditional academe to be reviewed. Faced with declining numbers of 'traditional' students coming directly from school with good A level scores and faced with the distinct threat of institutional closure or merger as a potential result, many have begun to embrace the idea of widening access since it might just be a way of avoiding redundancies and of staving off the closure notices. Conversion can be as convincing as it can be dramatic when the threats are real and, of course, it can produce its own special breed of new zealots who readily join the march for Educational Salvation under the revolutionary banner proclaiming 'Wider Access is A Very Good Thing'!

But no matter, even if it may be as much a case of 'the right deed for the wrong reason' as anything else, access *is* now being widened and very rapidly too. First, great changes have been made in terms of 'getting in'. Access courses of many different kinds have been developed and continue to be developed for those who do not have the so-called 'standard' A level qualifications; some are subject specific, others offer a 'general' passport of entry into higher education, and there is now a transbinary system in place to give national recognition to such courses. 'Alternative' qualifications (ie alternative to the old benchmark of two A level passes) have been recognised and continue to be recognised as acceptable for entry and, much more importantly, it is becoming increasingly commonplace for institutions to offer potential students the possibility of assessing their prior experiential learning (APEL). In effect APEL means that *all* forms of *relevant* learning, whether certificated or not, can now be taken into account as a means of gaining access to the higher education system and this, in turn, means that it is no longer necessary for people without passes at A level to be regarded as, or to regard themselves as, 'special cases' at the margins of the system. The CNAA dropped the terms 'normal' and 'standard' as applied to entry qualifications two years ago, preferring to list many examples of the qualifications and experiences that might be deemed appropriate for entry to higher education (of which but one was A level passes!). Many institutions, more especially the polytechnics, have taken over this particular CNAA beacon with great zeal and have re-thought their whole admissions strategy as a result. Gone, or at least rapidly going, therefore, is one of the main cornerstones upon which access to higher education has been traditionally based. 'Getting in' is no longer as restrictive a practice as once it was.

Nor does the process stop with the reassessment of qualifications. Every bit as important has been the way in which far more flexibile systems of delivery have been developed. In this context, the Open University can take much of the credit for literally opening up higher education to people who would otherwise have been unable to benefit from it, and other institutions are now following suit. 'Distance learning' in various forms is at the heart of the Open University and it operates within its modular credit accumulation and transfer system. Both these features have been seen as enabling features whereby students can study at their own pace, in a more convenient way and with greater flexibility. It is scarcely surprising, therefore, that these are the very features that are now being actively developed in most of the rest of the higher education system.

Modular systems of course delivery are becoming increasingly commonplace and, as such, represent a major change in the way in which higher education can be perceived. Such systems are based on the assumption that learning programmes can be disaggregated into meaningful short 'blocks' (commonly of about a term's length) each of which will be examined or assessed at their completion with the student being accorded 'credit' for successful completion of the module. The student can then follow successive modules as and when required, all the time accumulating academic credits until such time as sufficient credits have been gained to acquire a named award, such as a diploma, certificate or degree. In a fully developed credit system, the student can determine which modules to take and when, thereby allowing far greater flexibility of opportunity to complete a particular course of study. Furthermore, academic credit can be awarded for learning experiences in a wide variety of locations and situations, including learning completed successfully at work or elsewhere. Hence, in-company training can be assessed for credit purposes and thereby allowed to count towards academic qualifications. In turn, this means that modules taken in higher education institutions can be fully integrated with learning experiences from other contexts – that is, it makes higher education all the more accessible and 'relevant' and all the less of an 'add-on' to be pursued in remote, unknown, ivory towers. In this way higher education is beginning to reach out to the very parts from which it has traditionally been regarded as somewhat irrelevant and that very act means that access is indeed being widened in an important way. Nor does the process stop with the system of modularisation and credit accumulation; the adoption of distance learning processes, whereby students do not necessarily have to attend the institution of higher education, simply means that educational 'modules' can be taken at home, at the place of work or at other 'centres' which may be (and invariably are) more convenient places in which to study than in the established headquarters.

In effect, as distance learning and credit systems and their many derivatives become more widespread, it is less a question of people 'getting in' to higher education than of higher education 'getting out' to people – and that, of course, means that access really is being widened dramatically.

Whether 'getting out' or 'getting in', there is no doubt that there is also a great deal of change taking place in terms of what is actually being offered to prospective and actual students. It is increasingly less a case of 'come and study what we have to offer' than of 'tell us what you need to study and we will try to provide it'. In short, we are witnessing the beginnings of another revolution – this time one with massive implications – of higher education changing perceptibly to being more of a customer-orientated business than a producer-orientated service. In its own way, this may well turn out to be the feature that brings about the greatest widening of access of all since it is self-evident that it is no use making all kinds of 'instrumental' changes (such as those to entry qualifications and methods of delivery) if the 'product' itself is not attractive, or seen to be attractive, to the new students for whom access is being widened.

Conversely, the more the product is perceived to be 'right', the more likely it is to be desired and the instrumental changes will then certainly enable more people to gain access to it. A more overt customer orientation must surely be an important concomitant to widening access and there is increasing evidence that this message is, at last, beginning to be understood in the system.

In turn, this means that widening access is, as much as anything else, about attitudinal change: it is not simply a matter of producer-led instrumental change, but about fundamental changes in attitudes both inside the institutions (the producers) and in the market place (the customer). Traditional values and attitudes die hard – perhaps especially in academe? – and it will take a great deal of visionary determination to do more than tinker instrumentally at the edges of the system (which is arguably all that has happened so far) if the potential new customers are not to be turned away, or more likely turned off by what they are offered. Wider acess will only be achieved on a large scale if attitudinal change is taken as seriously as instrumental change: it must be believed in if it is to be practised and preached successfully. All the evidence suggests that, in this respect at least, there is a long way yet to go. The 'conversion' of institutional staff and of future customers has only just begun.

So, despite its relatively recent development and despite the long road that lies ahead before it changes the face of higher education yet more dramatically, a great deal has already been achieved in widening access – even if it has not been proclaimed in the popular press. And what has been achieved to date *is* revolutionary since it means that there are already not just more but very *different* people, courses and methods of delivery in the system than hitherto.

Gone are the days when higher education was confined to the universities and traditionally to students going up to universities for three years from school (often public school in particular) to read for single honours degrees. The post-Robbins expansion not only created more institutions (more universities and, later, the creation of thirty polytechnics) it created more places for people with the 'ability to benefit'. The polytechnics and colleges, in particular, opened up part-time and continuing education programmes on quite a large scale, thereby widening access from various socio-economic groups hitherto largely unrepresented in the system. 'Mature' students now form a sizeable element of the total student population with the result that the popular image of what constitutes an undergraduate student is out-of-date. The courses themselves are much more diverse than they were even a few years ago and, again, it has to be said that most of the progress here has been made by the polytechnics and colleges as they have tried to respond to the needs of their 'new' clients. Thus, alongside the traditional single honours degree, there are now not only many forms of honours degree, but also many certificates, diplomas and other qualifications on offer. 'Product diversity' is now real, and the system is no longer homogeneous in this respect.

The method of delivery of these varied study programmes has also been widened. Modular systems have increasingly been introduced since they offer greater flexibility of access for part-time and mature students in particular; credit accumulation and transfer has become respectable – again in response to customer need; distance learning packages which enable students to study more conveniently at home or elsewhere than the institution itself have become more widespread; and some institutions do their teaching in local community centres or at the workplace as part of schemes developed in partnership with major employers (eg Oxford Polytechnic and W. H. Smith), thereby not only creating partnerships between academe and the world of employment and skill training, but also enabling students to put together educational packages geared to their needs. All this means there is now greater variety, greater choice, greater customer-responsiveness and greater outreach than in the past – and, that, surely, should be good news for all, even if we know that there is a long way yet to go before we achieve an 'access for all' approach to higher education.

But let us return to the customer since it is all too easy to get carried away into self-congratulatory euphoria about present achievements. It is at least arguable, as was suggested earlier, that much of what has been achieved recently has stemmed directly from institutions' determination to find new customers in order to survive. This is not in any way to belittle the more laudable, more principled efforts of those with a long-standing commitment to widening access for good educational and social reasons, but to recognise that the pace of change would not have been as great, or as transbinary in nature, had the demographic 'closure' threat not been present. In the event, the very pressures for institutional survival have tended to lead to the kind of 'instrumental' changes outlined above and many, if not all, of these changes have tended yet again to be 'producer-led'; that is, based on perceived assumptions about customers' needs rather than on direct evidence of those needs or aspirations. The literature, such as it is, is long on so-called 'barriers to access' as perceived by institutional leaders, government officials and influential decision-makers but relatively short on hard evidence of potential and actual students' perceptions of such barriers as may exist. Notable exceptions to this pattern are to be found in the reports of the two NAB working groups on continuing education (NAB 1984a) and widening opportunities (NAB 1988), since both these groups went out of their way to discuss the issues of barriers with such potential and actual customers. In recent years, too, some (more progressive) institutions have also made great efforts to assess perceived customer need, usually by means of questionnaire survey or direct interview. One of the more frequently stated barriers is 'inadequate information and guidance' about the opportunities that may be available. This, incidentally, is a rather generalised characteristic which masks a number of more specific points. It is not simply a question of people not knowing what is available, but also of their feeling that they may be unqualified for higher education since they simply have not got the message that there is now much greater flexibility about qualifications and experiences. The old idea that courses in higher education are three years full-time and for people who have at least two A levels dies hard: meanwhile, the idea that courses can be made to reflect individual need is only just beginning to gain wider currency. The basic perception and assumption seems to be that the system is remote and operates 'from the top down' and displays a 'take it or leave it' attitude. Prospectuses are rarely seen to be 'user-friendly' and institutions do appear still to have the 'ivory tower' image. More worrying perhaps is the assumption that 'higher education is not for me' or 'it's not relevant'!

If wider access is to be achieved then surely we should begin by examining in much more detail precisely what it is that puts people off higher education and why it is seen to be so irrelevant. Indeed the NAB report on continuing education concluded tersely that we have an 'insufficient market orientated approach' (NAB 1984a: 29). Such an approach would enable institutions to assess more directly what the customer's needs are in terms of course content, length, level, delivery and mode of attendance. After all, the same NAB report concluded, our 'courses [are] not suited to meet continuing education objectives in terms of mode of attendance, content, length, level and delivery' (ibid). That conclusion was reached on the evidence of student perceptions. Is there any wonder there is a long way to go in achieving wider access if that is the perception of the customer? Wider access will only follow if that which is accessed is perceived to be worthwhile and geared to the client's need.

This then is a fundamental barrier to be removed. After all, what is being said is that the *product* is not right. It needs to be radically redesigned in practically ever aspect. Fortunately, as we have touched on already, a number of changes are being introduced in response to these perceptions. Thus, for example, course content is increasingly being matched to client demand and more flexible delivery systems based on modular credit accumulation and transfer schemes are increasingly being adopted by institutions, regional consortia, open college federations and the like. Increasingly, too, much more attention is being paid to the way in which students can learn most effectively. The days of 'talk and chalk' and of 'spoonfeeding' through lectures are beginning to diminish as Her Majesty's Inspectorate and others encourage academic staff to begin the process of course design by putting the learning needs of students before the traditional teaching assumptions and fancies of the teachers. This again reinforces the need to be customer-orientated rather than producer-led and as such it is highly challenging and revolutionary. Many staff are only too pleased to face its challenge but tradition does die hard and it will no doubt be some time before the system as a whole makes this major change in approach. On the other hand, as ever, pragmatism will out and the ever-increasing pressure on student/staff ratios may well mean that this educationally laudable, customer-desirable change in emphasis will happen more rapidly than it might otherwise have done.

Closely related to the new emphasis on learning as opposed to teaching is the need to match another of the new customers' perceived needs: that of adequate guidance and counselling services. Among the barriers perceived by students in the NAB reports were those of 'lack of confidence . . . and general educational preparedness' and 'inadequate information and guidance' (ibid: 30). Part-time and mature students need help in adjusting to academic work but all too often institutions do not provide it. This may be simply because there is an assumption that the existing student counselling and educational guidance facilities will be adequate; more likely, since such services are not inexpensive to provide and resources are scarce (as they have been and continue to be) other priorities have a higher claim. Either way, if wider access is to be achieved, such facilities must be provided since they are perceived as necessary by the customer. It could be argued that not to provide them when it is well known that they are required is tantamount to abdicating responsibility; but, be that as it may, if they are not provided in response to customer need the customer will not be so prepared or able to buy the product on offer – and thus, inevitably, access will remain restricted.

In so many ways, higher education needs to learn to put its customers first – and that means responding to their needs rather than responding to 'institutional need'. In that sense, a well-conceived customer-care programme might not go amiss. And such a programme would need to address a whole series of other matters, many of which may well be regarded as 'sacred cows'. For instance, if wider access is to be achieved, the plant must be open for business at times when the customer can use it – not at times dictated by historic patterns of demand or well-enshrined working practices. Libraries, computer facilities, counselling services, educational guidance services, crêches, refectories and academic staff need to be available at the customer's convenience, not their own. Importantly, too, everyone in the institutional organisation needs to be reminded that they are there for one purpose only – to serve the customer – and that without the customers there are no jobs and no institution. A friendly, welcoming and helpful reception can make all the difference, as we all know from our own experience, yet one of the criticisms often levelled at higher education institutions is that they are unfriendly, unwelcoming and unhelpful – especially near the front door. What chance is there of widening access if clients are put off before they even get in?

Finally, from the customer's point of view, it is not infrequently claimed that it is the well-established traditional 'business' that gets pride of place in institutional priorities. The three- or four-year honours degree full-time students straight from school often occupy the heartland of institutional thinking, with the result that part-time mature students on different kinds of programmes feel somewhat marginalised. This, of course, is no new phenomenon; for years, those who taught in the extra-mural departments of universities found their efforts to be perceived by their senates and peers as somewhat 'add-on' if not actually irrelevant. Even today, when so much is changing for the better, many of those who are pursuing increased access with great vigour still find that, given half the chance, their colleagues would much prefer to have them concentrate on 'mainstream' activities. It is still *seen* as and *felt* to be peripheral and its funding tends to reflect that too (see below), and so long as it is perceived in this way it will remain at the margins of institutional portfolios. But 'it' in this context is 'increased access' – the very lifeline of institutional survival for the Doubting Thomases of pragmatism. Is it too much to hope that the message will soon get home and that work in the field of widening access will be put at the very heart of institutional missions and priorities? If it is too much to hope, then we had perhaps better forget about the dream of 'greater access for all' since, unless such a change does occur, access work will remain, at least for the foreseeable future, at the edges of acceptability with specious, vacuous rhetoric lavished upon it as its sole major resource.

Having said all of this about the marginal place of increasing access, it is not at all difficult to see why it is extremely hard to bring about significant institutional change. It is not only tradition and entrenched attitudes – though they must figure as major causes in many institutions – it is more to do with staffing and funding.

The NAB report on continuing education came to the worrying conclusion that higher education is characterised by 'negative staff attitudes and inappropriate staff skills' (ibid: 24) and by a 'lack of recognition and other incentives for staff who promote continuing education'. We have already touched on negative staff attitudes and seen that they both stem from and contribute to the continuing perception of wider access as a peripheral activity. But there is more to it than just that. Behind the veneer of peripheralism there lies perhaps something more fundamental and it has to do not so much with people's deep-seated beliefs about the nature of higher education, as with their worries about having to make radical changes to the way in which they operate. Self-evidently the skills that are needed for working with part-time and mature students are very different from those with which most staff are familiar for dealing with 'traditional' 18-year-old students from school. This alone poses a potential threat to the status quo: it is yet another pressure on an already pressurised but well-motivated staff. Similarly, the introduction of modular credit transfer systems is another perceived threat: at the very least it invariably means re-casting all the well-rehearsed material in a radically different form and there are many who still regard it as a totally suspect and unwelcome phenomenon likely to lead to a serious decline in 'standards'. Closely allied to that is the even greater threat for some of the change from an emphasis on teaching to an emphasis on learning; for those who pride themselves on good lecturing and those who have been brought up in a system where straightforward 'talk and chalk' is the established way of teaching, the prospect of such a change is daunting.

Indeed, this may well be one of the reasons why so much concern was expressed by the relevant trade unions when the employers in the polytechnics and colleges sector of higher education tried to bring about a change in the lecturers' contract of employment. At the heart of that dispute was the issue of 'class contact hours' – a concept seen by the employers as outmoded (the more so if radical change in the system is to be implemented) and by the unions and employees as essential for their 'protection'. The worry was expressed that the employers, wishing to meet the challenges of widening access, wanted to have the academic staff available for more time and more flexibility and there was no protection in the so-called 'professional contracts' against an unscrupulous employer. That said, however, no one denied the fact that massive change in this respect was required. It is easy to see why it is difficult to effect such a scale of change when deeply-cherished conditions of service are threatened. Indeed, it appears that change on this scale is seen much more as a threat than as a potential opportunity.

This situation is exacerbated, as the NAB Continuing Education Group pointed out, by the fact that there have been few rewards and incentives for those who *have* made massive changes and taken up the cause of widening access. Indeed, such colleagues are often perceived as working all the hours God sends, well after others have gone home and their research and scholarly activity seem to suffer as a result. Is it any wonder, therefore, that great caution is expressed about changing the conditions of employment to enable the 'new' approach that stems from widening access to take place? The incentives need to be more tangible than those stemming merely from 'job satisfaction' – important as that alone must be. Promotion prospects, for example, need to be increased for those involved in widening access; as it is, especially in the university sector, promotion tends to relate primarily to research prowess and there is little prospect of active promotion for those who, as we have said before, are perceived as working 'at the periphery', and not pursuing much research *per se*. Promotion is, however, about cash as well as status and it is both these commodities that need to be made more fully available for work in the field of widening access if such work is to be seen as central to the functioning of the system.

All of these changes, whether perceived as opportunities or threats, point to the self-evident need for a sizeable programme of staff training and development to underpin and nurture them. After all, as we have seen, scarcely any of the established traditional assumptions about how the higher education system is managed and operated are left untouched. Change on this scale, and in so short a period, can only be effected if it is to be believed in and 'owned' by those who have to operate it; furthermore, it requires (and is predicated upon) new ways of dealing with the new clients and their needs. That means that staff development simply has to be higher on the institutional agenda. But the plain truth of the matter is that it rarely is. Staff development is itself all too often seen by institutional managers as a kind of luxury, that can be cut at a time of tight resourcing (ie it is perceived perhaps as an 'add-on' to be sacrificed, albeit reluctantly, when the financial going gets tough). Patently, successful businesses in the 'real' world have learned the folly of such an approach and have actually invested even more heavily in staff training and development precisely in order to guarantee that change is 'owned', taken to heart, and delivered to the full. Would that higher education institutions might follow their lead; a sign outside the university, polytechnic or college proclaiming, as our better stores do, that they are closed for staff training, for example, every Monday from eight-thirty to nine-thirty would at least be a step in the right direction (assuming the staff were actually there and going through a sensible, agreed and targeted training programme). In this respect there are cogent lessons to be learned from the systematic introduction of 'total quality management' in higher education and it is encouraging to see this being taken up by at least the leaders in the field of widening access. They have realised that widening access will be achieved the more readily and speedily if it is underpinned by a well-considered, institution-wide programme of staff development related to quality assurance. But then, that costs money!

Research is another perceived problem since the change in emphasis on learning and the changes in conditions of work implied in the 'new order' point to what is seen by many as yet another attack on research – for long a cornerstone, even a *sine qua non*, of a serious higher education system. As research funding gets more difficult, and as various exercises attempt to assess the extent to which research can and should be funded in the future, the very bastion of higher education may appear, to some, to be not just under threat but also beginning to crumble. Many staff joined higher education precisely because it offered the opportunity to pursue research. Teaching, for many, was secondary. Either way, that old order is now changing and again therefore there are some understandable fears, and thus opposition, to much of what is now being enacted.

And so we come, inevitably, to funding; there can surely be little doubt that, despite everything that has been said about the need for changes in attitude, the need to be more customer-orientated and the need to press ahead with the various 'instrumental' changes related to getting in and getting out, one of the main barriers to access must relate to funding. Both the UGC and the NAB recognised the need to introduce better and more flexible funding arrangements as a concomitant of encouraging continuing education and it is at least encouraging to see that some progress, albeit limited, has been made in this area.

First, the whole question of student financing has been under active review and there have been many revolutionary proposals to change the now somewhat historic system. Much advice has been proffered as to how a better student financing system could be developed. The NAB Continuing Education Group, for instance, made three particularly important recommendations; first, that the Department of Education and Science should 'agree to grants being made available for any part of a designated course studied full time' (this was in order to allow credit-transfer students to benefit from a grant); second, that the DES should 'undertake as a matter of urgency a review of the financial support arrangements for mature students . . . with a view to providing a larger measure of support and adjusting arrangements which cause particular hardship'; and third, that the DES should 'undertake a comprehensive review of the purpose and effects (both financial and educational) of fees in higher education, and that in the meantime the fees for part-time students across all sectors should be set at a lower level' (ibid: 7–8). Clearly these last two recommendations were taken up seriously, in principle, and the DES has indeed conducted the very kind of review envisaged. Whether the results of that review are what the NAB Continuing Education Group had in mind is another question, for what is now being introduced is a shift in funding *to* fees; the aim of which is to put purchasing power in the hands of the customer and to encourage institutions to take more students in order to secure higher levels of funding. Certainly it can be argued that this, of itself, could well be a major incentive for institutions to become more customer-orientated as required. The simple logic is that the customer will be able to shop around and purchase the right product at the right price and the effect of that would be that institutions would simply have to respond to customer demand; the net effect of this, in theory, should be that wider access would indeed be achieved. We shall see, only time will tell; but it is certainly a bold scheme that should ultimately reduce significantly the role of the two funding councils (UFC and

PCFC) as so-called 'surrogate customers' – a concept that was never fully understood.

Coupled with this change in funding are the various proposals to introduce student loans and/or vouchers to replace the established grant system for maintenance. Opinion on this is clearly divided; those who favour the notion of loans argue that it will actually help more people secure access to higher education, and those who disapprove of it argue the exact opposite. Whatever else may be said, it is clear enough that if access *is* to be widened, a system of student support that is *supportive* rather than punitive is required, otherwise the already existing financial barriers will only get higher. This is a particularly important matter when it comes to people who have not traditionally seen higher education as offering any potential interest for them or who have been put off already by lack of finance. In this respect, the promotion of equal opportunities in access to higher education could be significantly disadvantaged by the introduction of a system that requires people to take out loans and thereby become saddled with debt.

A greater difficulty in widening access may, however, yet turn out to relate to the attitudes of employers and of society in general. Both the NAB and the UGC studies on continuing education pointed to what they saw to be important barriers caused by employers. Commenting on the reports' conclusions Fleetwood-Walker and Toyne concluded:

> Four problems are laid firmly at the feet of the employers: first, it is said that they display a 'reluctance or inability to pay high costs for retraining or updating' their workforce, and it is alleged that they are similarly reluctant or unable 'to provide staff with leave of absence or paid leave for approved educational purposes'; there then follows what is in reality the most worrying charge, that they have 'inadequate longer term awareness of their own needs for updating and retraining'. That statement has to be read several times over before the jargon begins to crack and its true message appears – and when it does it is nothing short of alarming, for it really means that employers have no idea what they want or need. In the circumstances the academics might perhaps be forgiven their sins of academic omission and commission in attempting to provide anything at all. The last 'employer' barrier is seen to be 'inadequate longer term support for employees and educational institutions' and, again, when stripped of its committee-speak, the conclusion is every bit as alarming as the previous observation. Taken together, these four barriers attributable to the employers are particularly disturbing, since collectively they strike at the very heart of the problem and simply tell us that unless something is done very soon to rectify the situation all the best efforts of the providers to put their house in order will be to little real avail, since the employers will neither know what they want nor have the means of delivering the students. So much for *fostering* continuing

> education. Of course, many employers have rushed in to deny the charges when they are writ large in black and white, but neither the UGC nor the NAB group dreamed them up – they both went to considerable lengths to consult widely with employers and to identify their perceived needs and difficulties and the four observations merely stem from those consultations (Fleetwood-Walker and Toyne 1985: 109–110).

It is encouraging to note the way in which progress appears to have been made on all four of these observations, but there is still a long way to go. Certainly, however, employers have begun to address the ways in which updating, retraining and development of employees can be effected and there are many encouraging examples of closer cooperation between employers and academe in attempting to provide relevant 'packages' for employees. But the constant pressure in business to be cost-effective and to reduce employee costs does not exactly facilitate the widespread acceptance of providing training leave on a regular basis. The situation is arguably exacerbated by other traditional attitudes of society as a whole to the way in which working lives and home lives are separated and structured. Greater flexibility, for example in work and job-sharing both at work and at home would potentially enable more people to take up courses in higher education because they would have more time at their disposal. Such radical developments may be a long way off and difficult to achieve but there can be little doubt that wider access would be the more achievable if *some* steps in these directions were to be taken earlier rather than later.

At the institutional level also, as opposed to the 'customer' level, there are many serious funding issues to be tackled. In the main, it can be said that the funding of part-time work has been problematic for long enough. In the polytechnics and colleges sector (where most of this kind of work has taken place) institutions have until recently been funded on a 'full-time equivalent' basis in which part-time students have been counted for funding purposes as either 0.4 or 0.2 of a full-time student (respectively according to whether they were part-time day and evening, or evening only students). This has been a major bone of contention for long enough, since most of those with experience of dealing with part-time students know full well that these weightings do not in any way reflect the amount of work involved. Indeed, some would even claim that part-time students represent no different a quantum from full-time students. The NAB Continuing Education Group, for its part, came to the conclusion that the full-time equivalent weightings should be revised upwards but subsequent attempts to quantify by how much they should be revised produced no real agreement and, thus, very little change. However, the new PCFC has now gone in where previous angels feared to tread, and has produced a system for bidding for students which has completely scrapped the notion of full-time equivalent weightings. This should be good news – and it is in principle – but since the total amount of money to be allocated is not increased overall it simply means that there will be an 'internal' reallocation towards part-time at the expense of full-time student funding. Furthermore, the PCFC decision to go in for what it calls 'marginal funds' (whereby for 1990–91 institutions must bid at marginal prices for five per cent of the available funds) means that while there is an incentive for institutions to take on more students (thereby potentially widening access via an increase in places) the unit of resource for funding the extra students will be lowered. In other words, the institutional funding system is designed to achieve a widening of access at lower cost.

Whether this will be possible clearly remains to be seen, but there must be serious doubts about how far it will really deliver increased access. Certainly the Committee of Directors of Polytechnics, who have encouraged the widening of access and have done so from a consistently lower resource base than their counterparts in the universities, have now begun to make it clear that it is only possible to go so far in this regard, and that they have now got about as far as they can without a more realistic funding base.

It has often been argued – and indeed was by the NAB – that if institutions really believed in widening access they would make internal resource allocations that offered sufficient 'carrots' for taking part-time students. That really means that they would ignore the system-wide institutional funding mechanism of counting part-timers as 0.4 or 0.2 and offer higher levels of resource support for that work. Again, however, to do so is merely to rob Peter to pay Paul, ie to fund full-time work at less than its allocated rate. Some institutions have indeed adopted such policies with apparent success but most have shied away from them because of the self-evident potential for mayhem they might create. On the other hand, that *is* a way of rewarding these activities and for that reason alone it must be taken seriously as a possible mechanism. In practice, the new funding methodology (of bids at marginal prices not related to full-time equivalent weightings) does at least provide the opportunity to kindle the bonfire for this particular sacred cow since the methodology is based on actual prices and costs. Again, only time will tell, but there is at least a real chance now of establishing a more realistic resource allocation mechanism to encourage the widening of access, even if the overall funding available remains inadequate.

Naturally, there is great debate about whether funding overall is adequate or inadequate for higher education as it faces monumental changes in the nature and scale of its business. The basic governmental philosophy is essentially that the customers will buy the product, provided the product is right, and therefore the system need not be as dependent on public funds as it has traditionally been. If this analysis is correct, then the key to the survival of the system does not lie in trying to cling to the cherished practices of the past, but of responding further to the market place by establishing new courses, new programmes of study and new methods of delivery to new kinds of students or customers.

As we have seen, some great strides have already been taken along this particular road, but it has to be said that they will have to be regarded as but the first tentative footsteps along a very long and tortuous road ahead. Before the next steps are taken, a very careful and close assessment needs to be made of the needs of the customers and that means that the 'market-orientated approach' recommended by NAB really will have to be taken on board with great vigour. Market research will undoubtedly need to be one plank of the development, but so will marketing generally. Again, there have been some interesting examples in recent years of institutions redesigning their 'shop windows' (usually their prospectuses) and trying to sell their wares to the new customers with all the razzmatazz of a serious marketing campaign.

And that is nothing less than an anathema to many in higher education who claim that market-orientation merely treats education as no more than a can of beans: be that as it may, the point is that beans are sought after; arguably, at least, if higher education were sought after neither the nation nor the institutions themselves would be in the state they are. A mass higher education system in which higher education is not regarded as a boring 'add-on' may be something of a dream but it is now potentially achievable if the providers begin to take the customer seriously, sell their wares effectively, and make the system more responsive to demand. That way, there is a real hope that wider access will indeed be achieved; and then, who knows, higher education may make the positive headlines in the popular press it needs to make if it is to take its place as a much sought-after, popular commodity.

4 A levels and the future

Gordon Higginson

Throughout its life the A level has been, and remains, the dominant interface between school and higher education, and the future of A levels must be examined in the light of the widespread aim to increase access to higher education. This aim was discussed at length by the then Secretary of State for Education and Science, Mr Kenneth Baker, in an address at Lancaster University in January 1989, 'Higher Education – 25 Years On' (Baker 1989a). Mr Baker speculated on the issues associated with an increase in the participation rate in higher education from its present value of about 15 per cent to 30 per cent. The Council for Industry and Higher Education see expansion as imperative:

> The UK's prosperity, vitality and international standing depend on its becoming a more highly educated nation which recognises skilled brainpower and applied ingenuity as its distinctive assets. Government, higher education and industry need to become partners in developing a different kind of higher education system to provide for larger numbers, recruit them from a much wider segment of the population, and offer them a diversity of learning methods and opportunities, often work-related, at different stages of their lives.
>
> We need more educated people. The officially projected four per cent increase in student numbers by the year 2000 is at odds with the UK's ambitions for renewal and growth. Company total workforces may shrink as industry becomes more 'brainpower-intensive', but many more educated, adaptable and versatile people will be needed at lower levels. (Between 1978 and 1985 engineering company workforces fell by a third while graduate employment rose by a half.) Demand for graduates is rising with a more down-to-earth view of their roles and as the retail trade, service, and leisure industries, the developing professions and (particularly) the financial sector compete with traditional graduate employers. In an information economy, company success is a function of ability to attract, train and deploy highly educated talent constructively (Council for Industry and Higher Education 1987: 1).

The view is widely shared that the United Kingdom must educate more of its men and women for longer if it is to hold its place in the forefront of developed nations. There are two aspects to this: first, increasing participation in all sectors of higher education; second, and just as important, recognition that a degree or diploma does not mark the *end* of education, nor even the beginning of the end, but the end of the beginning of a lifetime of continuing education. The first we shall examine at some length.

Growth has been a characteristic of higher education during major parts of this century; the approximate numbers in the university and non-university sectors have been as follows (thousands):

	1900	1939	1963	1988
University sector	20	50	120	300
non-University sector	5	20	100	300

The participation rate in higher education among eighteen-year-olds is at present about 15 per cent. Before we look for ways of increasing that to 30 per cent or more, let us see who the 15 per cent are, and how they get into higher education, what they want to study, and what they do afterwards.

Table 1 shows the social classes of home students admitted by universities over the years 1984 to 1988. Corresponding figures are not available for polytechnics and colleges. Table 2 shows the division of admissions by sex

Table 1 Social class of accepted home university candidates, per cent

	1984	1985	1986	1987	1988
I and II Professional and Intermediate occupations	70.3	69.1	68.6	68.3	69.1
III N Skilled non-manual	10.1	10.4	10.7	11.1	11.0
III M Skilled manual	12.4	12.7	12.5	12.9	12.5
IV Partly skilled	6.2	6.6	6.9	6.6	6.3
V Unskilled	1.1	1.2	1.2	1.1	1.1

Source: UCCA Statistical Supplements (various)

Table 2 Sex of accepted home university candidates

	1984	1985	1986	1987	1988
Men %	57.7	57.5	57.2	56.0	56.5
Women %	42.3	42.5	42.8	44.0	43.5
Total	71,768	76,181	76,896	78,344	80,496

Source: UCCA Reports (various)

Table 3 Home entry qualifications, per cent

	UCCA		PCAS	
	1986	1988	1986 (sample)	1988
A levels	82.4	80.9	72.2	69.5
Scottish	10.1	10.1	0.5	0.5
BTEC & SCOTVEC	3.6	4.2	9.3	10.5
UK degree	0.6	0.7	17.4	19.2
Other UK	2.5	2.9		
Overseas or not known	0.9	1.2	0.6	0.3

Source: UCCA Statistical Supplements and PCAS Annual Reports (various)

over the same period. In 1986 the home admissions to the polytechnics of England and Wales were 58.5 per cent men and 41.5 per cent women.

The entry qualifications of home students to United Kingdom universities (through UCCA) and to the polytechnics of England and Wales (through PCAS) are shown in Table 3. The dominance of A levels is plain to see, especially in universities, where A levels in England, Wales and Northern Ireland and the equivalent in Scotland (Highers and Certificate of Sixth Year Studies) account for more than 90 per cent of the entry.

Table 4 shows the age distribution of the entry to universities of the United Kingdom and (by sample) to the polytechnics of England and Wales. 80 per cent of the polytechnic entry and nearly 90 per cent of the university entry are under twenty-one. A clear picture emerges of the typical British freshman: middle class, eighteen or nineteen years old, with A levels, and slightly more likely to be male than female.

Table 4 Ages of accepted home candidates, per cent

	UCCA		PCAS	
	1986	1988	1986	1988
Over 40	0.7	1.0	1.2	1.6
30–40	2.1	2.4	3.8	4.6
25–30	2.4	2.8	4.3	5.3
21–25	5.0	5.3	10.7	12.0
20–21	4.5	4.4	9.5	9.7
19–20	21.7	20.1	28.1	28.2
18–19	57.4	58.0	41.7	38.1
under 18	6.2	6.1	0.7	0.5

Source: UCCA Statistical Supplements and PCAS Annual Reports (various)

Turning now to what they want to study, we should note first that there is a bewildering range of degree and diploma courses available in universities, polytechnics and colleges. They include single honours courses in subjects studied at school: English, history, physics, chemistry and so on; joint and mixed courses in school subjects: French and German, mathematics and physics for example; subjects not generally studied in school: the various branches of engineering, accountancy, law and many others; creative arts; all manner of combinations of arts, sciences and social sciences. Table 5 shows the demand by home students for the twenty most popular university subjects. It is a big table but rewards study; it shows the trends in popularity over the years 1984 to 1988, and the proportion of applicants who were accepted. The demand for accountancy rose by 50 per cent but under a third were accepted throughout the period; the figures for management studies are similar. Psychology applications rose monotonically throughout the period (and are up by a further 30 per cent for 1989). The engineering disciplines are struggling, but still accepting only about two-thirds of the applicants. The physical sciences and mathematics are currently accepting more than 80 per cent of those who apply, but it is well worth noting that the average A level score of those accepted to read mathematics (85 per cent of applicants) is slightly higher than that of those accepted to read management studies (28 per cent of applications).

Choosing a course at a university or polytechnic is a hazardous and sometimes complicated business for a school-leaver or a mature candidate, but applicants are enormously helped by UCCA (The Universities Central Council on Admissions) which was set up in 1961, and by PCAS (The Polytechnics Central Admissions System) which came into operation with admissions to courses starting in autumn 1986. Many candidates apply

Table 5 Home demand in twenty most popular university subjects

	1984		1985		1986		1987		1988		1988–1984 %
	App	% acc	App	% acc	App	% acc	App	% acc	App	%acc	
1 Law	8,501	37.3	8,834	38.6	9,061	37.8	8,695	38.3	9,515	35.9	+11.9
2 Medicine	8,763	42.8	8,442	46.3	8,249	46.6	7,955	47.8	7,691	49.7	−12.2
3 Management Studies	4,442	25.1	5,532	28.5	5,477	28.0	6,040	28.6	6,379	27.7	+43.6
4 English	6,465	42.7	6,340	44.4	5,840	46.5	5,371	50.0	5,831	48.1	− 9.8
5 Economics	4,414	48.0	4,207	49.3	4,324	50.1	4,733	47.8	5,326	41.7	+20.7
6 Psychology	3,627	39.8	3,872	39.6	4,010	41.5	4,610	39.2	4,963	36.8	+36.8
7 History	5,003	58.0	4,677	63.9	4,575	64.8	4,734	63.8	4,961	57.9	− 0.8
8 Geography	4,683	43.1	4,343	48.4	4,054	54.3	4,060	52.8	4,240	52.8	− 9.5
9 Computer Studies	3,726	34.6	3,667	41.2	3,237	48.0	3,486	53.1	3,854	53.7	+ 3.4
10 Mathematics	4,115	67.4	3,677	74.0	3,100	79.3	3,238	81.8	3,420	84.7	−16.9
11 Chemistry	3,040	80.7	2,804	85.4	2,700	86.8	2,753	90.2	3,032	86.1	− 0.3
12 Physics	3,260	78.7	3,016	84.4	2,718	86.3	2,628	90.0	2,989	86.0	− 8.3
13 Biology	3,461	50.9	3,305	55.6	2,882	61.3	2,883	65.5	2,840	68.0	−17.9
14 Accountancy	1,717	26.3	2,057	30.2	2,541	31.3	2,658	30.2	2,617	30.8	+52.4
15 Mechanical Engineering	2,886	51.9	2,650	60.4	2,716	63.6	2,493	66.9	2,500	69.6	−13.4
16 Pharmacy	2,832	22.0	2,987	23.2	2,640	25.8	2,679	26.3	2,333	30.0	−17.4
17 Electronic Engineering	2,666	50.8	3,155	53.5	2,687	60.2	2,492	64.4	2,221	70.8	−16.7
18 Sociology	1,489	53.2	1,527	48.1	1,609	47.7	2,019	52.0	1,737	45.0	+16.7
19 Civil Engineering	2,378	52.8	2,295	54.6	2,065	62.8	1,766	66.3	1,723	68.1	−27.5
20 General Engineering	2,251	48.8	2,069	51.4	1,998	53.6	1,964	56.7	1,415	66.1	−37.1
All undergraduate courses	156,488	45.9	157,085	48.5	152,588	50.4	152,520	51.4	156,981	51.3	+ 0.3

Key
App = Number of applicants
% acc = % accepted

Source: UCCA Reports (various)

through both organisations, and Figure 1 is a flow chart showing very clearly the applications and success rates; the numbers include overseas candidates. It should be noted that the PCAS figures relate only to the polytechnics and a few colleges in England and Wales; many more people enter full-time study in colleges of higher education. In answer to a Parliamentary Question on 1 February 1989, the Department of Education and Science gave figures for the 1988 entry to higher education as follows: universities 87,000; polytechnics and colleges 124,000.

Finally in this section we look briefly at what all these people do after graduating. About 127,000 men and women are expected to graduate with first degrees in 1990. We can see from trends in recent years what they are likely to do. Over the last few years 50–55 per cent of (university) graduates

Figure 1 Flow chart: Candidates applying through UCCA and PCAS, October 1988

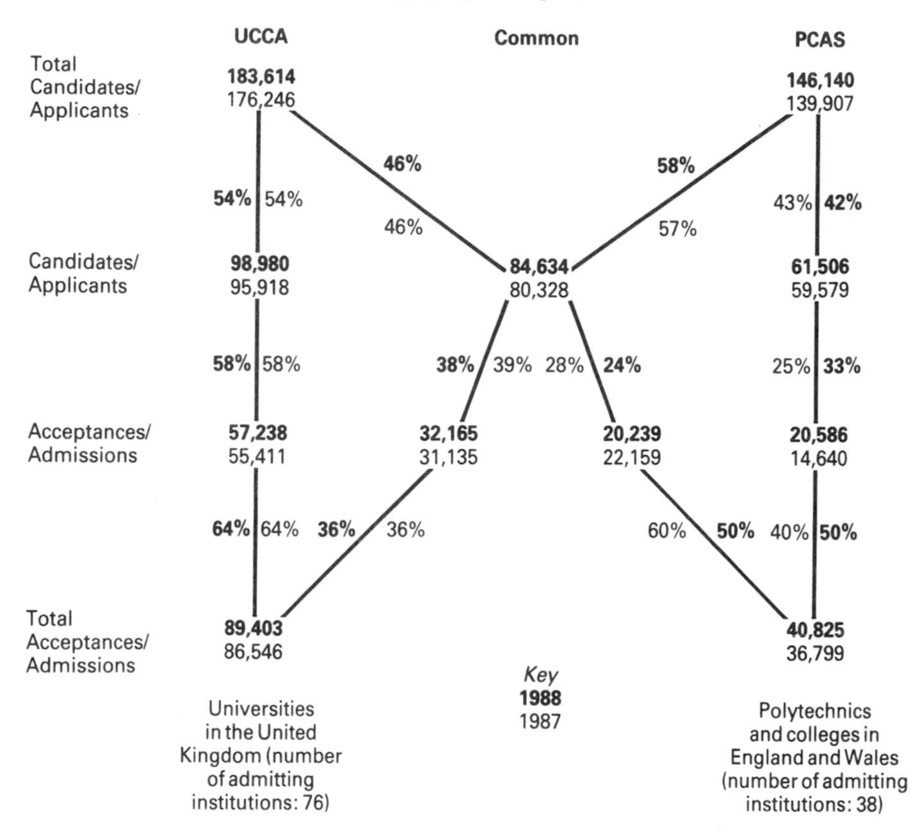

Source: UCCA Statistical Supplement to the Twenty-sixth Report 1987–8 (UCCA 1989)

have gone straight into permanent employment. The remainder have gone into further study, research, short-term employment, and quite a few describe themselves as 'not available for employment'; some of those spend six months or a year in travel and casual employment before settling down to a career.

The roughly 50 per cent going into permanent employment are made up largely of those entering the industrial sector, 15–20 per cent of the total, shown in Figure 2, and those going into commerce and accountancy, 20 per cent and rising as shown in Figure 3. Of those going into further study the proportion taking courses in teacher training is diminishing as Figure 4 shows. That trend is worrying enough, but the subject variation within the diminishing total is also a cause for anxiety; the proportions wishing to train to teach mathematics and physics are falling seriously.

Figure 2 University graduates into industry, per cent (United Kingdom)

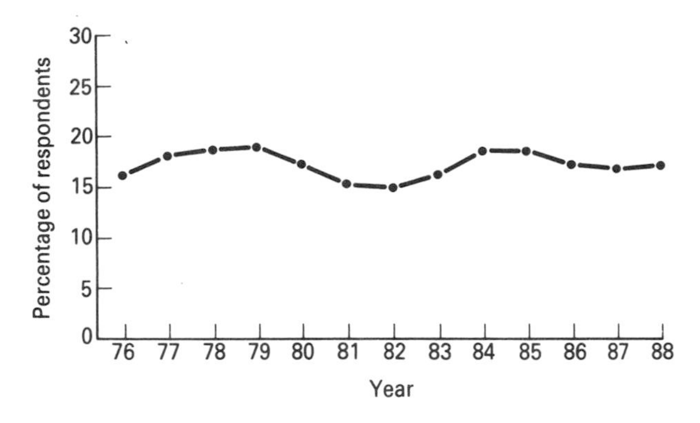

Source: Derived from UGC University Statistics Volume Two – *First Destinations of University Graduates* (various)

Figure 3 University graduates into accounting and commerce, per cent (United Kingdom)

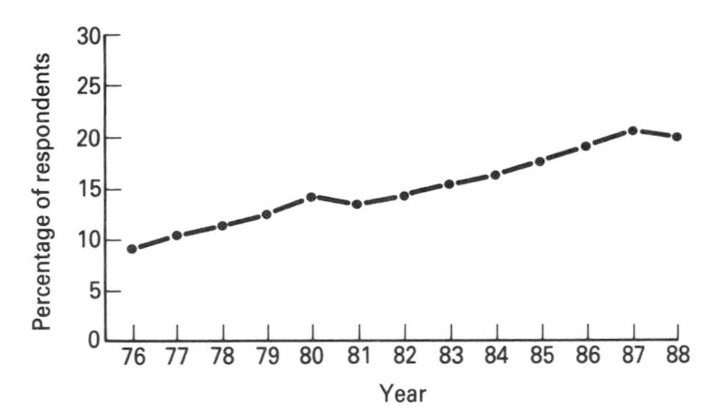

Source: Derived from UGC University Statistics Volume Two – *First Destinations of University Graduates* (various)

Increasing access

Now that we have discovered the shape of the 15 per cent who enter higher education before the age of twenty-one, we next look at the size of the pool of young people qualified to embark on degree courses. If we interpret 'qualified' in the conventional sense – two A level passes – the outlook is not good; in

Figure 4 University graduates into teacher training, per cent (United Kingdom)

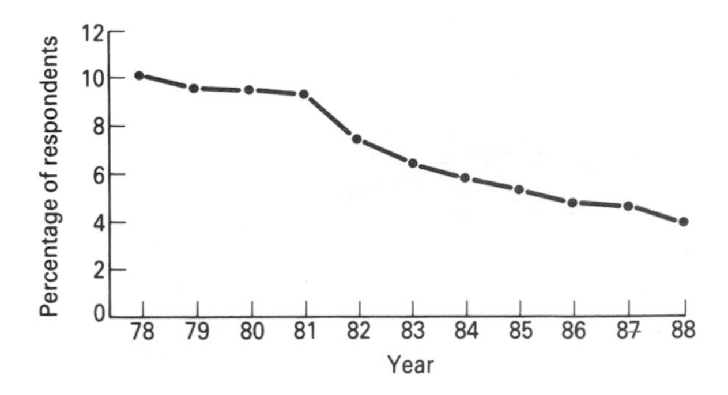

Source: Derived from UGC University Statistics Volume Two – *First Destinations of University Graduates* (various)

Figure 5 Live births, 1960–80, United Kingdom (thousands)

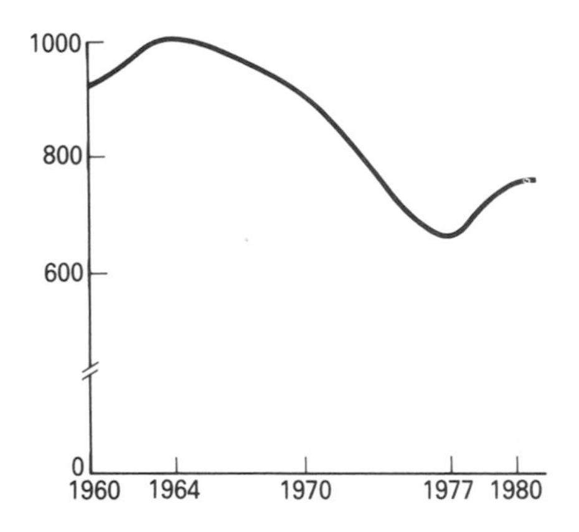

Source: Derived from Royal Society (1983)

1986 only 14 per cent of the age cohort obtained two or more A level passes. What are the chances of even maintaining the present numbers in higher education as the 18-year-old population falls? To do that alone will require an increase in the participation rate to 20 per cent in the mid-nineties. Hopes on that score are high; applications are increasing and the demography is not as adverse to higher education as it appears at first sight. The reduction in the number of births in the United Kingdom between 1964 and 1977 was 35 per cent and the figures are well known; the most spectacular act of self-inflicted social engineering is shown in graphical form in Figure 5. (Since 1980 the

Figure 6 Supply of 15 to 19-year-olds 1984–2000

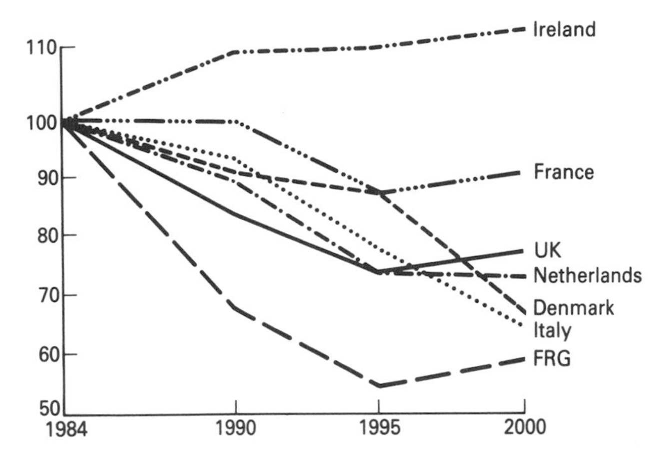

Source: Derived from Statistical Office of the European Communities (1988) and UNESCO (1988)

Figure 7 Live births by social class, 1960–80, United Kingdom (thousands)

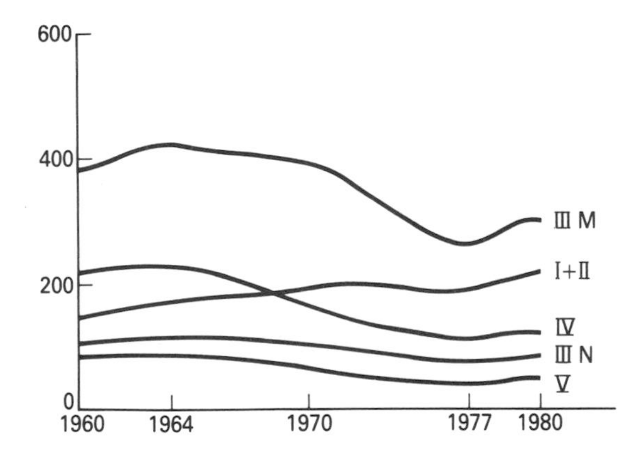

Source: Derived from Royal Society (1983)

number of live births has remained roughly constant at 720–750 thousand per year.) The United Kingdom is not unusual in this; Figure 6 shows in a slightly different form similar trends in several other European countries.

A detailed examination of the births in terms of social class is described in a working paper of the Royal Society published in 1983 and entitled *Demographic*

Figure 8 Eighteen-year-old population by social class, 1978–98, United Kingdom (thousands)

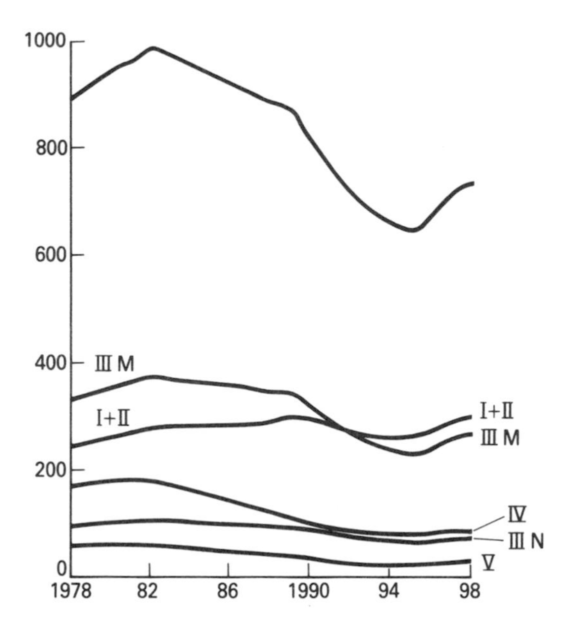

Source: Derived from Royal Society (1983)

Trends in Future University Candidates. The paper first divides the births into the social classes I to V described in Table 1; they are plotted in Figure 7, and show that the number of births in I and II was increasing during most of the time that the overall fall was occurring. These figures for births can be accepted with some confidence, although they do embody a number of (reasonable) assumptions. Rather more speculative are the estimates of future numbers of 18-year-olds in each social class.

> This cannot be equated simply with the numbers born into each class 18 years earlier: mortality, immigration and, above all, social mobility during the intervening period ensure that the social structure of the 18-year-old population will differ substantially from that of the new born population 18 years earlier (Royal Society 1983: 18).

The estimates are given in Figure 8 and show the numbers in classes I and II running between 250,000 and 300,000. Now Table 1 shows that about 70 per cent of university entrants come from classes I and II, so there is reason for optimism that the present recruitment will be maintained.

But how can we double the participation rate? Although a substantial increase in the recruitment of mature students can be expected, the main input

Table 6 Pupils in UK schools

	Pupils in UK schools thousands									
	1960–61	**1969–70**	**1979–80**	**1981–82**	**1982–83**	**1983–84**	**1984–85**	**1985–86**	**1986–87**	**1987–88**
Total	8,847	9,956	10,892	10,367	10,094	9,876	9,702	9,565	9,392	9,273
Aged 16	172	268	266	306	312	297	289	286	285	293
Aged 17	86	151	160	181	188	182	174	169	174	170
Aged 18 and over	29	51	19	24	27	28	28	28	27	26

Source: DES Education. Statistics for the United Kingdom (various)

to higher education must remain school-leavers and recent school-leavers, that is under-21-year-olds as at present. The numbers of boys and girls in schools in recent years are given in Table 6, with those aged 16, 17 and 18 shown separately. There are in addition many boys and girls pursuing sixth-form studies in further education colleges. The total number taking A levels can only be estimated, because the figures that are published for the number of A level candidates are the conflated figures of all the examining boards; many candidates take examinations with more than one board and so count as double or even triple entries in the grand total. The number of genuine home candidates – school, further education and private – is probably about 250,000 of whom about 134,000 are in schools (the latter figure is fairly accurate). Of those in school about half gain two or more passes. It would appear therefore from these and earlier figures that the universities and polytechnics are already absorbing the vast majority of qualified school-leavers.

The major problem in increasing access is that so many boys and girls leave school at the earliest opportunity: at age 16. Table 6 shows 170,000 17-year-olds in schools in 1985–6 when the number of people of that age was nearly 950,000, so fewer than 20 per cent stayed in school when they had access by right. The total numbers in all full-time education between 16 and 18 are shown in Table 7, which was presented by the DES in answer to a Parliamentary Question on 27 July 1988. Of the United Kingdom 31 per cent, a few are in higher education, roughly 20 per cent in schools and 10 per cent in further education colleges. Why do so few of our boys and girls stay at school after 16?

Alan Smithers has studied this issue at length and spoke in 1989 about the cohort that reached A level age in 1985–86 (which he described as not atypical):

> Figure 5,* following the flows through from 1981, shows that at least 40%, and more often nearer 45%, of those entering O-levels (in any case, with the exception of English, below half the age cohort) in the major subjects failed, and when the cream of these, usually obtaining A or B at O-level, went on to A-level, a further 30% were failed.

* Table 8 is based on Smithers' Figure 5.

Table 7 Participation in education and training of 16 to 18-year-olds, 1981

	Percentage of age group		
Country	**Full-time[2]**	**Part-time[1]**	**All education and training**
France	58	8	66
Germany, Federal Republic of	45	40[3]	84
Japan [4,5]	69	3	73
USA[5]	79	–	79
United Kingdom[6]	32	32	63
(1987)	(31)	(33)	(64)

1 Including apprenticeships, YOPs, YTS and similar schemes.

2 Including higher education for some 18-year-olds.

3 Including compulsory part-time education for 16 and 17-year-olds in Germany.

4 Estimated from new entrant and enrolment data; excludes some 18-year-olds, in 'special training schools' which provide certain types of vocational training for those aged 18 and above.

5 Including private sector higher education.

6 Includes estimates for those studying only in the evening. Excludes private sector full-time further education and training, estimated as 2 per cent for 16 to 18-year-olds.

Source: Derived from DES Statistical Bulletin 10/85 (DES 1985c) and DES Education Statistics for the United Kingdom (DES 1988d)

Only 14.1% of the age cohort in 1985–86 obtained at least two A levels at grade E or above. The others had been rejected or failed at various points. The English educational system is a process of cumulative failure, demoralising to individuals and inefficient for society. Is it surprising that so many of our young people are alienated?

Those discarded by the education system find their futures in a variety of ways. In 1985–86, in addition to the 31% in full-time education, 13% were studying day part-time (including an estimate for employer-based or private), 8% were attending evening only (including leisure classes), and 10% were on

Table 8 Quality through failure (after Smithers)

Subject	Entries	O Level Passes	% Fail	Entries	A Level Passes	% Fail
Maths	321,653	183,202	43.0	78,838	53,327	32.4
Physics	176,235	104,734	40.6	55,468	38,943	29.8
English	503,933	273,539	45.7	64,315	46,361	26.4
Biology	233,205	128,708	44.8	46,107	31,866	30.9
Geography	200,280	113,506	43.3	35,030	25,046	28.5

Source: Royal Society and Engineering Council (1989)

YTS programmes, with their variable quality of provision. About 40% therefore appeared to be following no systematic training at all.

> Education and training 16–19 is an amazing muddle, with no clear sense of direction. There is a bewildering variety of academic and vocational qualifications under the auspices of a number of different agencies. These often seem to be pulling in different directions (Royal Society and Engineering Council 1989: 41).

There is clearly a need for a national strategy for education and training for the 16–19 age group. The introduction of the General Certificate of Secondary Education (GCSE) and the National Curriculum up to age 16 are important steps in the right direction; at the same time major changes are taking place in higher education post-18. Action is needed to sort out the important period in between.

There is an early indication of the effect of GCSE. In answer to a Parliamentary Question on 26 July 1989 about the effect of GCSE examinations on staying on in full-time education, the Under-Secretary of State replied:

> Provisional statistics collected by my department indicate that in January 1989 there were some 382,000 pupils aged 16 and over in maintained and independent schools in England, an increase of 5 per cent on the previous year. This represents a staying-on rate of 32.4 per cent in all schools (29.5 per cent in maintained schools alone) compared with 29.4 per cent and 26.6 per cent respectively in 1987–88. These are the highest-ever rates for staying on in school. . . . Of these pupils, some 314,000 are following A level courses, an increase of 8 per cent on the previous year. The proportion of the age group on first year A level courses in schools has risen by 3 percentage points to just under 24 per cent; again, the highest figure ever.

But we cannot look to an expansion of A level numbers alone to provide the candidates for a much bigger higher education system, for reasons that will become clear later in this chapter. There must be a huge increase in the number of people qualifying through other routes, especially the Business and Technician Education Council (BTEC) and access courses. Very many more young people must be encouraged to remain in full-time, or substantial part-time, education after the compulsory years. It is earnestly hoped that the GCSE and the National Curriculum will play an important part in this encouragement, and the quotation above suggests that a good start has been made.

A levels

The first examinations for the General Certificate of Education (GCE) at Advanced Level (A level) were held in 1951. Unlike the Higher School Certificate (HSC) which it replaced, GCE A level is a single-subject examination. Candidates may enter for one subject, or for combinations of subjects, on as many occasions as they wish. It is administered by several GCE Boards in England and Wales; they are independent bodies, but there is some collaboration between them, and they are subject to scrutiny by the School Examinations and Assessment Council (SEAC), a statutory body established as a result of the Education Reform Act of 1988. This single-subject system is in contrast to the schemes in many other countries, where there is a compulsory mix of subjects. The French baccalaureate, for example, lasts for three years and is a multi-subject examination; typically candidates take written and oral examinations in seven subjects. In the USA the High School Diploma requires that, of the subjects studied, seven (English, social studies, mathematics, science, a foreign language, health and physical education) are compulsory.

Higher School Certificate was designed as a preparation for study at university, usefully filling the time between matriculation and undergraduate work. When A levels were introduced, there was little doubt about intended candidates; they were grammar or independent school pupils planning to become undergraduates. A levels were the means of assuring universities of the intellectual capacity of entrants, and a basis on which degree courses could be founded.

In 1951 there were just over 100,000 subject entries and about 37,000 candidates; the corresponding figures now are well over 600,000 subject entries and about 250,000 candidates. With the emergence and growth of comprehensive schools, sixth-form and tertiary colleges, A levels are now taken at a much wider range of institutions. More and more candidates study for A levels, full-time and part-time, at colleges of further education. Over the years an increasing number have taken the courses and examinations as stepping stones to employment, although of course very many embark on degree courses.

It is felt by many people that the needs of universities have had too firm a control over the sixth-form curriculum; indeed the aspiration to an honours degree course has had a strong influence on the curriculum well below the sixth form. This view was put by many who submitted evidence to the Committee appointed by the Secretary of State for Education and Science and the Secretary of State for Wales 'to recommend the principles that should govern GCE A level syllabuses and their assessment'. It was captured in a passage written by one of them:

> The most fundamental error in the traditional GCE/A level system was that each stage was designed to be suited for those who were going on to the next. Schoolchildren who were not good enough to go on were regarded as expendable. The other view, which seems to be held in every other advanced country, is that each stage of education should be designed for the main body of those who take it and the following stage has to start from where the previous stage ended (DES 1988b: 2).

This and the view of Alan Smithers recorded earlier constitute an indictment of the whole system which cannot be dismissed. Indeed, tacit acceptance of the criticism is embodied in the creation of the National Curriculum 5–16, the work of successive Secretaries of State. Before we look at the future of 16–19 provision, and A levels in particular, it will be rewarding to look at the present state of A levels and their new companions, AS levels. What follows in this essay draws heavily on the evidence submitted to the A level committee and its report *Advancing A Levels*.

Purpose

A good deal has been written about purpose already, but in summary the purposes perceived by different individuals and groups include the following:

1 An A level is a syllabus and a process of assessment, usually including a written examination, in a single subject.

2 It is aimed primarily at the 16–19 age group, following success at GCE O level, and now at GCSE.

3 It forms part of a coherent sixth-form curriculum.

4 It provides basic knowledge for courses in higher education and for employment.

5 It is a measure of achievement.

6 It is a predictor of future performance.

These are superficial, and it is necessary to look beneath the surface to identify the qualities of mind needed in this rapidly changing world. These are the ability to think, to apply as well as to acquire knowledge, to identify links between different forms of knowledge; they can be embodied in the single word: understanding.

These perceived purposes are also in some respects incompatible, or at least there are tensions between them.

Strengths and weaknesses

A levels are widely regarded as setting standards of academic excellence. The best syllabuses are seen as intellectually challenging and stimulating, confronting able students with the central concerns of the discipline. They develop analytical and interpretative skills, as well as imparting important factual knowledge. But many syllabuses fail to identify with sufficient clarity their aims, objectives and criteria for assessment. Furthermore, over the years, syllabuses have become too voluminous and pupils over-burdened with a large amount of information to the exclusion of other important demands. Above all, there are far too many syllabuses: more than 400 in England and Wales.

The strongest long-standing criticism of A levels is that the typical programme of study (three subjects) is too narrow and unbalanced, and that the system encourages premature specialisation. On the other hand, the proportion of candidates combining science and non-science A levels in their three-subject programme increased from under 10 per cent in 1963 to almost 30 per cent in 1985 (Smithers and Robinson 1988). The strongest recent criticism is that A levels are not continuous with GCSE, either in subject content or style of teaching and assessment. The pupil has a much more active role than hitherto in the GCSE, in contrast to the active teacher/passive pupil style which is customary in most A level courses.

AS levels

The recent introduction of Advanced Supplementary (AS) level syllabuses is a step towards broadening students' experience and is therefore welcome. AS levels are designed to occupy half as much teaching time as an A level but to be *of the same standard* – indeed at the *same level*; to quote a recent School Examinations and Assessment Council (SEAC) report to the Secretary of State

> Both examinations are of the same standard and both are intended for students able to cope with the demands of A level study (SEAC 1989).[1]

But despite the reckless proliferation of AS level syllabuses (more than 170 are published by the examining boards for 1990), the rate of take-up is slow and there is much suspicion that AS levels will narrow the choice of the candidate in higher education. Consequently, among the relatively few who are taking AS levels, far more are taking three A and one AS than are taking 2 A + 2 AS, so the minimal broadening being achieved is at the cost of increasing the total burden.

AS levels are designed to offer syllabuses which are complementary or contrasting to a candidate's A levels; for example, biology taken alongside mathematics and physics, or together with English and history. Contrasting

AS levels have the virtue that they afford the opportunity to bridge the arts/science divide, but the evidence suggests that so far relatively few AS level entries represent a genuine attempt at curricular broadening, and that most students are taking AS levels in subjects similar to their A levels, or even in the *same* subjects. A combination of existing A and AS levels is unlikely to produce a stable, lasting system.

A levels and the future

Before examining the future of the 16–19 provision it is worth looking at some likely developments pre-16. If we are to expand higher education greatly we must have a school system that does not 'turn off' the majority at or before 16. There is some evidence already that GCSE is encouraging more to stay on, and we must assume for this discussion that in the years it will take for the GCSE to mature, and for the National Curriculum to be established throughout the age range, we shall see the major increase in the number of 16 to 19-year-olds in education that is vital to the future of the nation. If the National Curriculum and the GCSE do so succeed in motivating 70 per cent or so to stay on, then one wonders how long GCSE will remain a public examination: a major industry with the associated bureaucracy. By the time there are 70 per cent of 16 to 19-year-olds studying full-time it will be more appropriate for schools and colleges to be accredited as examining centres by SEAC.

Turning now to A levels, it is important to see them as part of the 16–19 provision. They must be compatible with, and overlap, other elements in that provision. And they must provide continuity with GCSE and with employment and higher education. The whole 16–19 provision must be an enriching and rewarding experience in itself; for those not going into full-time higher education it must not leave them with a feeling of frustration or failure.

Compatibility with other elements of the provision is not as elusive as many people imagine. For example, the 'gulf' between A level and BTEC is not as wide as often perceived; there are many people in colleges of further education taking a mix of A level and BTEC courses. There are even a few brave experiments in which modular A level and BTEC courses have some common modules. The artificial distinction between 'academic' and 'vocational' courses must go.

The case for reform of A level syllabuses and examinations is now overwhelmingly made, and in most quarters accepted. The A level committee set up by the Secretary of State for Education and Science and the Secretary of State for Wales (DES 1988b) and the School Examinations and Assessment Council (SEAC 1989) reached many common conclusions. The committee consulted widely in education at all levels, industry, commerce, and many professional institutions and organisations. SEAC consulted

> all schools with sixth forms, sixth form and tertiary colleges, colleges of

> further and higher education and a wide range of educational organisations with an interest in post-compulsory education (DES 1989b).[2]

The principal common conclusion is expressed by SEAC:

> As the consultation showed, support for broader curricula post-16 is virtually universal (SEAC 1989).[3]

Another common conclusion is the need to develop general principles to govern A level syllabuses and their assessment.

The general principles must cover rigour, motivation, breadth, depth, and balance within and between subjects. Rigour involves notions of difficulty, of stretching pupils to the limits of their ability without demoralising them, of encouraging them to work hard and show what they can do. And rigour in the assessment of achievement is as important as in the content. Assessment is an important part of the whole process of education, not simply a one-off trauma at the end of the course.

Pupils and teachers must be motivated by a course if all are to give of their best and derive maximum benefit. Syllabuses must be interesting and stimulating, applying fundamentals in a variety of contexts to bring understanding as well as knowledge. They must not be over-burdened with factual information; learning facts is very important, but so is analysing them and making sense of them.

Despite the 'virtually universal' support for broadening the 16–18 curriculum, a central controversy surrounds the way in which broadening should be achieved. The typical programme for the able sixth-former at present is three subjects at A level, usually in fairly closely related subjects – mathematics, physics, chemistry for example, or English, history and modern language – with some broadening provided by general studies and/or non-examined material. About 30 per cent of A level students now take an arts/science mix in their three subjects, but that cannot be described as giving breadth and balance.

Some breadth comes from within individual subjects. Each syllabus should make connections with the content and skills of other subjects, and with the study and work methods of other subjects. But more important is the breadth that comes from studying a balanced spread of subjects. If young people lose contact early in life with the various broad aspects of the civilised world – the humanities, physical sciences and life sciences, the environment – they are unlikely to gain a thorough grasp of them later. The education system should provide and encourage a selection of courses which reflect those aspects of life.

Breadth in these terms should not be at the expense of depth. It is unfortunate that breadth and depth are seen by many as being in conflict. Breadth should increase understanding by enabling students to see the contrasts and relations between a range of subjects. In education, breadth and depth should be complementary.

Syllabuses

There is now general support for the development of general principles to govern A level syllabuses and assessment. In the interests of coherence, effectiveness and accountability, the basis of the system must be set out for all to see. The search for standards which are high and acceptably consistent can be pursued effectively only if the basis is described openly and clearly.

The overall aim should be to promote rigorous, broad and stimulating courses for a wide range of able pupils. An essential feature of any syllabus is that it should develop understanding and those skills and attitudes which come with understanding – initiative and confidence, creative thinking and adaptability. Understanding must be the dominant theme. The ability to memorise and recall facts, important as it is, must be a companion to understanding rather than an end in itself.

There must be a drastic reduction in the number of A level syllabuses on offer; the present number of around 400 is ludicrous. For each subject there should be an identified and compulsory common core; employers and higher education institutions would then be able to depend on people arriving with some skills and knowledge in common. The extent of the core will vary with the nature of the subject, but it should be defined in terms of skills and not simply as a list of content.

All these considerations apply equally well to AS levels for as long as they exist; the DES and SEAC insist

> that the system embraces only one 'level' – the advanced level – subsuming both A and AS examinations (DES 1989b).[4]

AS levels will turn out to be a transient phenomenon, but they will have a useful role to play during the period in which a rational and stable system is evolving. One important potential feature of AS levels could endure in the evolving system; that is that some syllabuses could be both contrasting and complementary for the same individuals. For example, a modern language course aimed at students taking primarily science would provide a broadening and useful extra set of skills. The course would be contrasting to the main subjects of study, but it would take into account that the students were looking towards further education or a career involving science; it would be slanted towards the needs of scientists and in that sense complementary to the science subjects. Similarly, a statistics course aimed at students of the humanities would provide breadth and would contrast with the main subjects, but by being designed for the needs of those studying primarily the arts/humanities, it would be complementary and truly supplementary (which is what the S in AS stands for).

Assessment

Assessment is an important and positive part of a well-designed course. It consists of very much more than a major written examination at the end of a two-year period of learning. It should, and in most cases does, involve a continual exchange of ideas and oral and written work between pupil and teacher, and often collaborative work between pupils. This exchange provides invaluable feedback to pupils and teachers, and is an indispensable feature of a good course. The extent to which the assessment of this work contributes to the final grade of the individual candidate varies widely across the range of A level syllabuses. But what is universally true is that all the information and assessment accumulated during the course of two years study and hard work, and an end-of-course examination, is encapsulated in a single letter-grading, A–E. How much more rewarding it would be to all concerned if an A level result portrayed both strengths and weaknesses in terms of agreed criteria. This descriptive assessment could supplement the single grades by a simple system of profiles of performance. These profiles could be recorded on individuals' certificates, together with any necessary explanation of the terms and gradings used. The certificate would be a self-contained record of the strengths and weaknesses of the student in each subject attempted.

Certificates prepared on these lines would be more informative and more helpful in selection for jobs or further education. They would also help to explain to those outside the educational field (and some in it!) the nature of A levels and what might be expected of those who gave gained them.

Other options

The A level is a single-subject examination. It could of course be embodied in other structures, such as the Higher School Certificate which it replaced. To obtain a HSC it was necessary to pass at one sitting either three principal subjects or two principal subjects and two subsidiary subjects. In the School Certificate, the forerunner of O levels, it was necessary to obtain passes in certain groups of subjects. A similar structural requirement could be imposed on the A level system (much as in the baccalaureate for example), and there are advocates of such a course. It is in many ways an attractive idea, but not timely when we are aiming to persuade many more people to stay in education full-time; but it could easily be incorporated in time into an evolving system.

Another possible feature of a 16–19 programme is a common core in the whole curriculum. For example, it should be decreed that all pupils in sixth forms and their equivalent should devote, say, 50 per cent of their examined timetable hours to mathematics, science, English and a foreign language; the remaining time would be devoted to a selection from a wide range of options, including advanced specialisms for high fliers.

Whatever options emerge as our educational system for 16 to 19-year-olds develops, they must be able to attract and retain a much larger number than the present system does. They must stimulate and satisfy a much wider range of the community than are at present in full-time education in their late teens.

Notes

1 The quotation is taken from paragraph 16 of the supplementary paper, entitled 'Advanced and Advanced Supplementary Examinations', attached to the main report.

2 Covering letter, dated 12 July 1989, to the Secretary of State from the Chairman and Chief Executive of SEAC accompanying the Council's report and published as an attachment to Department of Education and Science (1989b), Press Release 268/89 (22 August 1989).

3 The quotation is taken from paragraph 1 of the supplementary paper (see note 1 above).

4 Secretary of State's reply, dated 22 August 1989, to the Chairman and Chief Executive of SEAC. DES Press Release 268/89 (22 August 1989).

5 The changing relationship between schools and higher education

Michael Duffy

I want to start on an anecdotal note. In May 1984, when the government produced its 'firm proposals' for Advanced Supplementary (AS) level examinations, I was chairman of the Secondary Heads' Association (SHA) committee that was asked to draft the Association's formal response. A term of meetings and consultations followed, and a brisk and lively correspondence. On the basis of those sentiments and soundings we came to the conclusion that the proposals were deeply flawed, and we said so. The new examination was unlikely to be widely adopted, we said; even if it was, it was extremely unlikely to achieve either the curriculum broadening that was intended, or the widening of access to education post-16 that was so clearly needed, 'We do not accept,' we said, 'that there is a case for developing and introducing an AS examination *in the form and under the conditions* (my italics) outlined in the Statement of Intent' (SHA 1984).

Among the universities, and among those of my Headmasters' Conference (HMC) colleagues who had privately and unwisely assured Sir Keith Joseph that his proposals would be acceptable to the schools, our response caused ripples of concern. The Standing Conference on University Entrance (SCUE), which had strongly endorsed the Statement of Intent, met us in October, and we were able to recapitulate our reservations. It is fair to say, I think, that the members of SCUE were not convinced. The SHA position (not, at that time, generally shared by the independent schools) was that real broadening meant changing A level expectations, syllabuses and teaching styles; that the government's proposals would only tinker with the problem, and would tinker (unless universities expressed a clear preference for the new examination) without effect. The SCUE position was that universities would want to welcome AS levels in principle, but would not express a preference. The great merit of AS levels, it was said, was that existing A levels would not be in any way affected. Just how committed SCUE was to the maintenance of existing

A levels became clear a few months later, when it issued a leaflet for schools called *Choosing A Levels for University Entrance*. The tenor of the advice to students it contained was simple:

> the choice of A levels, it said, was crucial. The choice of 'the third A level' was must crucial of all. Students should be wary of choosing 'less conventional' subjects, and should be particularly wary of choosing 'subjects which predominantly involve practical skill' – though design and technology was 'increasingly considered to be intellectually demanding in a way that is not true for the craft subjects' (CVCP/SCUE 1985: 2).

The purpose of this anecdote is not to reopen old arguments, and still less to reopen old wounds. I quote it because it helps to illustrate the nature of the relationship between higher education (still thought of, I think, as predominantly university education) and the great majority of the nation's secondary schools, as it still was five years ago; and because it shows clearly how quickly and how considerably that relationship has changed.

In 1984, the universities' view of the relationship still rested on certain long-standing assumptions. Not all of them were made explicit: in my anecdote, it is necessary sometimes to read between the lines. But there was certainly a commonly held assumption that universities should have a major voice in sixth-form education. This was no more than a recognition of actuality; all but one of the A level examining boards were university based, and the great majority of A level syllabuses reflected (besides the need to offer something slightly different from the other, competing, boards) the universities' perceptions of what entrants to their courses needed to know. A level grades were seen then, as they still are, primarily and inevitably as pre-university qualifications. A levels were designed by universities, for universities; that had to be so.

In that design, factual content was paramount. The quantity of knowledge that a syllabus demanded was seen as the key to its quality: content provided the basis on which first degrees would build. Inevitably, therefore, there was a tendency – particularly in the natural and social sciences – to push more and more content into syllabuses, and the agreement of the GCE Examining Boards in 1980[1] to identify the essential common cores of the most frequently taken subjects was in part a reaction against this uncontrolled syllabus inflation. But common cores were still specified in terms of content; and when university departments determined the entry requirements of their courses, it was specific content that they had in mind.

In practice, however, the real importance of A levels to the universities lay in their use as mechanisms of selection. When the ratio of applicants to places was three or four to one – and sometimes higher – such a mechanism was imperative. Board by board and grade by grade, A level pass rates had the advantage of being remarkably consistent year by year. Among the boards, admissions tutors privately recognised – or claimed to recognise – gradations in standards and variations in the quality of syllabuses, and when they made their offers to selected candidates they took due account of these. Overall, their system seemed to work. Admissions tutors claimed a close correlation between a candidate's A level grades and the class of his or her degree.

Just as boards were held to vary in their standards, so, it was claimed, did individual subjects. The test was academic rigour: syllabuses not based on the conventional grammar school curriculum were viewed with great suspicion. There are clear overtones of this in SCUE's reference, already quoted, to the increasing acceptability of design and technology, a subject previously frowned upon by most departments of engineering as insufficiently theoretical in content, not intellectually demanding, and not a safe predictor. A lot of A level subjects came into this category, not least (because of its lack of specific syllabus content) general studies.

All of this meant that the universities exercised considerable control, not only over the sixth-form curriculum and the examination system that legitimised it, but also over the amount of choice available to individual students within this curriculum and the sort of advice that schools were free to give. It was still possible in 1984 to see such control as necessary and inevitable; to see the primary function of the sixth form as the supply of qualified customers for higher education, first for the universities as autonomous degree-awarding bodies, then for the polytechnics and the colleges. Each in turn would make their choice; for each, that choice would be determined by the A level subjects taken and by the grades obtained. From the universities' point of view, it was a sellers' market. Demand for places would always outstrip supply. As the very first sentence of the SCUE pamphlet said, 'Entrance to university is becoming more competitive and it is clear that the chance of securing a place will be improved if you make a careful choice of A levels' (CVCP/SCUE 1985).

That, in a nutshell, was the prevailing point of view; it neatly summarises the assumptions I am describing. Higher education, particularly at university, was of necessity exclusive: it was the role of schools to provide a supply of candidates appropriately qualified in subject knowledge for it, and it was the function of A levels to certificate that knowledge, grade candidates for selection, and set high standards.

Such assumptions affected, as they were bound to do, the great debate on breadth. That debate has run and run: it spans almost the whole of my professional career, from the 1961 agreement to broaden the curriculum, through the Schools Council's 'Q and F' and 'N and F' proposals for a two-tier sixth-form curriculum in the 1970s,[2] to the AS examination with which I began this chapter. For the whole of this period the universities and the schools have paid lip service at least, as they must, to the cause of reform. Most academics believed by 1984 that the typical three-A level diet of the Welsh and

English sixth former (they order these things better in Scotland) was damagingly narrow. Most schools did, too; but academics belonged to departments conditioned to the belief that specific A level subjects and specific A level grades were essential for their courses; and schools (especially those deemed influential, with track records of university success) were reluctant to change a system which worked to their (if not always to their students') advantage. The broader view comprehended the need for change; self-interest, more sharply focused, argued for the status quo.

It was precisely this tension, of course, that AS levels were invented to resolve. The new examination was deliberately and categorically planned to have half the content of the old, but be equivalent in standard. That, if it could be made to happen, would sell it to departments and hard-pressed admissions tutors. Two AS levels would be the same as one A level; there would be no loss of standards; selection for admission (particularly if students could be encouraged to take an AS level in addition to their A levels) would not be compromised. AS levels would be either 'complementary' or 'contrasting'; breadth would be achieved without the sacrifice of content; A levels themselves, the key to access and to standards, would be maintained. That was the universities' reaction.

The schools were much more cautious. Their scepticism was not due to a lack of commitment to broadening: many of them made costly provision for general studies, for instance, in spite of the reluctance of admissions tutors to give such studies credence. Nor, on the whole, was it due to the failure of the government to put any new resources behind the new examination. The cost of starting and staffing new free-standing courses (which most schools could only meet by dropping existing ones, always a highly speculative venture) was certainly a deterrent; so was the justified suspicion that the universities' theoretical welcome for AS would be less than whole-hearted at admissions tutor level. And the prospect of teaching AS within existing A level groups, on a side-by-side basis so to speak, was demonstrably absurd. But the real basis of the schools' concern lay in their developing perception that the traditional assumptions about sixth-form education no longer held true; that the ground rules, so to speak, were changing.

In this chapter I want to highlight that perception, and to show how it had become by 1989 much more widely held, not only in the schools and in the world of work, but in colleges and polytechnics also, and in universities themselves.

The argument for change

The extent of the change is striking. It was demonstrated most clearly in the recommendations of the Higginson Report (DES 1988b), and in what happened when the central recommendation was rejected by the Secretary of State. That story is told elsewhere in this volume; what matters here is that the Higginson Committee was set up (in the strictest sense of that useful term) to maintain the A level status quo, and to hear evidence from all users of the A level system as to whether that could or should be done. The tenor of the evidence – even from the universities – was that the answer to both questions was firmly 'no'. The rejection of the report was essentially political; an act of deference to an influential strand of conservative opinion that held A levels to be the gold standard of English education, the last bastion against the reforming radicalism of a minister in a hurry. It was certainly not an issue that was argued on educational, economic, or even demographic grounds.

In the schools, the educational arguments for change were gaining adherents throughout the 1980s. Callaghan's 'Great Debate' of 1976 had orchestrated, rather than initiated, concern about the nature of the secondary curriculum, and that concern was reflected in a brisk series of enquiries and reports to which the National Curriculum proposals of the Education Reform Bill were an inevitable (though not always logical) conclusion. The thrust of the enquiries and reports was remarkably consistent: that 'subject choice' operated against balance and coherence; that too many students got a second-class curriculum; that the all-powerful examination system locked students into courses that were narrowly conceived and often narrowly taught and whose outcomes – because they were 'norm-referenced' – were essentially predetermined. The curriculum still reflected university assumptions about the nature of knowledge and the primacy of the theoretical over the applied; the examination system reflected university assumptions about its essentially selective purpose. The result (and this was beginning to be perceived) was a bottleneck effect: a flow-through education system designed, not to permit access to the next stage, but to constrict it. Just as this happened at 16-plus, so, inevitably, did it happen at 18-plus. In all the concern about the shortcomings of our secondary schools that the Great Debate foreshadowed, there was an undertow of professional conviction that the *real* effect of the system was that it was designed to deal in failure – and did so rather well.

It was easy, particularly for those with limited experience of ordinary secondary schools, to write this off as the left-wing egalitarianism of teachers who wanted, in John Rae's words, 'an Alice in Wonderland world where everyone is in the top set' (Rae 1989: 117). My own belief is that it was nothing of the sort. Surveys in *The Times Educational Supplement* in the 1970s and early 1980s showed teachers predominantly conservative in politics and attitude. But they had discovered how difficult it was to motivate ordinary children with the carrot, at the end of their courses, of a CSE certificate to which nobody at all (including, often enough, the schools themselves) attached any credibility. Hence the impetus in schools towards Records of Achievement, which we conceived as a means of positively identifying a far wider range of learning, and in the process raising both motivation and attainment. The seminal Secondary Heads Association curriculum statement, *A View from the Bridge* (SHA 1983) reflected an influential belief that the curriculum was too narrow and the examination system too negative. So did the Hargreaves Report of 1984.[3] And so, much more important, did the government of the day.

Sir Keith Joseph's speech to the North of England Education Conference in January 1984 was at least as important as Callaghan's 1976 speech at Ruskin College, for it laid out a view of education to 16 that was bound to effect significant change both from 16 to 18 and from 18 onwards. The curriculum, he said, had to be broad, balanced, coherent and of practical relevance for *all* students, not just

> for those who are labelled (an interesting choice of word) non-academic; the technical and vocational aspect of school learning should have its proper place; . . . The quest for an improved curriculum and higher standards of attainment will require changes in the examination system (Joseph 1984: 7, 9).

A better curriculum and higher expectations would, he said, yield higher standards; and the examination system would have to change to reflect them. Sir Keith, in fact, was publicly nailing two persistent myths, neither of them unknown in the higher education world: the myth that 'pure' knowledge is superior to the knowledge of its application; and the myth that standards are maintained by restricting access to them. In this case, he was talking about those of the GCE O level examination; but the principle is more widely applicable.

All of this was consistent, of course, with the mounting chorus of concern voiced by industry, business and the professions about the performance of our educational system, and it was consistent too with the political rhetoric of the time. My point is that it was wholly consonant with what good teachers were beginning to perceive. Interestingly, it reflected very closely the parallel developments in curriculum and examination in Scotland, instigated (without the distraction of political flag-waving) by the Munn and Dunning Reports;[4] it certainly echoed the growing interest in many English and Welsh schools in specifically pre-vocational courses and certification.

The immediate outcomes of Sir Keith's Sheffield speech were, of course, the General Certificate of Secondary Education (GCSE) and the Technical and Vocational Education Initiative (TVEI), launched by the Department of Employment in 1983 as a provocatively well resourced magnet programme for a small minority of pupils, very rapidly turned into a much more thinly funded contract between the local education authorities and the Manpower Services Commission (now the Training Agency) under which agreed curriculum innovation within specified criteria received additional financial support. The criteria were almost all process-based: they had to do with the way that learning was (in the jargon of TVEI) delivered, rather than with its subject content. They put great stress on vocational relevance, the acquisition of transferable skills, the use of information technology, continuous 'formative' assessment as well as terminal 'summative' assessment, self assessment, the wide-span recording of achievement. Most significant of all, they insisted that any TVEI contract should apply to the age range 14 to 18. They explicitly challenged the deep-seated assumption of English and Welsh secondary education that most people's education finishes at 16-plus.

GCSE – by definition a terminal examination, targetted at 16-plus – had a rather different effect. To begin with, the effect was muted. The government's determination to introduce it quickly, at a time when the schools were riven with industrial action over pay, and concessions to teachers were politically unthinkable, created huge problems both for schools and for examining boards. Teacher and student overload were the most conspicuous early warning signals. By the end of 1987, however, with the first cohort of candidates halfway through their courses and the competing demands of their coursework programmes beginning to be resolved, schools all over the country were reporting better performance and better motivation from their fourth-form students. The new syllabuses were more sharply focused, more explicitly relevant. They put genuine stress on 'understanding' and 'doing' – as well as on the traditional 'knowing' – and their assessed coursework and practicals involved students in their own progress in a way that the all-or-nothing GCEs had not. The first GCSE results in 1988 showed a significant increase, grade by grade, in the number of certificates awarded, and this trend was continued in 1989. For teachers, this was a genuine – and deserved – improvement in standards. Forgetful of Sir Keith, however, government ministers – aided and abetted by some independent school heads who saw their market in exclusivity threatened – began to talk about 'dilution'; but they could not talk away what the schools themselves had experienced, and what they were beginning to describe as the 'GCSE factor'.

The GCSE factor, put simply, was that more 16-year-olds were staying on at school. In 1988, the overall rise was small – from 26.3 to 26.6 per cent. But it came after four years when the comparable figure fell.[5] In 1989, according to a survey of 33 local education authorities reported in *The Times*, staying-on figures rose very sharply indeed. In my own school, where the staying-on rate had varied, from 1981 to 1987, between 44 and 50 per cent, it rose steeply: to 55 per cent in 1988, and to 60 per cent in 1989.

No one disputes that other factors may be involved. No one, however, to my knowledge, disputes the primacy of the GCSE factor. And because an increased proportion of those who are staying on are taking A level courses, no one disputes the significance of these figures in the context of A level reform. There are two levels of concern. The first is what may be described as the pedagogical gap: the hiatus between process-centred GCSEs, taught with a heavy emphasis on practical work and applications, and content-centred A levels, taught with a heavy emphasis on theory and recall. There is a flurry of activity among the examining boards, in an attempt to close this gap; but examining boards have to look over their shoulders at the stance the universities adopt, and where content reduction is concerned, that stance is not always encouraging.

The second concern, of course, is the standards gap. The GCSE factor is confronting the examining boards, and through them the universities, with the 'more means worse' dilemma in a sharply painful form. Over the years A level standards have been maintained by the application of fairly consistent norms to the awarding of the various grades. In most subjects, for instance, the pass rate (the proportion of candidates getting grade E or above) is remarkably close, each year, to 70 per cent. And if the number of candidates, as a proportion of the age group as a whole, stays constant, we may assume that fairly constant standards are maintained. But what happens if the percentage of the age group staying on increases? The assumption may well be – must be, if the 'gold standard' argument holds true – that the failure rate will have to rise. And if that happens, we will be in the interesting position of having connived with our GCSE students to secure them increased access to education post-16, only to deprive them of commensurate opportunities at 18. Fortunately, perhaps, demography may come to their rescue.

I have shown how changes in curriculum and examinations pre-16 are indirectly affecting the nature and expectations of the sixth form. Meanwhile, however, there have been direct changes in the sixth form itself, targeted at that growing body of young people who want to stay on at school but who possess neither the intellectual ability nor the staying power to cope with the A level steeplechase. These are the 'new' sixth-formers, but there is nothing new about them at all. The term was coined in the mid-1960s, and the debate about the most effective provision for them has continued ever since. One of the schools' criticisms of the AS proposals was that they provided nothing at all for this category of student.

In the 1960s the debate centred on structural reform. Working Paper 5 of the newly instituted Schools Council[6] urged the adoption of 'major' and 'minor' courses, and in various guises this argument was to resurface over the next twenty years. Argument, however, still left the 'new' sixth-former without post-GCE or post-CSE qualifications to aim at, and it was not until 1979, under growing pressure from sixth-form colleges, that the experimental (and short-lived) Certificate of Extended Education (CEE) was instituted. This was conceived as an extension to CSE. Though it gained support in schools and colleges it was virtually unknown outside them. Meanwhile the GCE examining boards, identifying a gap in the market, began to produce 'Alternative Ordinary' (AO) syllabuses, aimed at a level midway between O and A. These carried greater credibility. They could be used, too, to leaven the over-specialised diet of the typical A level student – though few universities paid any attention to them. The result of all this was that the average non-A level student was following, by the early 1980s, a partial and disjointed curriculum of individual and unrelated subjects examined (and, in the case of ubiquitous 'resits', re-examined) at a profusion of levels.

Meanwhile, however, a genuine alternative was appearing based – for the first time – on the learning needs of the student rather than the credibility of the qualification. Some larger sixth forms were experimenting, by 1979, with the General Diploma course of the Business (later the Business and Technician) Education Council – a unitary course rather than a list of subjects, vocationally directed but by no means narrowly conceived. In the same year the Further Education Unit published an influential report, *A Basis for Choice* on what is called post-16 pre-employment courses. They prescribed a common-core curriculum, defined by learning objectives and not by traditional subjects, with additional modules of general and specific vocational study. Assessment would be by profiling: 'formative' as well as 'summative'. The report's language was heavily instrumental, but it was language that employers, parents and students respond to, and it was no surprise that the DES should echo it when it introduced in 1982 the Certificate of Pre-Vocational Education (CPVE), targeted at young people:

> with modest examination achievements at 16-plus, who have set their sights on employment rather than higher education, but . . . are not yet ready to embark upon a specific course of vocational education or training (DES 1982b: 1).

That was a useful reminder that large numbers of traditional sixth-formers, too, came into that latter category.

CPVE has had a somewhat chequered career. Welcomed in the schools, it was cold-shouldered by many further education colleges, as a rival to existing further education provision. The further education examining bodies which comprise its Board introduced competing courses; the Youth Training Scheme cut into both its clientele and its credibility. For all that, it has had considerable impact in schools. Students enjoy it, and respond to it positively. Employers value it for the skills and self-confidence that its students acquire. Teachers discover in it a challenging new methodology. Syllabus planners observe it, and build on what they see. CPVE's style – experiential, process-based, modular, continuously assessed – is diametrically opposed to the traditional A level approach. It is an implicit recognition, not only that sixth-form education is more than a pre-university obstacle course, but also that it may be the more effective for it. As a model for the organisation and assessment of education post-16 it has been surprisingly potent.

It is, however, only one exemplar of the influence of vocational awareness on secondary schools and on their teachers and students. 'Relevance to the world of work' – in Sir Keith Joseph's words at Sheffield – is built into the resourcing of schools through TVEI, into the in-service training of teachers through bodies like the School Curriculum Industry Partnership, and into the expectations of students through work experience. Increasingly, it is built into the management of schools as well, through industrial and business representation on governing bodies. Superficially, the message to schools from employers has been about 'standards': there has been a *naïveté* about some of these predictable criticisms and about the narrow vocationalism that accompanies them that it has been easy to discount. But the underlying theme has been more persuasive. Sir Peter Parker identified it in his 1986 Smallpeice Lecture:

> We have lost sight of what we are educating for. . . . Education should be designed for the pursuit of learning in all the walks and works of life. . . . a medium in which the vast majority learn how to learn and to go on learning throughout their lives (Parker 1986: 17).

Sir John Harvey-Jones, ex-Chairman of ICI and Smallpeice Lecturer in 1987, elaborated on this theme:

> We seem to have fossilised our country into a rigid pattern in which, if you end up in the bottom left-hand corner of the noughts and crosses module, there is no way of moving anywhere else. You start life with a nought or a cross, and that is apparently where our current systems aim to leave you. I have to say that is the absolute opposite of what an educated flexible society which could cope with tomorrow's world should be capable of doing (Harvey-Jones 1987: 21).

Capability, indeed, has become the key word; the Royal Society of Arts 'Education for Capability' movement focused both the philosophy and the practice. When Corelli Barnett was invited to address the annual meeting of the Headmasters' Conference in 1986,[7] it was an indication of how persuasive the concept had become. Deep-seated assumptions about the nature of the schools' curriculum task were dissolving, because the climate of expectations was undergoing change.

When the Secondary Heads Association called in 1987 for a more flexible, modular curriculum, including pre-vocational experience, for *all* students from 16 to 18, it was responding to the sentiments of its own members as well as to the rhetoric of change. Heads were influenced by what was actually happening in their schools. The growing vocational emphasis was beginning to affect not so much A levels themselves, which were still seen as the hard currency of education post-16, as the way that that currency was spent. Both student guidance and student choice were getting harder headed, and the content and vocational immediacy of a given degree was beginning to be more of a factor than the perceived status of the institution that offered it. The more lavishly universities and polytechnics marketed their wares, the more thoughtfully the customers surveyed them.

The demographic factor

That emphasis on marketing was in part a response – on the part of the universities, a strangely delayed response – to demographic change. It is difficult to overstate the importance of this factor; it has adjusted the balance of power, so to speak, not only as between the universities and the polytechnics but also between higher education as a whole and the schools. Schools, of course, were familiar with it. They had lived with falling rolls since the mid-1970s; they knew perfectly well that the number of 16 to 18-year-olds was going to fall sharply from 1982, and that the number of 18-year-olds would fall by a third between 1985 and 1995. Polytechnics, knowing that the number of conventionally qualified candidates available to them was going to fall, recruited vigorously and successfully in schools and among students with further education qualifications. Universities tended on the whole to take comfort in the fact that the age-cohort decline among social classes I and II was much less marked – a complacent and revealing attitude, it may be thought – and were more inclined to base their marketing strategies on what they saw as their market strength, their continuing ability to attract the best A level candidates. It was only when that ability, in some institutions, began to weaken (most dramatically and ironically, among the engineering faculties which had been most prescriptive in their demands) that the question of wider access began to be voiced. There was an obvious element of self-interest in this. Even so, it looks to schools as if some universities and departments have not yet grasped the way in which their market is changing. In higher education as a whole, the demographic down-turn in the post-16 age group means that, even to maintain the present output of graduates (estimated to peak at 124,000 in 1992) will involve raising the age participation rate from its present 14 per cent to almost 20 per cent. Maintaining the present output is clearly not an option: the government has told higher education to admit 50,000 more students to degree courses by 1990. That means that universities and polytechnics will be trying to increase their catch of students, from a rapidly shrinking pool. Unless they change their nets (which seem to many of us in the schools to be full of holes already) their catch is going to fall. It is going to fall in any case, because there are a lot of other predators gathering at the water's edge. Belatedly, business and industry (especially service industry) have woken up to the fact that they face an acute manpower shortage, as well as a skills shortage. Their ability to survive it depends on their ability to recruit from the same diminishing cohort of young people. The approach is increasingly competitive. Schools in all parts of the country, but especially in the south and east, report new pressure. From the employer's point of view, the vogue for school-industry liaison and work experience has, too, an element of self-interest about it. Early access to bright 18-year-olds (and, in the case of the big financial services companies, to 16-year-olds tempted by the short-term attractions of a wage) is seen as critically important, and offers of financial incentives to selected students are beginning to appear. Post-16 'compact' schemes will impact very considerably on higher education.

What is happening – and it is very difficult for the blue-chip universities to comprehend it – is that the market for higher education is being transformed. Potential customers now cover a wider spectrum of intellectual ability and (at last) a broader social background. Their educational background is broader, too, and this is beginning to be reflected in their choice of higher education options. Increasingly, they find themselves in a buyers' market. If they are going to be persuaded to commit themselves to higher education, it is going to take more than an A level points score to do it.

Inevitably, the cry of 'standards' will be raised. The old obsession with exclusivity, with academic rigour as the boundary between the cultured and the philistine, lives on in the schools as it does in the universities. The Matthew Arnold plaint, 'We can't have Heav'n crammed', has echoes in every common room, and it does not go unheard in Downing Street. 'More means worse' has bedevilled English and Welsh education for over a hundred years. But the majority voice from the schools – and the majority is large – is that this proposition is wrong. More does not mean worse: more means different. And different can often mean better. We have our own experience to support us. We have seen BTEC and CPVE provide a ladder to higher education for students for whom the conventional examinations route was an obstacle course of insuperable adversity. We have seen the success of the Open University with students (many of whom have been our teachers) who failed to make the stipulated grades at A level. And we are beginning to see real motivation to learn among 16-year-olds who, though they may know less in terms of syllabus content, most certainly understand more. We are beginning to see, in other words, that the enemies of real educational reform may be specialisation and exclusiveness, the proud badges of the A level system and the universities.

That message no longer comes from schools alone. The current preoccupation with access, in all sectors of higher education, is revealing in this context. Access means, by definition, the admission to higher education of students who have previously been, or have been held to be, excluded – who have failed to squeeze through the old bottleneck at 16, or the one that remains at 18. Such access has not – in spite of the pressure it brings on costings and units of resource – produced a lowering of standards. Her Majesty's Inspectors' report on the polytechnics,[8] where enrolment increased by 47 per cent over the period 1981–89, is emphatic on that point. It is an emphasis that the schools, with TVEI, GCSE and CPVE behind them, would welcome and endorse.

The question of finance

I have argued that four factors have significantly altered the relationship between schools and higher education: the momentum for change which built up, over a period of almost thirty years, around the perception that the universities exercised a narrow and narrowly élitist hold over the school curriculum; the introduction of major curriculum development through GCSE and TVEI; the advent of vocationalism; and the impact of falling student numbers at a time when the demand for educated and skilled young people has greatly increased. All these factors, I believe, have combined to change the expectations of each other that schools and higher education hold. The progress report of the Committee of Vice-Chancellors and Principals published, with the Standing Conference on University Entrance, in November 1988 was eloquent testimony to the extent of the change. It was also an interesting indication of the degree to which, in some departments anyway, it was not yet fully understood. The report

> records progress made so far by universities in reviewing their undergraduate courses, their teaching and their admissions policies and procedures in the light of changes to the secondary curriculum and the need for wider access to higher education.

It concludes: 'The work is not yet complete, is continuing and in a few cases has barely begun.' The report puts particular stress on the development of flexible and sensitive admissions procedures.

> The adoption of a 'wait-and-see' policy will not be fair towards future university entrants and will attract censure from schools, colleges, students and the wider educational community (CVCP/SCUE 1988:14).

The message is clear: universities (and by extension, polytechnics) must adjust to the changing market.

That used to be a metaphor. The government's drive, however, towards loan-funded higher education, and the obvious but short-term attraction to universities of financial autonomy through the levying of fees, are turning it into a literal description; and that is surely the most fundamental change of all. It is no part of my brief to analyse the tensions in that statement: the obvious contradictions between a government policy committed on the one hand to the exerting of control over funding and provision and on the other to the free play of market forces, and the uncomfortable contrast between the stated desire of the universities to extend access across the boundaries of class, income and ethnicity that now constrain it, and their stated willingness to charge students directly for tuition costs. At the end of the day, he who pays the piper calls the tune: it seems shortsighted of the universities to assume that financial autonomy is the way to safeguard academic independence, not least because (as schools have found out, under local financial management) there are going to be losers as well as gainers.

It would be difficult to exaggerate, however, the concern felt in maintained schools at the implication of the government's proposals for student loans and the suggestion in some universities that fees as well as maintenance should be funded in this way. Schools are familiar enough with the objections to the existing basis of student funding. We know that very many of our former students who are supposed to receive a parental contribution fail to get it, and that many students who receive a full grant appear to be more affluent at home than many of those who do not. Equally, we recognise that the present system is essentially a middle-class support mechanism: it is one of the arguments of this chapter that there is a growing will in the schools to see the advantages of higher education go to far more people, outside the charmed circle of those who currently enjoy it. But to move from the present position to one where access to a degree is determined by willingness to borrow, or by parental ability to pay, seems to carry major dangers. Less than 8 per cent of those who currently go to university are from low income families, ie social groups IV and V (UCCA 1989), in spite of the fact that their fees are fully covered and their maintenance costs (in theory) fully met. Increasingly, we believe, we are attracting youngsters from this background into our sixth forms, and pointing them towards degrees. Few teachers of these young people will believe that the prospect of having to borrow up to half the cost (more, if the universities' stance on fees is to be believed) will be anything but a disincentive. Many of them come from families where entanglement with credit is a factor in their poverty. Why pay for sixth-form education, they will argue (which in a sense they do) if it means indefinite indebtedness from 18?

The proponents of these schemes argue that a wide range of scholarships will be made available, on the American model, funded by the state and by individual or corporate generosity. It is these scholarships, they say, that will achieve the extension of access that is wanted. From the schools' point of view, there are two flaws in the proposition. The first is the weakness of the analogy. American higher education, in all its richness and diversity, is based on the universal provision of education for all, from grade K to grade 12 and high-school graduation. There is no equivalent in the United States of those barriers to entry which in England and Wales control, by convention or examination, access to the privilege of education post-16, and then beyond. Higher education in the United States is premised on access; in this country, it is premised on exclusivity and exclusion. The schools will argue that it will take both time, and explicit financial support to the 16–18 student, to change the cultural climate.

The second flaw in the scholarship scenario lies within the logic of the proposal. Scholarships, after all, are competitive: they have to be competed for. What will the basis of such competition be? The answer – given the value of the prize – is obviously 'outstanding ability and potential'. That is easier to say than to measure. The universities of Oxford and Cambridge have demonstrated, over years of experiment, how unreliable (and how socially regressive) selection-by-examination can be. So what is left? The answer, I very much fear, will be the use of A level grades – an effective reassertion of the status quo. The test of *admission* will become the ability to pay: market forces, so to speak, will rule. But the test of *access* will be outstanding performance in an examination which, because of its importance, will be . . . external, competitive, standardised, specialised. That examination – *pace* Q & F, N & F, AS, and all the rest – will become the gold standard of secondary education, and the wheel of exclusivity will have turned full circle. Matthew Arnold rules – OK?

Notes

1 The common cores themselves were published in 1983. See GCE Examining Boards (1983) *Common Cores at Advanced Level. A First Supplement* was published in November 1987 (GCE Examining Boards 1987).

2 Proposals for a two-level, *Qualifying* and *Further*, examination are contained in Standing Conference on University Entrance and Schools Council (1969) *Proposals for the curriculum and examinations in the sixth form*. Proposals for *Normal* and *Further* examinations are contained in Schools Council (1973) *16–19: Growth and response*. Schools Council Working Paper 46.

3 Committee on the Curriculum and Organisation of Secondary Schools (1984) *Improving secondary schools*. Report of the Committee on the Curriculum and Organisation of Secondary Schools chaired by Dr David H. Hargreaves.

4 Consultative Committee on the Curriculum (1977) *The Structure of the Curriculum in the Third and Fourth Years of the Scottish Secondary School* (The Munn Report). Committee to Review Assessment in the Third and Fourth Years of Secondary Education in Scotland (1977) *Assessment for all* (The Dunning Report).

5 Department of Education and Science (1989a) *Statistics of Schools in England – January 1988*. Statistical Bulletin 8/89, table 6.

6 Schools Council (1966) *Sixth form curriculum and examinations*. Schools Council Working Paper 5.

7 See Barnett, C. (1986) *The Audit of War*.

8 Her Majesty's Inspectorate (1989a) *The English Polytechnics: an HMI commentary*.

6 A higher education system fit for adult learners

Alan Tuckett

Adults learn best in contexts sympathetic to adult learners, yet the creation of such contexts in higher education has received comparatively little attention. Much of the debate about adult participation in higher education in Britain rests on the assumption that the problem is the recruitment of appropriately prepared adult students to full-time undergraduate courses in polytechnics, and to a lesser extent in universities. The debate tends to cluster around two questions: 'How can enough appropriate adult learners be identified, prepared and admitted to existing courses?', and 'who participates?' Both questions are clearly important, but they focus debate on access to higher education as if 'higher education' was a clearly identified and unproblematic set of functions and purposes, and as if it could be taken for granted that existing courses in higher education institutions provide sympathetic learning contexts for adults.

To some extent this is undesirable since there has been a significant increase in mature student participation, in particular in polytechnics, over the last decade. But the debate takes little account of the experience of the Open University, which now accounts for more than 10 per cent of university graduates in Britain, or of the experience of Birkbeck College, or of the long term residential colleges for adults. Those experiences suggest that provision in most universities and parts of most polytechnics needs to change to create a context sensitive to the needs of adults. This chapter seeks to examine the debate about access from the perspective of adult learners, and to propose changes that would make for a higher education system fit for adults to learn in.

The institutional case for increasing mature student participation concentrates on recruiting a sufficient number of adult students to compensate for the expected drop in 18-year-olds applying for courses. It complements a concern to encourage a higher proportion of young people to prolong their initial education. Government has recognised the potential impact of demographic change on the pattern of higher education provision in Britain since 1978 when the discussion document *Higher Education into the 1990s* was published.

Throughout the 1980s, ministers and officials have exhorted institutions to adapt to meet the challenges posed by the 35 per cent drop in 18-year-olds between 1983 and the mid-1990s.

> With the number of 18-year-olds set to fall sharply in the 1990s higher education faces both a challenge and an opportunity to broaden the range of those who have access to it,

Robert Jackson, minister responsible for higher education, argued in a speech to a Royal Society conference on Access to Higher Education in 1988, and in the same speech stated his belief that

> achieving a more open system is wholly compatible with maintaining high standards (Jackson 1988b: 1–2).

The government's policy in *Meeting the Challenge* that

> places should be available for all who have the necessary intellectual competence, motivation and maturity to benefit from higher education and who wish to do so (DES 1987: 7)

was developed in major speeches at Lancaster University and to the Association of Colleges in Further and Higher Education (ACFHE) by Kenneth Baker as Secretary of State for Education and Science (Baker 1989a, 1989b). His view was that Britain needed to move towards a mass system of higher education borrowing successful American experience.

This lead from government has been matched by a number of statements by the University Grants Committee and the National Advisory Body for Public Sector Higher Education, in the remit of the Polytechnics and Colleges Funding Council, by increasing recruitment of mature students in polytechnics, and by the development of more than 500 access courses preparing adult students for entry to higher education. However after five years of reductions in the number of 18-year-olds, applications for places in higher education continue to rise, though not in the sciences, with almost two applicants for every place in the system overall. In part this is explained by differential changes in family size between social groups, with the bulk of the fall resulting from the shift away from large families among manual, skilled and semi-skilled workers, and an increase in the number of children born to professional and managerial families from which higher education traditionally recruits heavily. In part, too, there seems to be evidence that Britain is moving towards an increased percentage of children staying on at school and applying to higher education.

The impact of these changes in student recruitment on adult participation is twofold. On the one hand, since there is evidence that the greatest single factor affecting adults' willingness to study is the length of initial schooling, if more children stay at school, they are, later, more likely to seek education and training opportunities as adults. The second consequence, mapped by Fulton and Ellwood in their study of admissions to higher education for the Training

Agency (Fulton and Ellwood 1989), is that, faced with the choice between admitting 18-year-olds with satisfactory A level points scores and the development of strategies to recruit mature students, most admissions tutors and admissions officers will persevere with the tried and trusted system. On their experience so far, most do not expect to face drastic changes in order to deal with a serious drop in applications, let alone to boost their intake substantially. On the other hand, there are few, if any, institutions in the country in which no departments feel any cause for concern. Fulton and Ellwood make clear that the debate about widening access is pursued sector by sector, with the polytechnics more sensistive to mature students than universities; institution by institution; department by department; tutor by tutor.

In part, this is because, as Alan Smithers and Pamela Robinson point out in their report on increasing participation in higher education prepared for British Petroleum (Smithers and Robinson 1989), there is a strong correlation between very good A level points scores and degree performance, and using point scores to ration scarce places is tidier and neater than developing systems to evaluate the fitness to study of mature student applicants. A Brighton Polytechnic team, summarising research on entry qualifications and first degree performance for the CNAA (Bourner with Hamed 1987), demonstrated that non-standard entrants on average fare better than other categories of entrant in acquiring 'good' degrees, and Smithers and Robinson also report on mature students admitted to the universities of Manchester, Liverpool, Leeds, Sheffield and Birmingham through the special scheme for people over 21 lacking formal entry requirements administered by the Joint Matriculation Board.

> The students admitted got as good, if not slightly better, results than A level entrants on the same courses and were no more likely to drop out (Smithers and Robinson 1989: 22).

Table 9 Degree performance by age

Age at graduation	% with 'good' degrees
21	30.1
22	35.8
23–25	36.1
26–30	37.7
31–45	40.8
36–40	49.8
41–45	43.1
Over 45	30.6

Source: Bourner with Hamed (1987)

However, they point out that the students were rigorously selected for their academic skills, and that 'only about 40 per cent of those embarking on the admissions process became eligible for entry' (ibid).

Bourner and Hamed's research also provides useful data about degree performance at different ages, irrespective of entry qualification (Table 9).

These results demonstrate that degree performance is likely to improve with age, up to the age of 40, after which students fall back towards the average performance of young people. Of course, degree results are only one measure of success. What is clear however is the evidence that mature students admitted for higher education in different contexts perform as well as 18 to 21-year-olds. At the conclusion of their study of admissions practices, Fulton and Ellwood recommend that:

> the ability to complete a course, not the highest possible entry grade, should be the basic criterion for admission (Fulton and Ellwood 1989: 6).

Smithers and Robinson disagree. They argue that to use 'capacity to benefit' as the sole criterion for entry to higher education:

> begs the question of how it is to be judged and competing claims resolved. If existing routes are to be superseded then better and fairer ways will have to be found (Smithers and Robinson 1989: 22).

It is in pursuit of such 'better and fairer' ways that the Unit for the Development of Adult Continuing Education (UDACE) has been working on the evaluation of learning outcomes in higher education through its *Student Potential Project* and *Learning Outcomes in Higher Education* initiatives (Otter 1988; UDACE 1989c) and working on ideas of competence that argue with the work of the National Council for Vocational Qualifications (UDACE 1989b). It is hard, at present, for many higher education institutions to say what knowledge, skills, competences, refinement of judgement and improvements in understanding a degree course seeks to impart. Without being clear about this, it is an inexact science to identify what experiences, skills and undertakings a successful candidate will need to have had to embark on a course. Without such an analysis adult learners are likely to be disadvantaged in the admissions process, and at best admitted under some exceptional arrangement. As Smithers and Robinson note:

> The institutions with the most 'liberal' admissions policies are usually under the least pressure from applicants (Smithers and Robinson 1989: 22).

From that, it is a short step to conclude that the recruitment-centred debate about access sees mature students as an optional extra, useful to fill undersubscribed courses, but not at all central to the needs of the system.

The case for adult learners is better made by a broader examination of the economic and demographic contexts in which higher education institutions function, and by examining issues of equity. A notable case for expanded adult participation was enunciated by the National Advisory Body and the University Grants Committee in their joint statement on *Higher Education and the Needs of Society* with its reference to continuing education as a fifth objective for higher education in addition to the four set out by Robbins. It neatly combined aspects of these arguments:

> Continuing education needs to be fostered not only for its essential role in promoting economic prosperity but also for its contribution to personal development and social progress. It can renew personal confidence, regenerate the human spirit and restore a sense of purpose to people's lives through the cultivation of new interests. In short, both effective economic performance and harmonious social relationships depend on our ability to deal successfully with the changes and uncertainties which are now ever present in our personal and working lives. That is the primary role which we see for continuing education (NAB 1984b: 4–5).

The economic arguments rest in part on the demographic ones. One consequence of the fall in the numbers of young people entering the labour market is that 70 per cent of the workforce who will be economically active in the British economy in the year 2000 are already in employment. If British industry is to adapt to the pace of change set by its industrial competitors, this must mean that adults are encouraged to update their skills throughout life. As Geoffrey Holland said to an Institute of Manpower Studies conference in 1988:

> The real skills gap is that our country is under-educated, under-trained and under-skilled. And that is because our approach to education and training is, and has been for decades too little, too narrow, for too few (Institute of Manpower Studies 1988: I).

According to a recent Confederation of British Industry report *Towards a skills revolution, a youth charter*,

> Only when skills are enhanced throughout working life will each employee's full potential be released (CBI 1989: 15).

However, concurring with Holland's view the report describes the extent of the problem:

1 Employers believe that top up training in the 1980s has proved to be very expensive because of an inadequate skills base.

2 Adult training in Germany pays back quickly and is highly effective because it builds upon the competence acquired in initial training to a level hardly matched by any other country.

3 Consequently British employers spend more on adult training than our

competitors but only because they spend so much less on youth development.

The CBI conclude that lifetime learning must be promoted. However, they also conclude that foundation skills for 16 to 19-year-olds must be an even greater priority. At a time when education is unlikely to maintain its overall share of gross national expenditure, because of the increasing demands on health and welfare services made by an ageing population, this may be arguing that lifelong learning should start, but not in our lifetimes. By contrast, workers in the German microelectronics industry are retrained every two years to adapt to the speed of industrial change. The life span of new industries has been calculated as fifteen years, yet the balance of expenditure in the British education and training system is still remorselessly wedded to the clockwork system, where young people are wound up with an initial education and training investment of differing length and intensity, and then sent out into the world until they wind down.

However, the greatest imperative for changing the balance of participation in the post-school education and training system comes from the ageing of the population. In the year 2012, if present working life trends and population forecasts are maintained, there will be, in Britain, more people retired than in the active workforce. Three possibilities for reacting to this situation exist: that we shall not be allowed to retire until we drop (since I would expect to retire in 2013 I have a vivid interest in this question); or that we skill our workforce so that each economically active worker generates enough surplus to keep herself, and one other; or that we find, as we did in Britain in the 1950s, that it is possible to feel positive about a multicultural society, and we renew large scale immigration to Britain at a time when because of the different age profile of black families in Britain, there is a proportionate growth in the number of black people in the workforce.

Each solution to this problem involves a heavy commitment to education and training, and to recruiting groups of people who have traditionally benefited little from post-school educational and training opportunities to train and to work full-time.

The White Paper *Employment for the 1990s* is clear about the implications:

> Employers will have to retrain their existing staff to adapt to changes rather than to rely on the market for ready-trained people. In addition, employers cannot expect to recruit as many young people, especially well-qualified young people, as they have in the past. They will have to tap new sources for their recruits. Provided, however, that we adapt and recognise that we are not yet using the full potential of all our people, these new sources of recruitment can help provide for tomorrow's needs (Department of Employment 1988: 7–8).

The groups of people the Department of Employment White Paper identifies as having a major contribution to play in this retraining and upskilling process are women, ethnic minorities, unemployed people – particularly the long-term unemployed – and older workers (it seems I may not be able to retire after all!). These groups, and the larger groups of working-class adults and people with disabilities, are underrepresented throughout the education and training system and in particular in higher education. Where they do study they have the greatest difficulties in securing employment. The growth of part-time employment and the increased segmentation of the labour force in the 1980s make the task of involving such groups in education and training particularly difficult where government sees itself bearing a decreasing responsibility for meeting full-time students' maintenance costs, whilst meeting fees, and sees the burden of funding part-time study as the responsibility of students or employers. Yet people in the least skilled jobs are least likely to have access to paid educational leave or work-based learning opportunities. They are also least likely to have ready access to advice or guidance about what opportunities exist for study.

The imminent creation of a single European market is already exacerbating the differential opportunities available to a highly mobile, highly skilled workforce and to a low skilled, immobile workforce. The move to afford freedom of movement to the professions throughout the market, and the intention of the European Community Commissioners to investigate the harmonisation of higher education entry qualifications over the next three years, will each have an impact on provision. Already the ERASMUS scheme (European Community Action Scheme for the Mobility of University Students) for student and staff mobility is starting to be felt, particularly in the universities. Since there is a dramatic difference in participation and completion rates between the United Kingdom and its European partners the gap between highly qualified and mobile workers and those who have neither qualifications or mobility is notable. In Britain, whilst a small proportion of school-leavers is offered access to higher education, a large percentage of them complete their studies. Differences in the pattern of participation will have an impact on the overall mobility of the European workforce. Since similar demographic declines are observable in the main northern European members of the European Community, with the exception of France, there will be a European market for qualified labour, and considerable shortages of skilled labour may be expected. As a relatively weak economy in the Community, Britain can expect to depend more heavily on recruiting the target groups identified in the Department of Employment White Paper into education and training, and to that end will need to forge closer links between institutions of higher, further and adult education, and between institutions and employers. The increase in institutional autonomy and the diminution in the effective coordinating role of local education authorities resulting from the 1988 Education Reform Act will do nothing to make that easier. The challenge will be to preserve the quality of education offered whilst increasing the number of adults and young people who can participate.

In his Lancaster speech, addressing this problem, Kenneth Baker argued:

> My expectation is that, as numbers and participation rates rise over the next 25 years, the relatively simple stereotypes around which British higher education teaching is still organised will lose their hold. The structures appropriate to higher education with 3% participation, or even 13% participation, simply cannot be sustained when participation rises to 30% (Baker 1989a: 7).

To some extent, these changes are already prefigured in the field of continuing professional education. Large firms already commit substantial in-house resources to the training of their workforce (IBM for example commits 4 per cent of its budget to staff training, and employs some 400 people in its training division), and responses to the government's Professional, Industrial and Commercial Updating (PICKUP) initiative demonstrate that employers are becoming more aware of the ways higher education can help them with technological updating. However, Her Majesty's Inspectors' report on PICK-UP initiatives in 1988, whilst praising the technical content and customised design of institutions' PICKUP initiatives, suggested that institutions were weak on teaching and learning methodologies appropriate to adult learners (DES 1988c). Altogether the combination of demographic change over 25 years, the sharply competitive economic climate, the pace of technological change, and the needs of industrial customers for a different pattern of course

Table 10 Social class of men and women by type of institution attended

Social Class (Men+ Women)	**Type of Institution**				
	Population	*Residential College*	*University*	*Advanced Further Education*	*Open University*
Men					
Service	28	20	77	70	70
Intermediate	28	26	12	18	15
Working	45	54	11	12	15
Women					
Service	19	30	74	70	74
Intermediate	54	65	24	29	24
Working	27	5	2	1	2

Note: 'Service' class covers professional and senior managerial occupations; 'Intermediate' covers self-employed, lower managerial and skilled workers; 'Working' covers semi-skilled and unskilled occupations.

Source: Adapted from Woodley, Wagner, Slowey, Hamilton and Fulton (1987)

support from higher education institutions each reinforce the argument that higher education institutions need to be doing more than filling their numbers. However, recruiting from the target groups identified in the Department of Employment White Paper involves many higher education institutions in new ways of working.

The access debate has been developed not only by those seeking to recruit enough appropriate students to fill existing and planned courses, or by those with a keen concern for the needs of the labour market, but also by those with a concern for equity. Successive reports have demonstrated the underrepresentation of working-class people in higher education, and though variously documented many of the same issues arise in relation to the other target groups identified. In *Choosing to Learn* (Woodley, Wagner, Slowey, Hamilton and Fulton 1987) the social class of men and women in the general population and in higher education institutions shows that the underrepresentation of working-class people in higher education is even more acute for women than for men (Table 10).

The same study makes clear, however, that if mature students are classified by their parents' social class, in the same way 18-year-olds are classified, there is a much closer match between class representation in the population and among mature students. The authors suggest that this may mean people enter higher education to confirm class change, but there is no doubt higher education is widely recognised as affecting class mobility, and existing working-class students do not think higher education is for them.

In the data presented by Smithers and Robinson, unskilled manual workers (who make up nearly 8 per cent of the general population) make up some 7.6 per cent of those entering higher education with non-standard qualifications, compared to 0.4 per cent of those entering with A levels and 0.5 per cent entering with vocational qualifications. There is, nevertheless, a massive underrepresentation of working-class adults in the system. Smithers and Robinson comment on this in the following way:

> Why there should be such a markedly uneven distribution across different sections of the community is not clear. Almost certainly it does not reflect conscious bias on the part of those admitting students. Where selection takes place, it is mainly on the basis of merit as expressed through A level performance. In general, too few from the underrepresented groups are coming forward . . . The social class effect could be due in part to differing abilities since there is some correlation between class and intelligence (Smithers and Robinson 1989: 11).

There is, of course, a continuing debate about the relationship between classes and intellectual performance, but it is clear from the above quotation that Smithers and Robinson see 'intelligence' and 'admission to higher education' as neutral constructions. For them the issue is for members of underrepresented groups to present themselves. Colin Griffin contests this directly:

> In fact barriers to access are collectively as much as individually experienced and culturally as well as materially constructed, and the paradox lies in confronting the individual learner with the problem of the socially and culturally constructed concepts of learning. Access (he says) does seem to be conceptualised in terms which ignore the cultural barriers to learning, which isolate and abstract the individual learner, and which tend to reduce the issue to one wholly resolvable in technical and institutional terms (Griffin 1983: 85).

Just how real the cultural barriers to access are, and how far apart the specific culture of academic study is from the lives many people lead, is highlighted in the testimony of women returning to study in adult, further and higher education collected by Bridger:

> I used to say to Fred, 'Would you like to read my essay?', but it was 'Oh, if you want,' but no enthusiasm. And one night I said, 'You must hear this, what I've written,' and I gets my paper and I starts to read and when I looks up, my husband and daughter are shuffling out the door making faces (Bridger 1985).

> I thought 'Oh, they won't have me!' I mean, me going to university! Well, I just never, never thought I would be (ibid.).

These experiences are amplified in the conversations with mature students reported in the recent research of Weil, where 'Janet' talks about access to knowledge in higher education:

> It has a way of keeping things from people. It is locked away from the average person. It's not that I am not up to it or not good enough. . . . Education should be about introducing people to things versus keeping people out of things. It's like a nice club. Why, TV lets people into places where they otherwise wouldn't go (Weil 1989: 133).

The issue of cultural barriers is examined again in the report of a committee of enquiry into higher education for Newham chaired by Peter Toyne:

> Newham lacks any effective 'grapevine' culture or general awareness about the possibilities of higher education amongst its young people and adults. Few pupils have any contact with anyone who has attended higher education, they do not know how the system works, and do not see its benefit (Committeee of Inquiry into Higher Education for Newham nd: 13).

One major initiative taken by higher and further education institutions to broaden mature student access to higher education, and to improve the participation rates of black people, women and working class people in particular, has been the development of access courses. Initially such courses were developed jointly between one further education institution and a receiving, or linked, polytechnic, and students satisfactorily completing the access course were guaranteed a place, or an interview for a place, on a higher education (usually degree) course. Much of the early impetus to develop access courses came in the inner London area, particularly following the Review of Advanced Further Education conducted by the Inner London Education Authority (ILEA 1983). As part of its equal opportunities strategy ILEA linked its top-up grants to the five inner London polytechnics to the extent to which they were successful in recruiting students from priority categories in accordance with ILEA policies. In 1986–7 these categories were: ILEA residents, part-time students, mature students, women, students from ILEA access courses, students from minority ethnic communities, and students needing concessionary fees. The dynamic for addressing the educational needs of groups underrepresented in the post-school education system was considerable and was paralleled in further education colleges and adult education institutes. A volume of demand was revealed that it has not been possible to meet solely through the provision of access courses, although there are more than a hundred access courses in the London area. The notable example of 700 applicants for a 25 place access course in law for black students at Vauxhall College throws up the question, what happened to the 675 disappointed applicants? It has been a major anxiety of the evolving debate about the dominance of access course provision as the major route for mature student entry that it may be removing decisions about who can participate from the higher education institution, and that for some students previously admitted as non-standard entrants it delays entry for a year where the completion of an access course is seen as a necessary 'qualification' for non-standard entry. The increasing centrality of access courses as an approved route to higher education was marked by their recognition in the 1987 White Paper as a third route alongside A levels and vocational qualifications for entry to higher education. The rapid growth in the number of courses offered (currently over 500 across 96 local education authority areas) has led to an increase in mature students more generally. However, a team from Wolverhampton Polytechnic reporting on the relative success of access and traditional courses in the Black Country in facilitating ethnic minority preparation for and entry to degree level courses concluded:

> Currently Access courses within this geographical area are not attracting any more mature working class students than other routes into HE. They are not automatically remedying previous educational disadvantage though they are clearly providing important second chance opportunities (Williams and Bristow with Green, Housee and Willis 1989: 19).

A final and major anxiety thrown up by access course provision is that it may provide a non-traditional route into traditional educational provision. As Parry has noted:

> After all, well-prepared can mean 'equipped to cope' or 'able to survive' in a system not designed to meet their needs (Parry 1986: 49).

A complementary initiative designed to facilitate progression and to add variety to the routes into higher education, by enabling students to accumulate and transfer credit in a variety of adult, further and higher education institutions, has been the development of accreditation-based open college networks in England and Wales. The UDACE report *Open College Networks: Current Developments and Practice* suggests that such networks spring from two roots:

> Firstly, there is a growing recognition that large scale expansion of education and training for adults requires a clear and comprehensible framework, where every individual can understand the opportunities available, can plan their own learning routes, acquiring and adding to their personal portfolio of credits throughout adult life. Secondly, there is the recognition that a vast amount of learning takes place outside the world of traditional qualifications. The accrediting of such learning through local consortia of experienced teachers and trainers can keep the opportunities relevant to learners' needs and provide 'real' qualifications (UDACE 1989a: Preface).

Although the open colleges involve an intense investment of staff time in moderating and validating courses, they are recognised by their participating organisations as above all else invaluable vehicles for staff development. The peer group moderation activity, the analysis of learning skills in contexts other than traditional academic settings, and the development of collaborative arrangements between institutions in different sectors of post-school education each offer something to the evolution of a post-school system sensitive to adult learners.

UDACE identify a number of benefits of an open college accreditation system: that it offers a learner-centred approach, increased mobility for learners between diverse institutions and organisations, enhanced progression opportunities, incentives for learning, the creating of a shared culture of learning, appropriate levels of learning, as well as staff development. Nevertheless, the credit system based on 'notional' hours of study seems still to be wedded to a system that measures learning by the time spent studying, and by the outcomes predicted in course design, rather than to a system which seeks to credit student achievement, wherever and however it has been acquired. However, the debate that evaluates the learning gained in groups alongside that measured in outcome-centred assessment systems is central to the developmental discussions within the open colleges, and touches on how each can be developed to give learners a measure of ownership of the systems by which they are credited.

Much of the work to accredit prior experiential learning in Britain has been developed in Friends World College and in the work of the Learning from Experience Trust, and UDACE is actively concerned with the implications of experiential learning for credit systems in its work on outcomes. The open college networks are a ground-upwards creation, which parallel in many ways the development of the CNAA's Credit Accumulation and Transfer Scheme (CATS) to improve mobility for students within and across higher education institutions, through the development of modular courses that improve opportunities for part-time as well as full-time students.

The development of special initiatives to recruit students from underrepresented groups has focused on access courses. However, the experience of the eight long-term residential colleges is important too. *Choosing to Learn* highlighted the success of the colleges in recruiting working-class adults to full-time and part-time study, and in offering an intensive period of education to raise their learning skills and confidence. Long-term residential colleges have shown over a number of years that for many students residence is valuable in providing respite from home pressures, mutual support, concentrated effort, access to good facilities, and collective support and encouragement to individual endeavour.

Students attending full-time courses at long-term residential colleges receive mandatory grant aid while many of the students on access courses depend on social security payments to finance their studies, under the '21 hour rule' (a convention where students were accepted to be available for work if their studies totalled less than 21 hours a week). Changes in government regulations affecting unemployed adults which introduce a need to demonstrate that individuals are 'actively seeking work' to qualify for benefit may, it is widely feared, weaken access to educational opportunity for unemployed adults. This, of course, illustrates the problems adults face as marginal participants in the education and training system. Because they are marginal, they suffer from the different and contradictory policy imperatives of different government departments. Whilst the Department of Employment is keen to see an educated and skilled workforce, and the Department of Education and Science is keen to widen access to higher education, the Department of Social Security has as its priority the filling of existing vacancies (however part-time and low-waged) as well as a reduction in expenditure on welfare, and is unwilling to fund mass participation in post-school education by what are sometimes described as 'work-shy' claimants. Even those adult students with full maintenance grants are at risk. In reporting the results of a survey of the financial circumstances of students at the long-term residential colleges, Bryant and Noble revealed that:

- Because of financial problems, 22 per cent of the students had to take on part-time employment during term time.
- Over half the students surveyed had to supplement their grants (which averaged £2,427) with funds from personal savings, loans and gifts from families and friends, and loans from banks.
- 60 per cent of the students had incurred debts as a consequence of going to college and 20 per cent of the students had debts over £500.

- Almost half of the students reported that financial problems had adversely affected their academic studies, undermining motivation and concentration.
- Almost a third of the students reported that financial difficulties had prompted them, at some stage, to consider leaving their course (Bryant and Noble 1989).

These experiences are shared by many adult students studying full-time in higher education, and part-time students get no grant to cover fees or maintenance. It is against this background that the government's proposals for top up loans for students needs to be seen. The existing mature student's allowance discriminates against the low paid, the unemployed and housewives, Bryant and Noble quote a Newbattle student as saying. For working-class adults, for women, or black people the loans scheme will be seen as a major additional barrier to access. Yet, as many commentators have recognised, Britain combines low overall participation rates in higher education with unusually high levels of financial support for students, in comparison with support for higher education students in other countries, or with students in further education in Britain. One argument for maintaining the value of grants is that without grants, working-class young people and adults are unlikely to participate in higher education – yet the current participation levels, with at most some 7 per cent of undergraduates coming from working-class families, scarcely argues for a universal grant.

An alternative argument has been put forward by McNair who maintains that

> The growth in participation which has been proposed is simply too great to be financed on the same basis as the old system . . . A rational overhauling of finances, towards a scheme based on weighted vouchers and loans, could open access to considerably more people, especially if linked to a graduate tax, which would minimise the financial discouragement to invest (McNair forthcoming).

He also recognises that changes in the balance of financing higher education between the state, the learner, and the employer, will give extra power in shaping the evolution of the system to employers as customers in a higher education marketplace. Sir Christopher Ball's address in 1989 inaugurating the Kellogg Forum for Continuing Education at the University of Oxford proposed a sharper solution: that there should be no universal grant but that people should pay the full costs of their education and that a generous scholarship scheme should be introduced which targeted groups underrepresented in the system. The successful experience of the Inner London Education Authority in encouraging black people, working-class people and women to participate through generous use of discretionary grants remains an argument for an active role for the state in funding. Nevertheless, unless there is a renewed enthusiasm for a high-taxation welfare-state economy, it is hard to imagine how a major increase in adult participation in full-time provision can be encouraged without a shift to targeted grant support, backed by a graduate tax.

However, more important than changes in the method of funding student support for full-time students is the distinction between arrangements for funding full-time and part-time students. Britain is the only country that discriminates against part-time study in its funding mechanism. Part-time students not only have to fund the full costs of their fees and maintenance to study, they often also experience the inflexibility of a system that remains only slightly modularised. Even in the Open University you cannot receive credit towards a degree programme from an associate student course. Yet there is no possibility of a major expansion of adult participation in higher education without recognising that most of any expanded adult student population will need to study part-time.

In reviewing some of the themes and debates about access to existing higher education institutions I have tried to show the extent to which there is an expectation that adults will fit themselves to the system, whilst at the same time I have argued that there are urgent economic and social arguments for increased adult participation in higher education, and indeed across post-compulsory education as a whole.

What then would a higher education system fit for adult learners look like? In the National Institute of Adult Continuing Education's policy discussion paper *Adults in Higher Education* (NIACE 1989), we argued that a system suited to adult learners depended on making continuing education central to the higher education system, and made specific recommendations in respect of access (with attention to 13 elements of an institutional policy: recruitment policy, needs analysis and outreach, publicity, selection procedures, prior qualifications and experience, curriculum change, access routes, collaborative systems, access to assessment, physical access, student support, financial access, planning and implementation), guidance, curriculum, course structure, funding, marketing and outreach, and staff development. Each area poses a challenge to some existing practice, yet it is possible to point to all the aspects of an adult-sensitive system in elements of existing practice.

The first need is for a system that recognises the distinctive experiences adults bring to their learning. Although there are no hard and fast distinctions between 'adult learning' and initial education, and although almost all undergraduates are technically adult, provision for adult learners needs to take account of the experiences adults bring to their learning, the complexity of their objectives, the discontinuity of their participation, and the financial complexity of their lives. By and large, adults learn voluntarily, with high levels of motivation, but they have little confidence in their abilities, particularly when embarking on a programme of study.

Victoria, another of the students participating in Weil's research, offers advice to tutors working with adult students:

> Don't assume that they don't know anything, but there again, this is a bit difficult. You can't assume that they know anything at all about your subject. . . . But without talking down to them and not going way above their heads so that they are saying 'What the hell are you going on about?' But it's amazing what life experiences, especially in groups of people, the amazing things they have done and been involved in and they add so much to the discussion. But you may assume that a student thinks that it's totally irrelevant (Weil 1989: 125).

Good adult education practice starts from where students are, from the experiences and skills they bring to their learning. Since these experiences are diverse and their starting points different, learning groups need to have a plurality of learning and teaching strategies, and the negotiation of what is to be learned, and in what way, is critical to making the process shared. Clearly, learner-centred learning is more immediately achieveable in the discussion-based curricula of the humanities and social sciences, and it may be that the absence of a discursive, experience-centred methodology inhibits wider adult participation in studying the physical sciences but, as the Open University has demonstrated, it is possible to foster active student participation, negotiating and discussing on the basis of experience acquired within the framework of a structured and sequential body of learning. Inter-disciplinary studies are also important in opening the curriculum.

In the Independent Studies programme at the Polytechnic of East London (PEL) the whole curriculum has been built around the experiences students bring to study:

> We have dispensed with pre-arranged syllabuses and externally imposed assessments and have made exclusive use of students' own Statements. These Statements cover students' own self-assessment of interests, abilities and achievements at the outset; their long-term aspirations and more immediate educational goals; their detailed plans for learning; and the details of their terminal assessment (Stephenson 1983: 169).

To design and build a racing car as a major part of a Diploma in Higher Education involves a combination of creative, intellectual and practical skills fitted to the specific purpose brought by the student. Just as the Open University's open-entry policy is so different from conventional higher education admissions policy that it has been effectively ignored by the system, so the experience of the School of Independent Study at PEL has been little imitated over the last decade. Yet it raises the question central to the purpose of higher education: What is the really useful knowledge universities, polytechnics and colleges are there to promote? How far can institutions shape what they offer to the needs of learners without jeopardising the research functions that complement the teaching activities of the academy?

> Because knowledge generally has been fragmented, artificially divided into subject areas, and then treated as the personal property of specialists, feminist learning intends to break down compartmental approaches wherever they act as a barrier to understanding:

the Network of Austrialian Women in Adult Education, in drawing up a list of feminist learning principles that reflected on the major curricular change resulting from the emergence outside the academy of the women's movement (paralleling the development of black studies), were clear that the curriculum can be a barrier to access (Network of Australian Women in Adult Education 1986).

The first major feature, then, of a system fit for adults to learn in is that it will be responsive in its forms of teaching and learning and in the curriculum offered to the experiences brought by adult learners and their purposes in learning.

This may lead to a major expansion in studies in the arts and social sciences and in business studies (perhaps unsurprising in a country where in 1988 the arts and tourism earned more than the motor industry). It is encouraging that employers increasingly recognise that it is the general flexibility, intellectual dexterity and quality of judgement of graduates that they need, and that technical skills can be taught at work.

A second major concern is that the system recognises that adults study part-time. An adult system would make no distinction in its funding arrangements between full-time and part-time students. All adults would have some form of learning entitlement or voucher to be cashed in when they wish, and this entitlement would take account of the different needs of, for example, students with disabilities. This proposal differs from the recommendation of the Confederation of British Industry on entitlement in that it would not be age-limited, and would apply not only to qualification-bearing courses, but also to assessable study. If I study Portuguese for pleasure and then demonstrate the extent of my competence in an assessment, I may choose to use the assessment for vocational purposes or towards other study. Adults need the opportunity to dip into, and out of, study throughout their lives. At work they will want to make use of educational programmes for technical updating, and in pursuit of personal development they may embark on a substantial programme of study in philosophy. To meet these needs, institutions will need to blur some of the sharp distinctions in post-school education. As McNair states:

> adult learners are clearer about what they want to gain from education than about what is labelled 'further' 'higher' or 'adult' and the providers' distinctions and organisational structures can themselves be a major barrier to access (McNair forthcoming).

If adults are to be able to dip in and out of study then the dominance of the three-year undergraduate degree course will gradually diminish. When students are all able to take modular courses (like the Open University's) some will decide that they have acquired the knowledge, understanding and skills they need without completing a full degree. In that context, leaving a course would not be 'dropping out'.

To achieve a system sensitive to part-time students it will be necessary to develop a credit system that recognises that adults will want to pursue their studies over a long time, in different places, and through a variety of modes of study. To do that it will be necessary for adults to be able to accumulate credits and to take them from one institution to another. As I noted in discussing the work of the open college federations above, there is much work still to be done to harmonise credit-award systems based on the measurement of outcomes with those based on the successful completion of a period of study. Even an institution with as much experience of modular credit-bearing courses as the Open University has still to find a means of including its associate student course programme within its credit-bearing system; and the Open University, the Council for National Academic Awards and the universities will need to seek a nationally agreed framework for recognising credit. Collaboration with open college federations will enable higher education institutions to harmonise these developments with initiatives elsewhere in further and adult education.

The existing post-school education and training system is complex. An adult system would maintain and increase the range of opportunity available, but would seek to clarify and simplify adults' ability to move around the system and to make effective choices about appropriate study. Because adults have such variety of experience and diversity of purpose, the provision of guidance services is essential to help them to clarify their own objectives and find the most effective ways of using the system to achieve them. In order to select the most appropriate strategy in a system offering modular courses, credit transfer, independent study, open learning, the accreditation of learning in the workplace, adults need access to informed and sympathetic guidance. Guidance is central, too, to the effective delivery of modular degree courses, as the Open University's experience shows.

For guidance to be an effective and central component of the system, there will need to be a shift in staffing resources away from face-to-face teaching, but learning contracts, learner-centred and self-assessed coursework and the potential of the new technologies for course provision offer opportunities for tutors to be released for this. However, it will also be important for guidance services in higher education to be linked in a network of guidance agencies. UDACE research on where adults seek guidance showed the vital importance of involving employers in this network, since a large proportion of the employed population turn to their employer for advice about education and training. Guidance systems can additionally contribute to the identification of unmet needs.

How you are assessed, and what can be taken into account in your assessment are central issues for adult learners. As 'Janet' suggests in the research reported by Weil:

> for adult learners you should abolish exams. And use continuous assessment. Look at your whole contribution over all your work. Rather than this [emphasis on final examinations] . . . The systems fails a lot of people who need not fail. If they are not taught to be failing, they wouldn't. It crushes the individual. It is all too rigid, too confining. You lose your creativity (Weil 1989: 131).

Again, as McNair observes:

> A system which exists to create an elite is by definition competitive and exclusive – it thrives on the failure of the majority, and sets its standards by comparison within the peer group, rather than by achievement (McNair forthcoming).

Adults need a system that can measure what students know, are capable of doing, can show they have learned, on course and off it. Employers may increasingly expect higher education institutions to validate learning undertaken at work, whether through conscious systematic training provision or through work experience. Applicants seeking entry to higher education will want to have what they know now assessed, so that where appropriate they may be admitted with advanced standing. Just how much work there is to do in this area is evidenced by the present arrangements in Britain to recognise qualifications gained overseas. To develop a coherent assessment-centred system, it will be necessary for higher education institutions to clarify the learning outcomes that are to be produced by particular courses. Then the enormously difficult task of devising tools for measuring such outcomes must also be confronted with energy and with a refusal to simplify the task. All this will take staff time; the effect of making the learner central to the system, and that is the key issue for adults, will be to involve tutors in a wider variety of roles and a different balance in the use of their time.

Once the enumeration of the purposes of higher education are clarified and tools for measuring outcomes developed, higher education institutions in a system sensitive to adults would undertake a marketing exercise aimed at employers. Just as black people have to apply for more jobs than comparably qualified white people, so adult graduates find it more difficult to secure employment than their 21-year-old colleagues. Demographic change is having an impact on employer attitudes, as evidenced by British Telecom's advertisement on the London Underground seeking engineering apprentices up to the age of 40, but there is an important function for higher education in changing employer attitudes: older students do have much to contribute to the workforce, as the Department of Employment White Paper recognises.

When it is clear what skills, knowledge and competence a degree course seeks to develop, the selection criteria necessary for effective admissions policies will also be clear, making it easier to secure Fulton and Ellwood's objective that:

> the ability to complete a course, not the highest possible entry grade, should be the basic criterion for admission (Fulton and Ellwood, 1989: 6).

Their second recommendation that:

> performance indicators should be used to assess and reward recruitment and successful graduation of non-traditional students (ibid.)

would be central to an effective adult system.

To be successful in recruiting adult students, particularly from groups underrepresented in higher education, will involve close cooperation between higher, further and adult education in developing outreach strategies, and supported return to study programmes. The enormous variety of access courses is evidence of the recognition of the importance of seeking wider participation already, but initiatives like the Sheffield experiment in taking higher education to the council estate (a literal re-creation of the extra-mural tradition of Tawney, Haldane and Mansbridge) will need to be built on elsewhere. In this area, the role of the Open University, offering academic education to viewers, free at the point of use, in their own homes is important, and initiatives like the Open Polytechnic, combining marketing and outreach strategies, have much to commend them.

Outreach needs to be accompanied by inreach. There is no point in persuading a single-parent woman to embark on a degree course unless the institution has a strategy for the provision of child-care, or in offering a place to a well-qualified recently arrived second language speaker, unless institutions can offer language support where needed. Physical access is denied to many potential students with disabilities, because learner support was low on the agenda of the architects and planners who built most of the sites on which we now study. Although the size of the task facing institutions at present in offering effective support to students is daunting, there is no doubt that much can be done by the effective use of institutions' planning and funding procedures over a period of time, and by more effective collaboration between institutions and other public services to meet learners' interests.

To move towards an adult learning system will involve many existing staff (academic and non-teaching) in considerable change. An adult system would recognise their learning needs and offer opportunities for staff to reflect on the impact of increased adult participation in admissions, guidance, course design, on learning and teaching strategies, information technologies and their applications. The national staff development centre in Sheffield has a vital role to play in building the experiences of those working with adults into the broader staff development programmes in higher education.

To achieve an adult system, government, funding councils and institutions need to make uninhibited use of targeted funding for change and to monitor outcomes. After all, the existing pattern of resource distribution is often the result of earlier targeting to meet other goals. But for that system to be truly worth studying in, the sense of intellectual adventure, energy, challenge and fun that characterises culture being made at its best must be preserved and developed, and this is in my judgement the great benefit of working with adult learners. 'If I can't dance I don't want to be part of your revolution', wrote Emma Goldman. To work with adult learners and to share their vitality and energy is to dance, and it makes the overhaul of the system worthwhile, as well as timely.

7 Access to and through further education

Geoffrey Melling and Geoff Stanton

The present situation

For one group of tutors and students in further education 'Access' is always given a capital initial. The tutors teach on special courses which have been designed to facilitate entry to higher education, and their students are usually adults (in their mid-twenties or older) who are without formal school-leaving qualifications and often lack confidence in their study skills and intellectual ability. Over the last decade Britain's 500 colleges of further education (CFEs) have become skilled at catering for such students. They now offer a recognised route to polytechnic and university for mature returners through these special access courses (FEU 1987). They are sometimes involved in collaborative initiatives which enable students to progress from a group of local colleges to named courses in a regional institution of higher education.

However, such work is only one aspect of the colleges' broad provision. Their traditional role has been to serve young people who leave school at the earliest opportunity. Together with the country's sixth forms, sixth-form colleges and work-based training schemes (for the young employed and unemployed) CFEs comprise what we might call a 'further education phase'. Because the most significant drop-out rate from the orthodox route to higher education occurs at the statutory leaving age, the colleges are agents of access for a much wider range of students than those who are taking A levels or retaking lower qualifications. Most young people who enter their doors after leaving school enrol on courses which traditionally have not been geared to higher education entry. These vocational programmes lead to qualifications for the world of work, and they constitute the main route provided by CFEs: the road to occupations which demand a planned preparation for entry.

The entire further education phase, as described above, is very diverse (Cantor and Roberts 1986; Russell 1989). It not only includes general education and recreational studies, but in the CFEs it comprises vocational education and training as well. Learning may take place full-time or part-time;

packaged in courses of two to three years' duration or of only a few weeks; and located in school, college, training centres, the workplace – or in some combination of these. Although it is usually described in terms of the 16–19 age group, the further education phase in reality has no upper age limit; it can also begin at 14 for those who are clearly on a track to higher education or on a progressive vocational course in the Technical and Vocational Education Initiative (TVEI), which was started by the government in 1982. It also has a commitment to furthering equal opportunities through education and to providing programmes and services for those with special educational needs. However, despite its diversity, most of further education has as its main concern the development of competence. It is developing the student's ability to perform to standards set by bodies outside the phase itself.

This distinguishes further education from both schooling up to 14 and from most full-time higher education. The coming of the National Curriculum, which is devoted to the cognitive development of pupils, does not alter that situation. It may produce greater uniformity among schools, but its targets (like those of most degree courses) are still related to the internal structure of the subjects concerned rather than to the demands of external agencies which wish to recruit people graduating from the system. Further education, on the other hand, is clearly *utilitarian*. Most participants have their sights set on destinations beyond the phase itself, and they wish to be sure that what they are learning will be approved by or acceptable to the 'gatekeepers' whom they have to pass.

In theory, a student's personal and career development might be furthered equally as well by learning related to academic subjects as by learning associated with a vocational interest. In practice, the many gatekeepers who are explicitly or implicitly setting the standards have their own priorities and work within their own different frameworks, as will be seen from the discussion of adult access below. And throughout recent educational history, one route – the academic – has had the higher status. That is not to say that either the curriculum design or the teaching is necessarily better in academic programmes than in vocational courses. However, it is the case that young people who possess A levels may enter higher education *or* a job whereas those with the nominally equivalent vocational qualifications find themselves restricted to a limited number of higher education courses (and an even more restricted range of jobs). It is no surprise, then, that those students who can take the academic route, with reasonable expectations of success, usually do so. The obvious corollary is that the gatekeepers tend to find A level graduates are indeed 'a better bet' than those with the vocational equivalents – and thus both the situation and their prejudices are perpetuated.

This leaves those responsible for vocational courses in a dilemma. They can ensure that their 'academic' demands are equal to those of A levels – but then they find not only that learners who would be quite competent in the vocation concerned fail the course (or even fail to get onto it) but also that their courses are the subject of adverse criticism from employers for 'irrelevance' of content. On the other hand, if they ignore the requirements of admissions tutors in higher education and concentrate on clarifying and meeting the requirements of employers, they narrow the range of future options for those who follow their courses, and so decrease the size and quality of their own market.

There are those who argue that this does not matter: we should simply accept that the brighter students will follow the academic route while we provide vocational courses and qualifications for the rest. There are several things wrong with this argument:

1 Neither set of gatekeepers has the development of the individual as a primary aim when they set their learning targets. Therefore, success at A level cannot necessarily be correlated with basic or developed intelligence.

2 Some able students find the structure and content of vocational courses more conducive to both their intellectual and their career development.

3 Many people choose a vocational route because of a clear intention which they possess at 16, but later change their minds about the gatekeepers they wish to satisfy.

4 Too great a polarity between the routes increases the likelihood of academic education being of little vocational relevance and of vocational provision being educationally narrow. Both these situations under-use the potential of our population, with serious economic consequences for the nation and unfortunate personal consequences for the individuals concerned.

5 It is not likely that we will get the right quality of entrants to technician courses and occupations unless a bridge exists from the vocational to the academic route.

The way in which we have approached access for older people in colleges of further education is in itself a case study of this polarised position. Over the last decade the colleges have become adept in attracting adults. This has been only partly due to increased effort, and more sophistication, in marketing their courses. True, they have had the foresight to look for new customers in the light of falling numbers of school-leavers, and have therefore targeted segments of society (such as unemployed adults, housebound women and ethnic minorities) which are different from the traditional 16–19 population. They have also encouraged employers to commission bespoke services and to support the attendance of workers on existing courses. But in particular, they have exhibited a positive response to government initiatives (and, of course, the associated finance) which have been devised to attract adults into vocational education and training.

Throughout the 1980s the government has been increasingly concerned with improving Britain's economic competitiveness, with keeping abreast of technological change, and with satisfying skill shortages in the labour market.

Much of Whitehall's comment has been to the effect that the country's workforce is under-educated, under-trained and under-qualified in comparison with our major competitors in Europe, the United States and the Far East (Department of Employment and Department of Education and Science 1986; Department of Employment 1988). Much of its action has consisted of ventures to remedy that situation at both national and local levels. Its programmes for young people – TVEI for 14–18s, and the Youth Training Scheme (YTS) for 16–18s (employed as well as unemployed) who have left school – have figured highly in the press, but there have also been a number of programmes to attract, and upgrade the skills of, adult workers. Among these are:

1 PICKUP (under the aegis of the Department of Education and Science), which helps colleges, polytechnics and universities to meet the updating and retraining needs of employers and their workers, usually at 'full cost' (ie without subsidy)

2 REPLAN (also under the Department of Education and Science) which promotes the development of education opportunities for the adult unemployed

3 the Adult Training Strategy, the Job Training Scheme and Employment Training (under the Manpower Services Commission, now the Department of Employment's Training Agency) which, in sequence, have offered unemployed people work experience and training opportunities

4 the Open Tech and, later, the Open College (also under the Department of Employment) which have promoted vocational education and training at a distance.

Teams of staff in various college departments have been involved in these programmes, and (at the time of writing) they are awaiting the advent of the Training and Enterprise Councils (under the Department of Employment but led by local business people) which will oversee vocational education and training and ensure that they meet the requirements of the local labour market.

In addition to initiatives which are designed to upgrade the competence of the workforce, colleges have undertaken activities of their own to benefit adults through education. Examples include:

1 adult literacy schemes

2 flexi-study and similar programmes which allow adults to pick up general qualifications through a mixture of private study and group work

3 access courses which offer an alternative to A level for entry into higher education

4 drop-in skill centres where adults can pick up a range of techniques useful in the home and at work

5 outreach programmes with community groups, prisons, hospitals and firms.

Again, such activities are often developed by different sections and departments in colleges. The staff who organise them, and teach the students, frequently have little contact with each other or with colleagues.

What is revealed by examining these ventures is not the conventional wisdom that we need to stimulate more kinds of access in colleges, but rather an unacknowledged waste of opportunity and human talent which is caused by fragmentation of provision. Current approaches to widen access not only confirm the problem of the academic/vocational divide; they also militate against a holistic approach to adult learning and to the rationalisation of its management. The real challenge of access, so far as managers in further education are concerned, is to make programmes more coherent in order to ensure that clients get the greatest benefits from the service in terms of advice, courses, qualifications and subsequent placement in either work or higher education. To leave matters as they are will only preserve an archipelago of opportunities in which learners find themselves on one island or another without a chance of taking the boat to places in which, subsequently, they would rather be.

Management issues

Although there are things to be done at the level of programme objectives and content, as will be discussed later, there are some major management decisions to be taken if we are genuinely to open up further education to many more adults. At present the emphasis is on establishing and maintaining discrete courses dedicated to a variety of ends. Although teaching staff are aware of the importance of treating adults as mature learners and of using their often considerable experience in the learning situation, the organisation of provision does not reflect the same concerns. Very few colleges have adopted a client-centred approach to the key areas of a student's life in college: entrance procedures, curriculum sequencing, and arrangements for assessment and exit. Were they to do so and to put clients – rather than programmes – first, they would be able to use the funds provided for those programmes in such a way as to meet the targets (of numbers and quality) set by the various sponsors while delaying the final choices by students until they had sufficient advice and guidance as part of the curriculum to be able to make well-founded decisions. The advantage of this approach should be obvious. Students would be able to acquire learning which satisfied particular gatekeepers, but would have the chance to confirm or change direction at a number of points in their studies. The gatekeepers would admit entrants through their portals who did not resent having had to walk down a road from which they could find no exit earlier. The colleges would have more successful and more satisfied students –

and they would be able to incorporate, *en route*, the kind of general education which they know would help access to higher levels of achievement later. Even with individualised advice, the service is likely to be more cost-effective.

The entry phase of an improved operation would have to address a number of concerns: getting through to potential customers, bringing them to an enquiry or admissions point, explaining the college and its offerings to them, assisting them to choose courses or activities which will satisfy their interests and requirements, enrolling them on a programme, and introducing them to college life. The traditional way of tackling these issues has been for departments or individual courses to undertake most of the jobs from advertising to induction, while contributing to some 'corporate marketing' in a general college prospectus and fitting in with the procedures laid down by the institution for its annual enrolment week in September. In this way students have been caught, for example, either by a science A level programme in one section of the college or by its technical equivalent in another department, either by an adult return-to-education course or by the Training Opportunities Scheme, depending on the area of their initial interest, or on the guidance they received from careers advisers or friends, or on the way in which they came across the college's advertising materials. Small advances have been made on this piecemeal approach over the years but it is only very recently that professional marketing techniques (in terms of both research and promotion) have been used to generate more attractive and informative ways of presenting the colleges. Though there are those in the education professions who see this approach not only as trivialising their work but also as treating it after the fashion of a commodity to be sold like any other consumer good, it must be admitted that the employment of marketing managers by colleges and the closer contact with different groups in industry, commerce and the community has paid off in terms of increasing enrolments and in getting to those parts of society which other methods do not reach.

Of course, marketing is not just promotion. It includes activities such as cleaning up public areas of the college, improving food service and eating arrangements, and having at least as welcoming a reception staff as the local department store. Access for adults would be increased by addressing these issues as it has been improved by holding open days on occasions throughout the year, by encouraging community groups to make visits, and by offering 'trial lessons' and seminars on aspects of the colleges' work. (Some ambitious colleges are now producing their own shopping bags, beer mats, bookmarks and items of clothing, which are meant to be useful as well as to serve promotional ends.) The point is that more needs to be done than merely enhancing the advertising budget.

A more obviously educational innovation for managing the entry of students into colleges would be a new kind of reception and assessment centre. Indeed, some of these are now to be found in a few colleges around the country. Where teachers have undertaken the job of advising and admitting students they have generally done so from the standpoint of people committed to particular courses or subject areas. To be more objective, the colleges would have to start with the client, to take a few personal details from enquirers and set about answering their questions partly through information held centrally (possibly in computerised databases) and partly through personal guidance sessions. The latter would involve diagnosing the clients' requirements in relation to their interests and/or ambitions, and explaining what was on offer to satisfy those desires in the college. This guidance would have to outline how the curriculum was structured, and what it entailed in the way of attendance and work from a student. Nor can colleges continue to act as the sole providers of knowledge and skill in the future. They will have to recognise that adults come to them with experience which can be both informative for guidance purposes and valuable in terms of educational worth. As pressure grows to recognise learners' achievements outside the conventional context of education so our institutions will feel obliged to offer some assessment of prior learning either through the examination of a portfolio of evidence or through something like computer-based tests. The results will be useful in terms of advice about entering programmes and could be used for credit.

Enrolment could be managed through a centralised admissions system which ensured that the same basic information about college procedures was given to all students, that they had all completed the appropriate records, and that each of them had been assessed for adequate financial support (and given guidance, if necessary, about sources of aid). The departments and academic teams could then take over for the induction process, though some of that could also be centralised through open learning packages which introduced students to college facilities and the use of library and resource centres. Some colleges have developed packages on study skills which provide a basis for further induction into learning by academic staff.

Managing the provision of courses and the appropriate teaching resource demands some form of 'curriculum audit': that is, a close look at the content, structure and support arrangements for some or all of the programmes in a college. Most institutions which are undertaking this kind of activity are doing so with the aim of identifying opportunities for saving costs; the more far-sighted are using the techniques of analysis to make both the structure of courses and the associated learning strategies more flexible and more client-centred. The result of the exercise is nearly always to produce disaggregated curricula, divided into modules of standard length, which facilitate combining elements from different courses into common units and allow the repeating of the most popular or necessary modules at a number of times during the year. Some units can be materials- or computer-based rather than dependent on teachers, which frees staff to take up other kinds of support role. The great advantage of such 'alternative' teaching methods is that they can be brought together to provide reinforcement learning in resource centres, skill centres, open learning centres and the like; these parts of colleges can offer drop-in facilities for people not enrolled on courses. Indeed, one of the keys to managing for increased access is to ensure the availability of a wide range of learning strategies. This not only makes sense when teaching time is the most costly item in a college's budget (and so must be used wisely), but it is also eminently desirable when institutions are setting out to attract clients through offering a variety of opportunities on an all-the-year-round basis and throughout the day. The technology is now available to provide flexible learning packages in many areas of the curriculum. Computer courseware is improving all the time, and more teachers have become interested in open learning. An increase in the use of learning resources and information technology-based learning would enable students to work at their own pace and to re-work material where necessary. In this way they would become more independent and more readily prepared for further study. They could also take packages home. However, the colleges would have to ensure appropriate tutorial support if they wished to keep the students committed, enthused and working at some pace.

Loosening the constraints of course structures might increase some types of opportunity for the student but it would also bring its own kinds of threat. Most courses in colleges are 'thematic': that is, they are built round content and experiences which relate to an occupation or vocational area. They are not like single-subject GCSE or A level programmes. However, converting them into modular format and juxtaposing their elements with units from other courses would entail the college's making provision for tutorials, advice sessions, 'integrating modules' and work experience or placements which could bring together the strands of what was learned in the classroom, workshop and resource centre. This is of a piece with the support which is necessary for alternative learning strategies. Personal assistance may be necessary, too, in the form of counselling, peer group meetings, child-care facilities, health care and careers advice. Those colleges which are seriously embarked on the access route are already building support networks of this kind. The implications for managers are clear: in the future they will need a range of administrative and professional staff in addition to teachers, to undertake these valuable roles in centres of various kinds. Working out the balance of staff to attract, teach and support learners is a task which will occupy many heads of colleges in the years to come.

A modular curriculum structure facilitates the combining of academic and vocational elements. With the right kind of guidance learners can ensure that they do not miss key subject areas which will prevent them crossing the divide either in the present or later. Similarly, they can all undertake periods of work experience (either in employers' premises, or in voluntary projects or in simulated conditions in college). The well-supported modular curriculum provides the bridges which link the islands of the archipelago, and it allows the student to add upgrading or updating knowledge to a previously acquired core if he or she wishes to change direction.

The ends of education are not all concerned with qualifications, but for many adults their gains in knowledge, skills and confidence will be invalidated by a failure to achieve recognition from an examining authority and/or a passage past the gatekeepers of work or higher education. The management issue here is the provision of ongoing assessments which are related to the requirements of examining boards. A modularised curriculum generally has tests for each unit, but that is not a necessary condition of modularisation if attainment over several units can be measured at once. What is required are opportunities for assessment which occur more frequently than once a year, and which can incorporate some 'testing on demand' for those who arrive at the college not knowing whether they are already competent in particular modules. Staff in charge of an assessment centre should also have a list of standard equivalences between what is on offer in the college and what can be accepted as its equal elsewhere. The corollary of all this for the students is that they should have records of achievement on which their various attainments are registered, and that the college should have a database which holds that information.

One of the last acts of the college for the student is likely to be helping with placement elsewhere. This kind of advice could be offered by specialist teachers or by staff in the guidance centres which were mentioned earlier. The centres could also undertake follow-up studies of a sample of students from each academic year in order to establish how useful the period at college has been in furthering the ambitions of the clients. Indeed, many colleges are already beginning this task much earlier in the learners' careers by undertaking surveys of students' perceptions of courses at regular intervals during their programmes. The feedback from these surveys is part of the evaluation of courses and other services, and helps in the improvement of provision for future customers.

Curriculum issues

Earlier in this chapter, we argued that the further education phase was 'utilitarian' in the sense that as far as that part of the learning which is accredited is concerned, learners wish to be sure that the outcomes they achieve match what various gatekeepers want. Some students may be studying A levels for their intrinsic value, but even here it cannot be denied that the major influence on the design of A level syllabuses is that of the universities, who wish them to be a preparation for degree-level work and a predictor of success as an undergraduate.

Rather than questioning the utilitarian nature of further education, perhaps we should embrace the challenge of enabling the learners to meet clearly defined targets – as long as they *are* clearly defined. The process is well under way as far as vocational qualifications are concerned. 'Industry Lead Bodies' are working at defining the standards of competence required in given vocational sectors. The obvious danger is that definitions may be of narrow skills relevant to only a limited number of jobs. However, many of those concerned with the task are determined that competence in broad roles (rather than skills in a narrow task) is what will be defined. Where this is happening, it is clear that a competent person requires a degree of 'personal effectiveness' which means that learning programmes not only have the chance to be educationally demanding but the requirement to be so.

Could not a similar process be followed by the gatekeepers in higher education? If they could specify as unambiguously as possible the competences required for someone to make a success of a course, then not only would this protect their own interests, it would also give clear targets for the learner to aim at. As in the case of the new vocational qualifications, it would promote access by recognising the attainment of any candidate however his or her competence had been acquired. At the moment, because no one is clear what prerequisites are essential, and to what level, or how they might be measured, recruiters tend to prefer students from the route they know, and whose hidden talents they can at least guess at.

It may be worth dwelling on the way in which the structure of vocational qualifications is currently being reformed (Manpower Services Commission and Department of Education and Science 1986; National Council for Vocational Qualifications 1989). The emphasis is being placed on the measurement of outcomes rather than the design of learning programmes. The 'Industry Lead Bodies' for each occupational sector have been asked to define what it means to occupy competently a vocational role at each of five levels within the sector concerned, from operative through technician to senior managerial or professional roles. Examining and validating bodies are asked to submit schemes for the assessment and certification of these competences to the National Council for Vocational Qualifications, who accredit the qualifications if they are satisfied that they meet the necessary criteria. Among these is that the certification process should only relate to the level and nature of competence achieved, and should not constrain the means by which it is or has been acquired. In other words, it will not, in future, be necessary to do a course in order to gain a qualification.

Although this might take away some of the power and influence of those responsible for the design and implementation of learning programmes, it also liberates them. They are now free to 'tailor-make' a programme to suit the needs and previous experience of the learners concerned. It is no longer the case that the 'quality' of a qualification might be put in doubt by unorthodox recruitment procedures, learning methods or means of recognising prior learning.

We are arguing, therefore, that, if admission tutors could specify the intellectual and other competences which are prerequisites for their courses, then this might

1 protect them against a slide in standards
2 give clear targets at which learners and tutors on preparatory courses could aim.

It might be that higher education would find that to specify prerequisites only in terms of 'competences' was inadequate. However, if some more general requirement for particular earlier learning experiences (for instance) were also identified, then it would be equally useful for those designing access courses. It would also raise interesting questions about the approach of NCVQ which assumes that this is not necessary in the vocational context.

This leads to the thought that adoption of a 'competence-based' approach with regard to admission to both academic and vocational courses would have other advantages. There is at least a chance that the questions raised on both sides of the 'divide' might cause us to realise that some of the abilities and qualities required by a competent person are similar whichever field he or she is in. There would doubtless also be differences, but identifying them would enable us to determine the kind of 'bridging' provision which would be necessary to enable people to gain access to higher education from their present courses or occupations (and also what induction training graduates would require before being competent in a given profession).

The effectiveness of all this would be much enhanced by the existence of a coherent system of record-keeping which not only embodied the crucial common competences in its summative reports but also tracked progress towards them, and therefore served to monitor both progress and the adequacy of learning programmes. This might also serve to systematise and make more reliable the preparation of UCCA and PCAS references.

If all this was put in place, one final difficulty could remain, and might even be exacerbated. If learning programmes on preparatory or access courses are increasingly tailor-made to suit the learning needs of individuals, then this is likely to increase the degree of curriculum discontinuity which can already exist between such courses and those in higher education itself. There is some evidence that learners who have prospered on specially designed access courses find the transition to higher education difficult (Osborne and Woodrow 1989), not because of any lack of ability but because of the inflexibility and unresponsiveness of teaching methods in much of higher education. The implication is, of course, that providing access to higher education for new client groups is not enough. The way to do this without compromising standards might be to follow the approach described earlier: to separate the definition of competence to be reached from any particular means of attaining it.

In curriculum terms, this means giving proportionately more attention to the diagnosis of learning needs and the design and monitoring of individual action plans, and less to standard methods of delivering or teaching 'performance'. In other words, institutions of higher education have to develop expertise in the management of learning, as well as maintaining their levels of academic excellence and research.

8 Enterprise, scholars and students

George Tolley

For the great majority of entrants, higher education is, academically, a continuation of the sixth-form. Most will continue studies in subjects that comprised their sixth-form curriculum. All those who enter higher education directly from school (and it is this direct entry from school that has shaped the ethos and the methods of higher education), whether continuing their sixth-form studies or not, will very largely continue in the same patterns of learning that governed their sixth-form work. In spite of the emphases in higher education upon student autonomy, responsibility and independence, two features predominate and deeply influence methods of learning, attitudes and relationships. There is, first, the notion of scholarship. The word 'scholar' has a clear progression of meaning from 'one who is taught in school', through 'one who is taught in the schools' (ie to pass university examinations), to 'a learned and erudite person'. Scholarship, denoting extensive and erudite learning coupled with a scrupulous and critical approach, is for the most part translated in higher education into mastery of a subject.

The second feature is directly related to the first and is the perception of studentship; in higher education there are the teachers and the taught. Students in higher education are there to be taught, to master a given corpus of knowledge that constitutes 'the subject' and to master certain intellectual skills that can be applied as logical and critical thinking. Contained within this perception of studentship are ideas and traditions about the methods and the content of learning that do much to formalise study in higher education and to prescribe methods of assessment that demand, all too often, the reproduction of what has been taught, rather than assessing what has been learned.

Now it is necessary that both scholarship and studentship should figure prominently in the objectives and the processes of higher education. What is not necessary, or justifiable, is that these features should override other necessary aspects and aims and, in particular, what is not acceptable is that traditions of scholarship and studentship should impose unnecessary rigidities upon the community of learning that is a university or a polytechnic. Pressures for the widening of access to higher education arise from the facts of demography and, more importantly, from the need greatly to improve the general level of education throughout the population. Responses to these pressures that concern themselves only with enlarging the door into a room that continues with the same furniture will in no way meet the needs of wider access. It is the aims, the content and the process of higher education that have to be changed if significantly wider access is to be achieved. Changing the requirements for entry will not, of itself, produce a wider access system.

If all that were at issue was overcoming the demographic plunge, then we need not concern ourselves overmuch with what goes on in higher education. A few changes here and there in admission requirements and procedures, a little more flexibility on the part of admissions tutors would be all that is required to move from a participation rate of 14 per cent to, say, 18 per cent. But surely that is no longer the central issue? We need to think in terms of something like a doubling in numbers in higher education (Baker 1989b). And *en route* to achieving that target, we need to ensure that graduates become better fitted to the changing world of employment. There are issues of quantity and also, to put it crudely, issues of how to change the product. Teachers and administrators in higher education are adept in directing most proposals or calls for change back to issues of quality; but it is quality in the narrow sense of largely maintaining the status quo in terms of scholarship and studentship. It is quality also largely in terms of the inputs of higher education rather than outputs. An élite system of higher education based upon these narrow notions of quality is no longer appropriate for a complex, competitive world.

If numbers in higher education are to increase substantially, the traditions of scholarship and studentship must take their place amongst other demands and other needs, and must not dominate, as they have done in the past. That domination has restricted entry into higher education, has maintained the rigidities of the single-subject honours course and has ensured that the pursuit of much mediocre research has taken precedence over the aim of good teaching. It has long been agreed or assumed that research and scholarship guarantee the quality of university teaching (Ashworth 1989). It is difficult to see how they guarantee anything of the kind, given the lack of attention to issues of quality in teaching. Conformity to the norms of a world in which scholarship and studentship take precedence over other demands and needs has maintained the narrow élitism of British higher education. Other needs, equally if not more pressing in a changing world, have not been addressed with the necessary urgency. They need to be addressed if higher education is to meet the needs both of a changing clientele and a changing world. I see the need to address five issues in particular and will briefly consider each of them.

Skills shortages

All sectors of employment are requiring more people with higher levels of skills. Even when numbers in employment have fallen drastically, as in manufacturing industry, the demand for people with high-level skills has increased. In engineering and science there are evident shortfalls in numbers of people capable of operating at the leading edge of technology in rapidly advancing technologies,notably in information technology and electronics. And there is a substantial and chronic shortfall at the higher technician level, which for so long has been the forgotten sector of British higher education, spurned by the universities, carefully nurtured by some polytechnics and maintained on sufferance by others. Whilst some jobs have been, and are being, deskilled by the development and application of new technology, there is clear evidence to show that higher levels of skills are necessary to meet the demands of new technologies and of global competition (Gallie 1989). But the most important factor to address is not that of specific skills shortages, important though that is. The nature of skill itself is changing; it is the ability, the competence, to cope with rapid change that is now a necessary concomitant of any specialist skill, without which overall competence cannot be delivered. That there have been, and are, specific skills shortages (notably in engineering and science) in the United Kingdom is clear enough. Remedying those shortages by providing more places in specific courses will not guarantee the flexibility and adaptability to change without which there will be neither personal effectiveness nor a sound economy.

Professionalism

Graduates take up jobs that, for the most part, call for the exercise of professional responsibilities. That does not mean that all graduates become members of the so-called chartered professions, that is, those that are governed by statutory or non-statutory requirements of entry and/or performance. But it does mean that, in addition to the exercise of specific skills and the application of knowledge, there are professional requirements that must be fulfilled. The professional must accept responsibility for work done; must exercise discretion and judgement; must work with other professionals; must exercise, in some form or another, the responsibilities of management. The acceptance and the discharge of professional responsibility need to figure in the aims and the outcomes of all higher education courses, not merely in some. Yet most graduates emerge with little or no acquaintance with the professional demands that will be made upon them. And the great majority of teachers in higher education take the view that the processes of professional formation and development have little to do with the essentials of undergraduate education but are matters for the professions themselves and for work experience subsequent to graduation. But subject knowledge and intellectual ability do not, of themselves, assure dependable powers of judgement or the proper exercise of responsibility, or the ability to work as a member of a team.

Personal, transferable skills

The University Grants Committee and the National Advisory Body sensibly and usefully identified, some years ago, the importance for the world of employment of generic skills that go beyond and underwrite subject knowledge and specific skills. Many employers are looking, in a wide range of jobs, for those generic skills, rather than for some specific skill or knowledge. To be able to communicate, to solve problems, to make decisions, to cooperate with others, to adapt to change; these things are more highly prized in the world of employment than performance in examinations that test the ability to master a subject. But it is not only in employment that personal, transferable skills are important. That generic skills are transferable means that they are of value outside employment in all activities that have to do with relationships or that require the application of knowledge and skills to achieve tasks. For personal fulfilment and personal satisfaction it is these generic skills that will be particularly important. The outcomes of higher education that really matter, in the longer term, are those that relate to personal, transferable skills. It is these outcomes that need emphasising more strongly and identifying more clearly. They need to be sought more directly and reflected in the process and content of higher education. The Joint Statement, *Higher Education and the Needs of Society*, published by the National Advisory Board (NAB) and the University Grants Committee (UGC) in 1984, puts it very well:

> The abilities most valued in industrial, commercial and professional life as well as in public and social administration are the transferable intellectual and personal skills. These include the ability to analyse complex issues, to identify the core of a problem and the means of solving it, to synthesise and integrate disparate elements, to clarify values, to make effect use of numerical and other information, to work co-operatively and constructively with others, and, above all perhaps, to communicate clearly both orally and in writing. A higher education system which provides its students with these things is serving society well (NAB 1984b: 2).

Enterprise

Enterprise means getting things done. To be enterprising is to be able to set goals for oneself and for others and to know how to set about achieving these goals. Enterprise is not necessarily a business-related skill or aptitude, nor is it necessarily about making money or profit. It is about taking and implementing decisions to achieve objectives, which will always involve some element of risk and will require an individual to live with the consequences of those decisions. In a narrow sense, every course in higher education requires the student to get things done and to strive to achieve goals, if only to complete essays on time and to pass examinations. But too many graduates, when they take up employment, lack enterprise and it cannot be said that their courses have encouraged the development of the qualities of enterprise. The tasks they seek to achieve in higher education are largely set for them; there is only one way – the 'right' way – to achieve those tasks; there is little opportunity for team work and even less for risk-taking; many of the tasks are concerned with abstractions rather than the real world. Because these are the common characteristics of so much in higher education, which is so often all about knowing rather than doing, enterprise is regarded as a foreign and unwelcome concept by many in higher education.

Regard needs to be had to three aspects of enterprise, to getting things done. There is education *about* enterprise, which will give to graduates some measure of economic awareness, will point up the need for application of knowledge in the wider context of setting and achieving goals. There is education *for* enterprise, which will introduce the undergraduate to the skills necessary for some aspects of management, in the context not only of profit-making organisations and small businesses, but also of all organisations that must be run efficiently if they are to achieve their purpose. Concentrating upon these two aspects – *about* and *for* enterprise – could well have a business-oriented slant which has little relationship to the mainstream curriculum of some subjects. There is a need also for education *through* enterprise, in which the undergraduate is given some real autonomy in learning, in which there is adequate opportunity for projects to be undertaken in a different environment to that offered in the lecture room, library or laboratory. Education through enterprise will touch the curriculum, not merely in its content, but in its process. This leads to the fifth issue to be addressed if higher education is to adapt to meet the needs of a wider clientele.

The learning relationship

The norm in higher education is still very largely that of the single-subject honours degree course in which most of the teaching is didactic, in which each individual student is responsible for their own work and the unseen, written paper stands as the supreme arbiter of performance. Group learning is largely extra-curricular, as is the exercise of individual choice in interests and activities. The purpose of learning is confined too narrowly to the acquisition of knowledge and skills in order to pass examinations rather than learning in order to apply knowledge and skills which must involve experience in a different learning environment and in the achievement of group tasks. The concept and the tradition of the solitary scholar, individually mastering a corpus of knowledge, solving problems in isolation, underlies so much of the tradition of learning in higher education that one forgets all too easily that this is not how we learn most of what we know and do. For, outside the artificial learning environment that constitutes so much of higher education, we learn by doing, by working with and reacting to other people in the joint achievement of tasks, by having to choose from a number of possible solutions to problems, all or none of which may be right. In higher education, the method of assessment – the examination – dominates the methods of learning. Once out of higher education it is the application, not the reproduction, of knowledge and skills that matters.

The major emphasis in the arguments and pressures for wider access to higher education has been upon changing the procedures and priorities for entry. Hence the development of access courses and the criticism (entirely proper) of the A level domination of entry. This emphasis continues the obsession, which governs so much in education, with inputs rather than outcomes. If wider access is indeed to be achieved on any substantial scale and the needs of both individuals and society are to be better provided for, then it is outcomes that must be more clearly expressed and more seriously sought than at present. One of the advantages of exploring the concept of enterprise in higher education is that it focuses attention upon outcomes and upon the changes that may be necessary if desired outcomes are to be achieved. It is difficult to see how alternative futures for higher education can be adequately expressed and assessed unless outcomes are stated, not merely in terms of output (numbers and broad classification of disciplines) but in terms also of curriculum aims. If, in addition to an understanding of subject knowledge and the development of certain cognitive skills, every graduate were required to develop and demonstrate the personal, transferable skills which the NAB/UGC Joint Statement emphasises and, at the same time, were also required to have the ability to apply knowledge and skills for the achievement of tasks and goals, then we could not rest content with much that goes on in higher education at the moment. Neither could we be satisfied only with changes in access that fall short of changes in teaching and learning methods.

It is changes in teaching and learning methods that have been the central concern of Education for Capability, which the Royal Society of Arts has been effectively promoting for some years. An extract from the manifesto of Education for Capability might be helpful here:

> The aim of Education for Capability is to encourage and develop in people four capacities that are currently under-emphasised in our education system.
>
> The great majority of learners – whether pupils at school, students at universities, polytechnics or colleges, or adults still wanting to learn – are destined for a productive life of practical action. They are going to do

things, design things, make things, organise things, for the most part in cooperation with other people. They need to improve their *Competence*, by the practice of skills and the use of knowledge; to *Cope* better with their own lives and the problems that confront them and society; to develop their *Creative* abilities; and, above all, to *Cooperate* with other people. It is these four capacities that we want to see encouraged and developed through Education for Capability.

The education system at present gives most of its emphasis to other educational aims – the development of the abilities to acquire and record specialised knowledge and to appreciate the values inherent in our cultural heritage. We call their achievement *Comprehension* and *Cultivation*, respectively, which by themselves are not enough; even for those destined to pursue a life of scholarship or contemplation, they do not alone afford an adequate preparation for life in the outside world (Education for Capability nd: 2).

More recently, the Royal Society of Arts, with support from other agencies, has launched the Higher Education for Capability Project with the aim of helping to bring about a fundamental change in the culture of British higher education to produce one in which all students can develop personal qualities of capability, irrespective of their area of study. In general terms capability is defined as the ability to take effective action, to live and work with other people, to explain what one is about and to continue to learn and to adapt. Today's rapidly changing world and increasingly diverse society demand these abilities and skills of all graduates irrespective of the work they will be doing.

I would summarise the task for higher education as a dual one requiring a progression from teaching to learning and from abstraction to involvement. If the task is to be undertaken than major changes in three particular areas are required.

Assessment methods

Examination methods in higher education are dominated by the written unseen paper and by the essay. Conventional examinations are tests of individual ability to write, to reproduce facts, to present a critical analysis, to demonstrate in writing knowledge and understanding and to perform under the pressure of time in an artificial environment. They do not test a whole host of abilities and skills that are absolutely essential to the application of knowledge and to getting things done. Conventional examinations test only that narrow ground of ability and interest that relates to scholarship and studentship. The wider ground of personal, transferable skills and of broad aspects of enterprise remains unexplored.

Assessment, to be of value, must satisfy requirements of validity, reliability and convenience. There is little doubt that conventional examinations have reliability in that results are, with the very occasional and explicable error, repeatable. They are convenient to administer and cheap to run. But they do not meet what should be the central, essential requirement of assessment, which is that of validity. An examination is valid if it achieves what it is designed to do. The conventional examination grades students and it does this clearly and simply, but it does not indicate potential, nor competence, nor effectiveness in applying knowledge, nor the ability to cope with change. Yet it is assumed by many, including employers, that possession of a degree, and in particular the class of degree awarded, does indicate these things. If capability and enterprise are to be developed then examination methods need to change. There is no need to get rid of conventional written examinations totally. They have an important place in assessment. But there is a need to extend and supplement the written examination with other, more valid, forms of assessment. Some degree courses, notably in engineering, take account, in the final degree award, of project work involving external clients, in which assessment is carried out jointly by teachers and the staff of the external organisation. In such a project, the tasks to be achieved will be set out clearly, there will be a choice of options for solutions and there will be time and resource constraints. The assessment of individual contributions to group projects remains a difficulty, although where there is the will to take advantage of the effectiveness and benefits of group learning, solutions have been found.

But assessment methods, and their impact upon learning methods, will not change significantly until the obsession with single-mark, single-classification awards gives way to a desire to present a fuller and clearer picture of a person's abilities and skills. The question 'What competencies are being developed and assessed?' is one that the higher education community refuses to face up to, taking refuge behind the tradition, with all its misleading assumptions, of classifying achievement by class of degree. A competency approach calls for a profile of achievement rather than a statement of class of award as a single summation of both performance and potential. It is encouraging to see interest developing in student profiles and in a competency approach to identifying the outcomes of learning. When the straitjacket of examinations begins to be released, then important freedoms will be offered in the development of learning methods.

Few teachers in higher education teach solely in order to ensure that students pass examinations, but all teachers in higher education must and will have regard to examination methods and those methods exert a considerable influence in the shaping of objectives for teaching methods. If one would change teaching methods, then examination methods must change also.

Learning environments

To press the case for the development of qualities and skills of enterprise in undergraduates is not a matter of constraining learning; it is rather to seek the enhancement of the learning environment. I have no wish to characterise universities and polytechnics as ivory towers; those who do so often have little idea of the reality of contemporary higher education. But it remains true that the environment of learning in higher education is for the most part narrow and exclusive. Yet it need not be so, and indeed must not be so, if personal, transferable skills are to be adequately and effectively developed to meet the needs of graduates. Sandwich courses, work experience placements, project work involving external organisations, team work that requires the solution of practical problems: all these broaden the learning environment beyond the confines of the lecture room, laboratory and library, whilst depending still upon activities in those places within the institution.

Higher education institutions, if they are to fulfil their role, must offer students access to a variety of learning experiences. Yet learning is dominated, unduly dominated, by the course and delivery of the course in classroom or laboratory. It is teaching, not learning, that controls the curriculum and its delivery. It is the acquisition of knowledge and not its application that stands central in the purposes of higher education. Yet learning is incomplete without application. And learning that is constrained by the narrow environment of classroom and laboratory will be narrow learning. It is not good enough to point to the variety and richness of extra-curricular activities in higher education. Certainly these contribute significantly to the quality of the learning experience. But a rich panoply of extra-curricular activities taken up for the most part in a random fashion by students does not necessarily enrich the learning process in the mainstream curriculum.

Interest in involving students in planned activities forming part of their course which bring them into contact with external organisations, with visiting staff and in settings that take them outside the educational institution has increased considerably in recent years. In part this has arisen from a desire to give to undergraduates some opportunity for exploration of the world of work; to give them an edge in the job market. In part it has been due to a desire to relate theory to practice and to do this in practical settings where the application of knowledge and skills can be tested out on real problems. Hence the growth in sandwich courses, in work placements, in projects requiring cooperation with external organisations, in the use of visiting lecturers and, here and there, encouragement for students to take a year off during their course to gain some relevant experience. What is lacking, still, in the great bulk of courses in higher education is recognition of the need to enrich the learning environment by establishing structures and requirements for the exploration of learning opportunities outside formal course teaching. In setting up these structures and requirements there has to be a serious examination of the shortcomings of formal teaching situations; of the need to provide adequate opportunity for the application as well as the acquisition of knowledge; of the need to provide opportunity for group work and for accountability to complete tasks within time and resource constraints.

The role of external organisations (whether private or public sector employers, manufacturing, profit-making or voluntary) in these activities is not merely to give opportunities for recruitment or for work experience and certainly employers should not be allowed to dominate the curriculum. The aim should be that of enriching the curriculum, so stimulating motivation and enhancing learning. Participation by employers in the processes of curriculum development, going well beyond the provision of work placements, has been found to be beneficial to the effectiveness of learning. Moreover, if the intake into higher education is to become more varied, with a greater proportion of mature students and of non-standard entrants, there will be a need for greater variety in learning methods and in learning environments. The artificiality and the limitations of so much of the learning environment in higher education will become more exposed as wider access becomes a reality. And the breadth and variety of the learning experience of those students who enter higher education directly from school is also now being widened considerably by new approaches in schools, notably through the Technical and Vocational Education Initiative (TVEI), and this new clientele will hardly be satisfied by the narrowness of much of the learning environment in higher education.

Course structures

The single-subject honours degree course provides, for the most part, the hallmark of quality in British higher education. Joint honours courses and modular courses have been developing in recent years, notably in the polytechnics and colleges, and interdisciplinary courses such as business studies have become important. But it is still the single-subject honours course that is regarded as a norm and governs entry and aspiration. And even in those courses that depart from that norm there remains, often enough, a good deal of rigidity in course structure and in methods of teaching. For purposes of scholarship, the single-subject degree course may well be a relevant and indeed a sound basis of preparation. It provides for depth, for penetration in a narrow field; it allows the student to appreciate and to understand recent advances in knowledge in parts of a narrow field; it can give the student confidence in achieving mastery of a small canvas of knowledge; it introduces the student to the intellectual challenges in striving for that mastery. The single-subject honours course must certainly not be written off. But should it have the dominant position it holds, exerting an influence across the whole spectrum of British higher education, setting a standard of academic excellence which goes unquestioned by so many?

The great majority of graduates will not be scholars and will have no cause to seek scholarship in the sense of mastery of a narrowly defined field of knowledge or the broad sweep of abstraction. That they should be aware of and respect standards of scholarship is entirely right and proper; that they should have to follow a course of study that seeks to develop attitudes and skills of scholarship is, at the very least, arguable. But, issues of scholarship apart, the great bulk of course structures in British higher education do not provide sufficient flexibility to allow for the developing interest of students and usually offer little opportunity for that eminently human characteristic, change of mind. The student is called upon to make a choice before sampling the goods and has to live with the consequences of that choice. If indeed there is to be a more varied and more mature entry in higher education this is a situation that is not likely to go unchallenged by those entrants.

But there are other reasons for challenging the all-too-monolithic structures of most courses. In the first place, intellectual challenge and academic rigour are not confined to an in-depth study in a relatively narrow field. The abilities to handle concepts, to pursue a line of argument, to analyse critically, to assemble and to present facts, to demonstrate logical and coherent thought are not solely dependent upon in-depth study of a single subject. And, secondly, other abilities of equal importance may not be developed adequately in a single-subject course: the ability to establish and to express relationships between cognate fields of knowledge; to assemble and analyse data of complex multidisciplinary and multidimensional problems; to appreciate and understand the insights of other disciplines and professions; to understand and to be able to handle the often conflicting priorities identified through those various insights. Pure scholarship may not be the best ground from which to develop and to apply such abilities; indeed, narrowly based convergent thinking may be a disability amidst the reality of complex, multidisciplinary problems which constitute the real world.

Course structures that provide for greater flexibility and choice and for multidisciplinary studies of value in a range of applications are justified on grounds of demand and relevance. There is no case for claiming that such structures lead to a lowering of standards or to a lessening of intellectual demands upon students. Where such courses exist at the moment, as they do quite widely, they are not of lower standard than single-subject courses. What is difficult to justify is the continuing domination of higher education by courses that develop skills of scholarship that are inappropriate to most of those entering higher education.

Excellence and competence

Pressures for widening access to higher education are increasing and can hardly be resisted. I have been suggesting that widening access, coping with greater numbers, is much more a matter of changing what goes on in higher education, than it is a matter of changing modes of entry into higher education as we currently know it. I have had nothing to say about funding higher education or about changing institutional structures or the future of the binary system. I will leave that to others because I have wished here to comment upon issues which seem to me to transcend finance, administration and structures. It seems to me that perhaps the greatest resistance to change in higher education comes from those within higher education itself. That resistance to change derives from notions of excellence that sustain ideas of quality. There is an institutional hierarchy within higher education that is based more upon perceptions of a tradition of quality than upon the effectiveness of learning. That hierarchy, the pecking order that governs the A level grades required for entry (a hierarchy that interestingly is increasingly irrelevant to the substantial and growing numbers of mature and non-standard entrants) reflects a concern for the most part with excellence in the narrow sense of the demands of scholarship and research. Narrowly based notions of excellence have bedevilled British higher education for far too long. The Robbins Committee missed the opportunity presented to it of establishing a higher education framework to meet the demands of a great and necessary expansion. Most of that expansion came about in institutions that the Robbins report ignored, precisely because of the constraining notions of excellence that governed their thinking.

It is entirely possible to have excellence in a system of higher education that provides for a great diversity of institutions. Indeed, some would say that it is only with such diversity that excellence can be sustained. What is not possible any longer is to pretend that excellence in the narrow sense of achievement in scholarship and research is the correct basis upon which to make decisions about a higher education system for the twenty-first century. There is another issue alongside excellence of at least equal importance and that is the issue of competence. For we must ask, not only what subjects will be studied in depth in higher education, but what competencies are to be developed in graduates. Amongst all the gloss and glitter of present-day prospectuses of universities and polytechnics there is a great deal about facilities (indicating the ease with which the student can get away from education) and about courses (the blocks of knowledge taught). But there is very little indeed about the competencies that a course seeks to develop. So we have many knowledgeable graduates who lack competence to apply that knowledge. We need in our higher education the commanding heights of excellence, however expressed. The thin stream of excellence could do with being increased from a trickle to something like a spate. But at the same time we need a flood of competent people, and higher education must direct its attention much more than it has done to encouraging and managing that flood.

The competencies that are needed, both for adequate and satisfying personal development and also to meet the needs of society, must include personal, transferable skills and the abilities and skills of enterprise. It is these competencies that higher education has so regularly ignored or taken for granted. It would be of great benefit to students, potential and actual, to employers and to the cause of seeking effective learning, if universities and polytechnics could be more revealing about the competencies they seek to develop in graduates and how they develop and assess them. Only when this is done can the question 'Access to what?' be properly addressed.

9 Need mathematics and science present a problem for access to universities?

Sinclair Goodlad

Initial assumptions

The argument of this chapter is premised on the assumption that education is an end as well as a means. Whatever use they may have, mathematics, science, and engineering are intellectual creations of the utmost fascination and delight; to participate meaningfully in the culture of contemporary society (to take political decisions; to read, look, and listen with discernment; to exercise imagination and enjoy the fruits of the imagination of others) people need to study mathematics, science, and engineering to high levels of achievement whether or not they are going to become practitioners.

It is not obvious whether competitive advantage in industry and commerce is effect or cause of a highly-educated population in modern society. Prudence suggests that it is best to work on the assumption that education leads to prosperity and to plan accordingly, not least because if we get it wrong, it will take a generation to put arrangements in place to educate the population.

From arguments of both use and delight, this chapter assumes that it is desirable that the greatest possible number of the United Kingdom's citizens study mathematics, science, and engineering to the highest possible level. If, as is the case, significant numbers of people do *not* undertake such study who *could* do so, this is a matter for concern.

The following pages show that mathematics, science, and engineering do indeed seem to present a problem for access to universities for women and for students over twenty-five years of age. The chapter argues that this need not be so if universities were to plan curricula and teaching methods in ways somewhat different from those which prevail at present. Although significant innovations are currently taking place in polytechnics and in colleges and institutes of higher education in the United Kingdom, the discussion in this chapter is confined to possible changes in practice at universities, not only because that is where most of my own experience has been gained, but also because universities are major centres for education in science, engineering and mathematics in which women and adult students should be made welcome.

Access in mathematics, science, and engineering: the problem

Despite fears of 'the demographic winter', there has been no overall decline in the applications to United Kingdom universities since 1983 (Fulton and Ellwood, 1989: 9). As in the United States (see Trow 1989), people who might not otherwise have applied for entry to higher education have come forward so that the decline in the age-cohort of 18 to 22-year-olds has not yet appeared to be the problem that was feared at first.

There are, nevertheless, some gross imbalances in the take-up of subjects. Table 11 shows that in 1988, students over 25 years of age represented 10 per cent of those accepted in social sciences and 13 per cent of those accepted in humanities, compared with 3 per cent of those accepted in physical sciences, 4 per cent of those accepted in mathematical sciences, and 3 per cent of those accepted in engineering and technology.

Table 12 shows that for women the situation is similar. In particular, women represent 68 per cent of acceptances in languages, 80 per cent in education, and 64 per cent in combined arts, compared with only 27 per cent in physical sciences, 25 per cent in mathematical sciences, and 12 per cent in engineering and technology. Despite major initiatives such as WIST (Women into Science and Technology), the situation does not seem to have improved significantly from what it was six years ago (see Acker 1984).

Those mature students who *do* get admitted to university seem to perform as well as their younger contemporaries (see Smithers and Griffin 1986; Clarke 1988). Likewise, in broad terms, women do as well as men in all subjects at university, although there are some notable areas of underachievement that are still the subject of research and debate (Clarke 1988; Rudd 1988).

Access courses in mathematics and science

With a view to encouraging more mature students and women students to apply for higher education, access courses have for some years been offered in a number of further and higher education institutions. In the early 1980s, there were very few courses in mathematics, science, and engineering (CNAA 1984;

Table 11 Home candidates aged 25 and over accepted by subject 1988

	a	b	
	Over 25s N	**Total N**	**a/b %**
A Medicine and Dentistry	149	4,662	3
B Topics allied to medicine	130	2,127	6
C Biological Sciences	360	5,877	6
D Agriculture and related subjects	52	1,201	4
F Physical Sciences	182	7,153	3
G Mathematical Sciences	207	5,694	4
H/J Engineering and Technology	264	9,466	3
K Architecture, Building and Planning	40	1,189	3
L/M Social Sciences	1,191	11,705	10
N Business and administration	100	3,922	3
P Mass communication and documentation	28	196	14
Q/R/T Languages and related subjects	597	8,642	7
V Humanities	652	5,186	13
W Creative arts	57	1,193	5
X Education	86	1,023	8
Combined sciences	79	1,888	4
Combined social studies	104	1,561	7
Combined arts	239	2,166	11
Science combined with social studies or arts	81	1,864	4
Social studies combined with arts	231	2,504	9
Other general and combined studies	150	1,277	12
Totals	4,979	80,496	6

Source: Based on UCCA 1989 Table B2

Lucas and Ward 1985). Although there have been some improvements recently in the number of courses on offer (Osborne 1988), there is little room for complacency. Parry (1989a: 24) discovered that of 97 access courses offered by or in association with United Kingdom universities in 1987–88, only seven were in mathematics, science and technology. As experience of such courses

Table 12 Home candidates by subject of acceptance 1988

	Men		Women		Total
	N	% Total	N	% Total	
A Medicine and Dentistry	2,475	53	2,187	47	4,662
B Topics allied to medicine	663	31	1,464	69	2,127
C Biological Sciences	2,659	45	3,218	55	5,877
D Agriculture and related subjects	654	54	547	46	1,201
F Physical Sciences	5,248	73	1,905	27	7,153
G Mathematical Sciences	4,274	75	1,420	25	5,694
H/J Engineering and Technology	8,305	88	1,161	12	9,466
K Architecture, Building and Planning	866	73	323	27	1,189
L/M Social Sciences	6,076	52	5,629	48	11,705
N Business and administration	2,322	59	1,600	41	3,922
P Mass communication and documentation	59	30	137	70	196
Q/R/T Languages and related subjects	2,745	32	5,897	68	8,642
V Humanities	2,778	54	2,408	46	5,186
W Creative arts	459	38	734	62	1,193
X Education	205	20	818	80	1,023
Combined sciences	1,189	63	699	37	1,888
Combined social studies	883	57	678	43	1,561
Combined arts	773	36	1,393	64	2,166

Cont'd . . .

	Men		Women		Total
	N	% Total	N	% Total	
Science combined with arts or social studies	1,128	61	736	39	1,864
Social studies combined with arts	1,110	44	1,394	56	2,504
Other general combined studies	573	45	704	55	1,277
Totals	45,444	56	35,052	44	80,496

Source: Based on UCCA 1989 Table G1

accumulates, it is to be hoped that other establishments of further and higher education will emulate the work described in the admirable case studies provided by, for example, the Royal Society (1988) and Strachan, Brown, and Schuller (1989). The establishment by the CVCP and the CNAA of a framework of national arrangements for the recognition of access courses (CVCP and CNAA 1989) may give added impetus to the movement.

Other initiatives have been taking place which may improve the situation. For example, foundation-year courses in engineering have been established in a number of universities by an initiative of the Engineering Professors' Conference. In the first year of these courses, the percentage of women in the intake was 19 per cent – more than twice the average for undergraduate engineering courses (EPC 1989).

The influence of modes of study on student motivation

This chapter will not deal with the relative merits of linked or open arrangements for admission to university following access courses; rather, it will focus on certain issues regarding course design which are emerging as significant in stimulating or reducing student motivation.

The underrepresentation of women in science and engineering at universities has been well-known for years; it has been convincingly shown to stem from influences at work, in the home and in the school which produce systematic discrimination against females from the earliest years (see, for example, the excellent essays in Kelly 1981). Similarly, the reasons for the underrepresentation of women in mathematics and mathematically-based subjects are very complex. Walkerdine and her colleagues from the Girls and Mathematics Unit of the University of London Institute of Education (1989) make a convincing case that the confidence of girls is eroded from their early years in the present education system. They offer no easy solution to the problem but propose a transformation in mathematical discourses themselves to produce a discursive practice which would not separate rationalisation from affect and from the social. They state (1989: 207):

> This would not be a femininst or female Mathematics, precisely because it would not be Mathematics as we understand it today. Its limit conditions and bases would be differently drawn.

Burton, who studied the experience of adult learners of mathematics, also identified confidence as the key issue. She urges a move away from traditional ways of teaching mathematics and mathematically-based subjects as follows (Burton 1987: 314):

Emphasis on	competition	changed to	collaboration
	individual work		group work
	knowing		enquiring
emphasis on	answers	changed to	questions
	formalisation		informality
	substantiation		conjecturing
	replication		creation.

In their major study of *Access to Mathematics, Science and Technology*, Osborne and Woodrow (1989) show how colleges of further education do indeed adopt the style of working recommended by Burton, but only in the early stages of access courses. In their section on Teaching/Learning Strategies (p. 34), they report that:

> The style of delivery is changed gradually towards a more formal approach, lecture-based to reflect the impersonal style of HE.

In mathematics, lecturers tried to promote student-centred, workshop-based methods using independent-learning materials, though the students often resisted or were suspicious of unfamiliar learning materials. Interestingly, Osborne and Woodrow also recommend (p. 58) that mathematics should be taught wherever practicable within the context of science.

Most significantly, from the point of view of the present chapter, Osborne and Woodrow note (1989: 60) that:

> Although it is not the primary aim of Access courses to change the delivery methods of HE, it may be that as increasing numbers of adults enter HE, traditional modes of teaching may be challenged.

Another pressure for change will almost certainly emerge within the next five years. The emphasis of the National Curriculum on a wider spread of studies at school level and the increasing use of project-methods in GCSE subjects will, despite the present government's rejection of the Higginson report, create pressure for a modification of traditional GCE A and AS levels; this will, in turn, produce further pressure on universities to modify their methods of teaching.

The thesis of the remainder of this chapter is that traditional modes of teaching in universities need to be challenged for a variety of reasons in addition to those already mentioned, and that if they are appropriately modified, mathematics, science and engineering need not continue to present the problems of access that they undoubtedly do at present. In short, courses could become more 'user-friendly' to both women and mature students (or both, bearing in mind that there is a significant overlap between these categories).

Universities in the 1990s: constraints and opportunities

Policy and practice in universities currently has to reflect and respond to a rapidly changing political, economic and administrative climate. Course design (in terms of curriculum and teaching methods) must, I will argue, be the principal instrument of that policy. Relevant issues include:

1. A projected decline between 1989 and 1995 of approximately one-third in the age cohort of 18 to 22-year-olds in the United Kingdom;
2. A move away from full grants towards a mixture of loans and grants;
3. An increase in fees for further and higher education courses (and possibly differential fees for different types of courses);
4. Changes in the curriculum, teaching methods and assessment procedures in schools;
5. Increased movement of students between countries;
6. The implementation of sophisticated credit-transfer arrangements in further and higher education (initially in CNAA-validated institutions, but now throughout further and higher education).

The consequences (many already evident) of these factors are likely to be:

1. Increased competitiveness between further and higher education institutions for their share of the 'market';
2. A pressure on institutions to take additional students at marginal cost (to get the benefit of the fee income which will compete singificantly with that available from the UFC or PCFC);
3. A possible desire among students for 'accelerated routes' to degrees, for part-time study (moving between the status of external and internal student

of the university), for 'stopping out'; for exercising credit-transfer options between courses and institutions – in short, for greater flexibility of study (on the model already familiar in many parts of the United States);

4 A possible associated pressure to make two-year courses the basic qualification in some subjects, with facility for transfer into the third year of three- or four-year degree courses (as happens in several community college systems in the United States);

5 A probable increase in the popularity of sponsorship of students with an associated interweaving of study and practical work;

6 A probable increase in the popularity of part-time study through which learning and earning can be combined;

7 The need to accommodate overseas students who wish to study in the United Kingdom for a year or part of a year to earn credit within their home degree regime;

8 A widening of the spread of achievement of United Kingdom students at entry;

9 Overall, an increased emphasis on the facilitation and assessment of learning rather than on the simultaneous direct instruction of relatively large numbers of students with homogeneous experience/knowledge – a movement, in short, from table d'hôte to cafeteria styles of academic provision.

The vision that this scenario may offer to already overworked academics may be of deteriorating staff/student ratios, progressive lowering of standards and 'academic entropy' (with the coherence of studies gradually disintegrating). The future need not, however, look bleak. What is required, in my judgement, is scrutiny of the fundamental aims and methods of degree courses to respond to the developing situation.

There is no doubt that some university courses suffer from an undesirable rigidity. For example, Fulton and Ellwood (1989: 11) report that some mathematics and electrical engineering departments in universities are reluctant to change their traditional requirements for admissions qualifications even at the price of empty places. Again, modular courses, although supported by employers, were resisted for fear that professional institutions might disapprove!

The following sections offer a possible approach to the design of university courses in science and engineering which might respond to the changing scene, and which might be more congenial to mature students and women students than much of what is at present on offer. I do not deal explicitly with mathematics because my judgement (reinforced by the observations of Osborne and Woodrow (1989) and Burton (1987) reported above) is that increased access to mathematical thinking is more likely to be achieved through applied forms of study than through pure mathematics. This notion is also consonant with the suggestion of the Cockroft Committee (DES 1982a, para 565, p. 171) that all A level mathematics courses should contain some substantial element of 'applied mathematics' so that all who are studying the subject, whether for its own sake or because of its usefulness as a 'service subject' for their other studies, are able to gain a balanced view of mathematics. With imaginative use of Independent Study options in universities (see below), students who show a propensity for pure mathematics can be re-routed later in their studies if need be.

The approach is to set aside for a while one's awareness of the complexities of present arrangements, and the upheavals implicit in any substantial re-appraisal of priorities and practices, and to concentrate on what things might look like if we instituted comprehensive adjustments to curricula and teaching methods the better to respond to the new constraints and opportunities. The issue of who should do what is addressed in the final section of this chapter.

The '4,3,2,1' approach to course design

In mathematics, science, and engineering departments in universities, it is common practice for a third-class degree to be awarded for a mark of 40 per cent. The implication of this is that there is an irreducible minimum of material, constituting some 40 per cent of that which a student could know, which it is required that a student should know to get a degree.

Taking this notion as a starting point, one could envisage a pattern of study emerging in which objectives are spelled out for different types of study, criteria of assessment determined for each objective, and the whole regime of instruction loosened up to permit and encourage a wide variety of routes to the degree. In that such an approach will involve serious attention to differences in learning styles between students, and appropriate for different types of subject-matter, it will seek to accommodate the interests of women and mature students.

At the heart of the approach is the idea that 40 per cent of the curriculum in science or engineering should be taught in such a way that all students achieve complete, or nearly-complete, mastery. This 40 per cent would be that which defines a degree as physics, chemistry, electrical engineering, or whatever.

The model I offer below I call the '4,3,2,1' approach because it is based on the idea of considering four elements of a degree course, each requiring specific methods, representing proportions of credit in the following ratios:

Element	% Credit	Proportion
Core study	40	4
Contextual and Professional study	30	3
Independent study	20	2
Reflective and Cultural study	10	1
TOTALS	100	10

The essence of this approach to course design is to consider the broad strategic function of substantial components of a degree course, rather than to define the course primarily in terms of content. The approach does not, of course, de-emphasise content (in terms of knowledge, skills, and attitudes to be acquired); rather it stresses what type of content is to be acquired by what method and for what purpose. In short, it is an objectives-lead or competency-based approach. For each mode of study discussed, the paper reviews existing practice, and relevant evaluative research, to indicate what could be done if we drew systematically and purposefully on the deposits of research about good practice laid down in recent years – but only too rarely used to best effect.

Core study (proportion of degree study-time: 40 per cent)

Core study is the irreducible minimum of ideas and information in a given discipline which a student should have mastered, not at a low pass-level, but completely. In practice, this material is likely to be concerned with the theoretical foundations of the discipline – the laws, theories, and intellectual methods by which the discipline is defined at an intellectual rather than social/operational level (insofar as the social and the intellectual can be separated).

Traditional modes of teaching in higher education, based largely upon lectures supported by tutorials (and laboratories), are not always entirely satisfactory for teaching such material. Lectures aimed at high-achieving students can leave low-achieving students bewildered, while lectures aimed at low-achieving students can leave the high-achievers bored and frustrated. The lock-step process does not allow for variations in students' capabilities, nor for temporary absences. Back-up tutorials (often distant in both time and place from the initial presentation of material) are not a sufficient remedy, not least because they are often badly attended, students being reluctant to expose their weaknesses to lecturers. In short, some current modes of instruction are often unsatisfactory even for 18 to 22-year-olds, let alone for mature students or women who lack confidence.

To cater for spread of interest and achievement, core material could be mediated by Personalised Systems of Instruction (PSI), such as Keller plan courses which require mastery of one module before the next can be undertaken. Such courses (which have been used successfully in a wide variety of disciplines; see, for example, Johnston 1975; Kulik and Kulik 1976) are often effectively 'correspondence courses taken in-house', and can be readily adapted to be taken in either internal or external mode.

If designed so that a student achieving complete mastery would be awarded at least a lower second class honours degree, such courses could be deemed the identifying core of degree studies in the particular subject, a core capable of being taken at different speeds and in different modes (part-time or full-time, internal or external, correspondence only or correspondence with personal tuition, etc.) depending upon the aptitude, previous education, and personal circumstances of the student. Such core material could be the basic currency of credit-transfer arrangements. There is evidence that PSI methods are highly effective for this type of study.

The basic features of a PSI course are admirably summarised thus by F. S. Keller, one of the pioneers of this type of instruction (1968: 83):

> (1) The go-at-your-own-pace feature, which permits a student to move through the course at a speed commensurate with his (sic) ability and other demands upon his time.
>
> (2) The unit-perfection requirement for advance, which lets the student go ahead to new material only after demonstrating mastery of that which preceded.
>
> (3) The use of lectures and demonstrations as vehicles of motivation, rather than as sources of critical information.
>
> (4) The related stress upon the written word in teacher-student communications; and finally:
>
> (5) The use of proctors, which permits repeated testing, immediate scoring, almost unavoidable tutoring, and a marked enhancement of the personal-social aspect of the educational process.

Courses in science embodying these features have been used in the United Kingdom both at school level (Daly and Robertson 1978) and in the Higher Education Learning Project (Physics) sponsored by the Nuffield Foundation (Bridge and Elton 1977).

Research (mostly conducted in the 1970s) suggests that PSI courses are both popular with students and effective. For example, in an analysis based only on studies systematically comparing PSI with other types of instruction, Taveggia (1976: 1029) concluded that:

> When evaluated by average student performance on course content examinations, the Personalized System of Instruction has proven superior to the conventional teaching methods with which it has been compared. Not one of the independent comparisons of PSI with conventional methods favors the conventional methods. This is true

irrespective of the type of course in which the study was conducted (eg physical science, natural science, social science, engineering), or the type of conventional method with which PSI was compared (eg lecture, lecture-discussion, group discussion).

In a meta-analysis of 75 comparative studies, Kulik, Kulik and Cohen (1979) come to a similar conclusion.

In a review study concentrating specifically on the use of the Keller plan in science teaching, Kulik, Kulik and Carmichael (1974) found that:

1 The Keller plan is a method attractive to most students. In every published report, students rate the Keller plan much more favourably than teaching by lecture.

2 Self-pacing and interaction with tutors seem to be the features of the Keller courses most favoured by students.

3 Although several investigators report higher than average withdrawal rates for their Keller sections, it seems possible to control procrastination and withdrawal through course design. (Hursh (1976: 98) reports a number of measures which have been found useful to prevent procrastination and withdrawal.)

4 Content-learning (as measured by final examinations) is adequate in Keller courses. In the published studies, final examination performance in Keller sections always equals, and usually exceeds, performance in lecture sessions.

5 Students invariably report that they learn more in PSI than in lecture courses, and also nearly always report putting more time and effort into the Keller courses. A similar study by Aiello and Wolfle (1980) supports these observations.

There is a strong probability that students coming to higher education in science and engineering by way of access courses might value PSI. Two of the features in particular seem attractive.

First, self-pacing. Robin (1976: 343) sees this as one of the keys to the proven effectiveness of PSI. If university departments used PSI for the core material in degree courses, the written materials could be used in access courses to ease mature students gradually into the modes of university work, as well as offering to all students a desirable element of flexibility (so that absence through illness did not prove so problematic as in conventional lecture-based courses where students can run the risk of never catching up if they miss a lecture or two).

Second, proctoring. The use of students to help students which is a regular feature of Keller courses has social as well as pedagogic benefits. Students who lack confidence can derive significant support from other students. Hursh (1976: 101) reports that the combination of this with study groups has proven highly effective. A group has to take unit quizzes and have them graded by a proctor at one time and is not permitted to advance to the next unit until all three members of the group have passed the current quiz. This version of PSI results in fewer withdrawals than regular PSI, and examination scores, grades, and ratings that are higher than those from the lecture section but similar to the grades and ratings of the regular PSI section.

Proctoring has proved popular in conventionally-taught engineering courses (see Button, Sims and White 1990 forthcoming). Combined with study groups, it has the potential to release the massive benefits known to be associated with many forms of peer tutoring (see Goodlad and Hirst 1989). Women and mature students (who sometimes feel beleaguered in science and engineering courses in universities) could be expected to flourish if methods such as these were to be more frequently adopted.

Contextual and professional study (proportion of degree studies: 30 per cent)

For engineers, such studies are all those concerned with problem solving and project management. They include all the knowledge and skills necessary for competent professional practice, such as management science, accountancy and finance, modern languages, group working and communication skills, familiarity with the political, social and economic constraints on the design of physical systems.

For scientists, such studies are those concerned with the design, management and execution of complex experiments.

The object here would be to specify precisely what a student should be able to do to merit a degree, but to be infinitely flexible about how the relevant knowledge and skills are acquired. The emphasis should be, accordingly, on the assessment of learning derived from experience rather than on prescription of precisely when and how that experience should be acquired.

One approach to the provision of contextual and professional studies is to provide them by a process of 'lateral enrichment' through specialised lecture courses in various commentating disciplines. Although this approach offers certain logistic merits in sustaining the 'turf' interests of the academic groups which earn full-time equivalents by it, it can seriously distort (by under-emphasis) the complex political, economic, and social context in which professionals have to take decisions. The problem has long been recognised (see, for example, Schein 1972), and some sophisticated approaches have been developed to deal with it (see Schon 1983, 1987).

One approach which has proved fruitful in medical education is that of problem-based learning (see Barrows and Tamblyn 1980; Neufeld and Chong 1984). Rather than having parallel lecture courses in a number of disciplines, students are presented with multi-dimensional problems (similar to those they will encounter in medical practice) in which they have to decide what they need to know (about the location of organs, possible regimes of treatment, the costs and benefits of specific courses of action, and so forth) and then acquire that knowledge by guided independent study. The approach has recently been spreading to other disciplines (see Boud 1985), including engineering (Cawley 1989). The common feature is that the teaching of organising concepts follows rather than precedes student experience of problems.

The significance of the method for the purposes of this chapter is that conceptually it overlaps with other types of experiential learning. It is, indeed, one of the 'villages' within experiential learning identified by Weil and McGill in their introduction to a recent (and important) collection of essays on the subject (Weil and McGill 1989); the 'village' where reside those concerned with changing the practice, structures and purpose of post-school education. One of the other 'villages' is identified with the assessment and accreditation of prior experiential learning as a means of gaining access and recognition in relation to educational institutions, employment, and professional bodies. The link idea is that some contextual and professional knowledge and skills (which it is the purpose of problem-based learning to supply) can be attained as readily off campus as on campus. In short, they are types of learning with which mature students may already be familiar.

Rather than concentrate on advocating any specific method (which it would not be profitable to do without a detailed statement of objectives), I will simply note here that there are whole areas of study in science and engineering which positively demand experiential learning styles (cf. Kolb 1984) and that the key issue to be addressed (which is common to both study undertaken in the context of a degree and in the accreditation of prior experiential learning) is how to assess what has been learned from experience (rather than a simple describing of the experience).

The basic formative thinking about Experiential Learning is usually attributed to Dewey's 1938 text *Experience and Education* (Dewey 1963), though some ideas go back to Plato. As with PSI (which flows from a different tradition – behavioural psychology – and is appropriate to different teaching objectives), the assessment of experiential learning relevant to professional and contextual studies is a field in which there is already substantial experience.

Over a decade ago, the organisation CAEL (then called Co-operative Assessment of Experiential Learning, but now, with the same acronym, Council for the Advancement of Adult and Experiential Learning) published in the United States a series of distinguished working papers suggesting specific ways in which learning derived from experience could be assessed for academic credit (CAEL 1975). (Willingham (1977) offers an admirable, brief distillation of the good practice developed by CAEL.) Since then, numerous studies have been published in the area: there is even a bibliography (Anderson

1985). Some publications offer case studies and analysis of issues (see, for example, Boot and Reynolds 1983; Boud, Keogh and Walker 1985; Boydel 1976; Brooks and Althof 1979; Chickering 1977; Conrad and Hedin 1982a; Further Education Unit nd; Keeton *et al.* 1977; Moore 1981; Weil and McGill 1989). Others concentrate on how experiential-learning programmes can be organised (see, for example, ACTION 1979; Davis, Duley and Alexander 1977; Duley 1978; Stanton and Ali 1987). Still others focus on how learning derived from experience can be evaluated and assessed (see, for example, ACTION 1978; Conrad and Hedin 1982b; Duley 1982; Hendel and Enright 1978; Yelon and Duley 1978). In the United Kingdom, Norman Evans has made a minor industry of promoting experiential learning (see, for example, Evans 1981; 1984a; 1984b; 1987; 1988).

The National Institute for Adult Continuing Education of the United Kingdom (NIACE) has supported the notion of building on the growth of experiential learning within the higher education curriculum, urging that institutions should consider whether potential adult students who are in full-time work could be enabled to negotiate a programme of action-based learning around their work-experience (NIACE 1989: 16). It is, indeed, probable that mature students (who often have substantial recent, relevant experience to draw upon) might be attracted to modes of instruction which celebrate (rather than set aside) their non-formal learning.

There is another reason why universities might wish to take more seriously than they have done to date the systematic exploitation of off-campus learning. It is becoming increasingly difficult for universities to keep at state-of-the-art levels with high-tech equipment (because the rate of change implies costs which are unacceptable). A prudent strategy might be for teaching within universities to concentrate on fundamentals (which can often be learned from somewhat simple apparatus, and/or by PSI methods), and to arrange for students to receive 'hands-on' experience of sophisticated equipment where it is in intensive use, outside universities (in industry) or in university research laboratories. For this purpose, it may be necessary to recognise that there will necessarily be differences in the detail of what individual students learn, although the teaching objectives can still specify particular types of experience to be gained.

Independent study (proportion of degree studies: 20 per cent)

To capitalise on the research-orientation of universities, and to offer ample scope for high-flying students, guided independent study could be promoted through schemes such as Undergraduate Research opportunities.

In addition to planning and designing their own projects (which comes under the heading of professional and contextual studies), students should be given opportunities to assist with the ongoing work of faculty and other high-level practitioners on campus or off campus, at home or abroad.

At the Massachusetts Institute of Technology, some two-thirds of the undergraduates are at any one time taking part in the Undergraduate Research Opportunities Programme (UROP) (MacVicar and McGavern 1984). Imperial College (London University) has had a similar scheme since 1980. The object of both schemes is to give undergraduates the opportunity to participate directly in the research activities of the university staff and postgraduates. Students make direct contact with staff whose research interests (and room and telephone numbers) are listed in an annual directory. The students then commit themselves to as many hours or days of work as they can manage while still keeping up in their studies. UROP is a very flexible system which encourages students to:

1 learn at first hand what research is all about;
2 learn at their own pace and actually do something (rather than just read what others have done);
3 contribute directly to knowledge in a field of research;
4 further interests which they have developed elsewhere (in industry or through personal initiatives);
5 cross disciplinary boundaries (by working in departments other than their own);
6 get their names on scientific publications;
7 find their way into suitable final-year projects;
8 arrange opportunities for PhD research when they graduate.

At present, much work both at MIT and at Imperial College is done either for love or for money. At MIT, however, students can get academic credit for writing up their experience of this form of independent study. Assessment is primarily by dissertation in which students describe the work in which they have shared: explaining its theoretical and/or industrial significance, identifying factors conceptual or administrative which aided or impeded its progress, reporting on what they personally have done, reviewing literature and indicating directions in which they think the work could/should be developed.

If UROP work became more widely accepted as a valid form of university study, the really brilliant student might spend substantial term-time hours on such work (undertaking the core work by private study). Achievements in this area undoubtedly provide very sharp discriminations between students for purposes of honours classification.

In a different, but related area, the School for Independent Study (SIS) at the Polytechnic of East London has had considerable experience with non-traditional entrants. SIS appraises the learning from previous experience of students who are required to write down detailed study plans before being allowed to register for the final (honours) year of the degree. The major part of the credit is assigned to a final product which can reflect students' interests and initiative in an enormous variety of ways.

Mature students seem to thrive on this type of study, and women students get opportunities to push their studies in directions which they value, thereby offsetting in some measure the perceived male-dominance of higher education. As chief external examiner for the degree by independent study for the last four years, I have been privileged to see the astonishing energy which this type of study can release. (The origin and working of SIS are described in, for example, Percy and Ramsden 1980 and Robbins 1988).

In the 4,3,2,1 scheme, 20 per cent of the credit would be set aside for this type of Independent Study. Many students of science, engineering, and mathematics would probably take more study in their chosen discipline in the mode of independent study. But, not least to encourage women students and mature students, the opportunity should be presented for study in any academically-coherent area.

Reflective and cultural study (proportion of degree studies: 10 per cent)

The final proportion of work could consist of study in the humanities (literature, history, philosophy, theology), social sciences (economics, political science, sociology), or arts (music, fine art) designed for personal enrichment.

At MIT, such studies constitute some 20–25 per cent of the degree; however, because some cognate areas are included above under professional study, and could, indeed, be included under independent study, I suggest 10 per cent.

We have already seen that both mature students and women are attracted to subjects in the arts and social sciences. Table 13 shows that in 1988 very considerable numbers of university applicants took a mixture of GCE A levels: science with social science 14,193, and science with arts 23,615. The majority of these students applied for courses other than those in the categories which include mathematics, physical science, or engineering: 58 per cent of those taking a mix of science and social science A levels, and 64 per cent of those taking a mix of science and arts subjects.

Table 14 shows that there are signs that universities are taking into courses in the categories which include mathematics, physical science or engineering, a reasonable proportion (53 per cent) of applicants offering a mix of science and social science subjects. But of applicants offering a mix of science and arts A levels, only 40 per cent are so accommodated. There is a huge pool of students who could take science or engineering courses if such courses were made attractive to them: some 7,179 students in 1988!

Table 13 A level subject specialisation by subject group of application. Home candidates 1988

A level subject passes	A to K+ Combined science		L/M to X+ other combinations		Total N
	N	%	N	%	
Science + Social Science 4 or more passes	1,907	42	2,631	58	4,538
Science + Social Science 3 passes	3,000	41	4,371	59	7,371
Science + Social Science 2 passes	1,009	44	1,275	56	2,284
Subtotals	5,916	42	8,277	58	14,193
Science + Arts 4 or more passes	1,558	43	2,045	57	3,603
Science + Arts 3 passes	1,438	31	3,177	69	4,615
Science + Arts 2 passes	415	34	789	66	1,204
Subtotals	3,411	36	6,011	64	9,422
Totals	9,327	39	14,288	61	23,615

Source: Based on UCCA 1989 Table D6

At Imperial College, the humanities programme offers courses in literature, history, sociology, philosophy, and modern languages which some students (whose departments permit it) may take as part of their degree studies. It is not without significance for the argument of this chapter that on a course which I teach on modern literature and drama, women students are disproportionately represented compared to their numbers in Imperial College as a whole. These women students are not dissenters taking refuge from science and engineering disciplines; rather, they are manifestly keen to combine reflective study with technical study.

To those who would say that such subjects would represent 'dilution' (contamination?) of the main discipline being studied, I would ask whether excellence is to be identified with quantity? Apart from the benefits of personal enrichment offered by reflective study, there is the added value of letting students see their mainstream studies in context, an aspiration which women students and mature students seem to share.

Table 14 A level subject specialisation by subject group of acceptance accepted home candidates 1988

A level subject passes	A to K+ Combined science		L/M to X+ other combinations		Total N
	N	%	N	%	
Science + Social Science 4 or more passes	1,665	51	1,592	49	3,257
Science + Social Science 3 passes	2,300	54	1,997	46	4,297
Science + Social Science 2 passes	244	63	145	37	389
Subtotals	4,209	53	3,734	47	7,943
Science + Arts 4 or more passes	1,283	47	1,430	53	2,713
Science + Arts 3 passes	925	33	1,845	67	2,770
Science + Arts 2 passes	70	29	170	71	240
Subtotals	2,278	40	3,445	60	5,723
Totals	6,487	47	7,179	53	13,666

Source: Based On UCCA 1989 Table D7

New patterns of study

It is not possible in this brief chapter to examine all the types of problems confronting mature students or women in higher education. Indeed, admirable studies already exist for adults, by Woodley (1981) and for women by Spender (1981). The essence of my argument is that both to meet the interests and needs of mature students and women students and to respond to the rapidly changing demands on higher education, certain changes in curriculum and teaching method are both desirable and necessary.

The '4,3,2,1' approach sketched above addresses the issues in primarily administrative terms, rather than at the level of fundamental pedagogic philosophy. My experience is that university people feel uneasy if not downright embarrassed at discussion of fundamentals; progress is made, as Schein (1972) predicts, when one concentrates on removing barriers (some of which are conceptual, but most of which are administrative) to what seems a sensible course of action.

In the next five years, students paying their own fees or sponsored may find it highly attractive to work in ways which are at present unfamiliar, such as:

1 concentrating on undergraduate research opportunities during the spring term and studying core material by directed-reading session during the summer vacation 'long vac term', or

2 concentrating on learning a modern language during one academic year, acquiring professional skills and undertaking independent study abroad during another year, and concentrating on project work in the final year, or

3 taking all core-study requirements in one year (having had a run-in during a period of pre-university professionally-related work), and concentrating on UROP work and project work in subsequent years.

Apart from the changes I have already discussed, there are other matters to be addressed which can only be hinted at here.

Assessment

With the loosening up of modes of instruction, there would be good reason to consider overhauling assessment procedures. For example, to facilitate the flow of students in and out of institutions, one might envisage take-when-you're-ready examinations (based on a computer database of questions) gradually replacing examinations taken in blocks once or twice a year.

Credit transfer

A move towards a 2+2 model for further/higher education might be an important way of combining élite with mass higher education (as is done in the California State system, for example). Already, experiments have been undertaken which set the scene for this type of development. For example, the PASS scheme (Polytechnic Associated Students Scheme) of Newcastle upon Tyne Polytechnic (see CNAA 1989b) allows adults to study units taken from a range of polytechnic courses without having to enrol for the courses as a whole. It is not a big step from this to allowing students to put together a degree in a 'pick'n mix' way.

I should, perhaps, emphasise that the 4,3,2,1 model I have advocated is not itself a modular scheme, although it has some similarities to some modular courses, and could be made compatible with them (see CNAA 1989a). Its intention is to retain the ethos and sense of purpose and coherence of a single honours course, but to widen the content of the single honours course; thereby, it is hoped, widening its constituency.

Fees

To take full advantage of a course which, while conceived of as a conceptual whole, was nevertheless an administrative mix, it would be sensible to develop a fee-structure based on the components of the degree, rather than on the degree as a whole. In a market economy, this might be highly attractive to students, and not overly difficult to administer.

Faculty role

Any one of these options would require pretty drastic changes to our present ways of operating, but ones that would 'fit' well with the research and consultancy obligations and aspirations of the faculty. The role of faculty would necessarily move from that of direct instructor towards that of course designer (with more emphasis, for the construction of 'core' material, on writing than on talking); in short, a movement towards a management role rather than one of performance.

Concluding observations: issues, research, action

The alternative model for higher education in science and engineering which I propose, and which would I judge be user-friendly to women and mature students is summed up in Table 15.

Table 15 Alternative model for higher education in science and engineering

	Present practice	Possible alternative practice
Core material	Heavy emphasis on lecturing	Emphasis on PSI, with more on paper
Professional and contextual	Parallel lecture courses	Problem-based study, experiential learning
Independent study	Mainly through final-year projects	UROP experience, research overseas, off-campus work
Reflective study	Very patchy Marginal	Open to all students
Examinations	Concentrated into fixed periods	Question-bank exams when students want them
Credit transfer	Unusual	Frequent
Fees	For a whole year	For an activity
Faculty role	Primarily direct instruction	Primarily management and consultation

Who should do what to bring it to pass? A few recommendations are here addressed to specific constituencies:

(a) UFC and PCFC

The Universities Funding Council and the Polytechnics and Colleges Funding Council could influence practice significantly by issuing 'design criteria' for those who make bids or tenders to supply courses (much as engineering concerns do for contractors making tenders).

(b) Professional bodies

Accreditation bodies could stimulate initiative in higher education establishments by imposing upon themselves a self-denying ordinance restricting their specifications of required content to no more than the 40 per cent of core material in first-degree courses. Subsequently, they could (as several already do – eg civil engineers) stimulate continuing professional development by recommending specific types of post-experience professional development.

(c) The Department of Education and Science

The DES could encourage flexibility by encouraging pay-by-unit schemes or, in the short term, defining degrees as attracting certain UFC/PCFC grant-levels in terms of a basic 40 per cent core of content in the main discipline to be studied.

(d) Individual faculties

Despite having their hands largely tied by the agencies listed in (a), (b), and (c) above, these can help by moving towards the 4,3,2,1 model as far as they are at present able – and by lobbying the UFC, PCFC, professional bodies and DES vigorously until an alternative future is secured for higher education which encourages greater access to university courses in science, engineering, and mathematics for women and for mature students.

10 Access and the media[1]

Naomi Sargant

We choose to use the media instead of conventional face-to-face teaching if we believe we can get to *more* people than we could using conventional ways, or if we can teach them better or more effectively, or if we can get to people whom we could not reach in other ways. Using media is not necessarily a cheap option, though if the numbers are large enough it is likely to be. Broadcasters have access to an extremely valuable technology which enables them to deliver programmes to large numbers of people very cheaply. It is not that the programmes are necessarily cheap to make, but that because the cost of programming and transmission is borne up front, and predicated on a very large number of viewers watching, the cost per person viewing is usually very low, and there is no cost to the viewer at the point of viewing.

Broadcasting is just one of many delivery systems and it is not realistic to talk about broadcasting as if it is somehow separate from other delivery systems. Our existing broadcast channels already engage in narrowcasting for part of the time, just as they increasingly make programmes which are designed *ab initio* to have a broadcast life and a video life. The same programmes may be available for direct copying off air or on video or even re-edited in a different structure for mediation by teachers.

And the *broadcasting television set* is also no longer just that. As Rupert Murdoch said in the MacTaggart lecture at Edinburgh:

> Perhaps surprisingly, television has so far been left unaffected by this information revolution, for that revolution involves digital technology, while the TV set has remained a doggedly analogue device. . . . All this is about to change. The television set of the future will be, in reality, a telecomputer linked by fibre optic cable to a global cornucopia of programming and nearly infinite libraries of data, education and entertainment. All with full interactivity (Murdoch 1989: 1–2).

Current arguments about broadcasting, he stated, will soon sound as if they belong to the Stone Age:

> These telecomputers will bring a huge variety of television channels including the ability to order up whatever you want to watch. . . .

> [they] will revolutionise the way we are educated, the way we work and the way we relax (ibid.: 2).

Of course we are not yet at that stage and most of us will not live to see it, though our children will, but it is clearly on its way and the successful launch of the Olympus satellite last July marks a punctuation point of some importance. I have chosen to quote Murdoch since he reiterates in an important forum what a small number of us have been saying for nearly ten years. What is more, he refers positively to the significance of education in this new dawn.

We are here less concerned with curricular and content issues than with issues of access. For broadcasters, as for educators, this divides into two parts: access for those who know what they want, most of whom are already in the educational system, and access for those who may not yet know what they would want if the opportunities were appropriate and appropriately offered. In parenthesis, we note that the first category divides into those who know what they want and will seek it out *themselves* and those who are still in a *subject* condition where learning decisions are taken for them by teachers or trainers. Schools Television for example still has a captive audience of children. It is the teachers who are the captors and who decide what schools programmes will be watched (not that that equates with what will be learnt, of course). And we shall continue to be happy with schools and teachers exercising their custodial and selection functions on our behalf for a long time to come, it seems to me.

We are here also less concerned with schools programming than with the education and training of adults.

Access to broadcasting

The basic argument about access to *broad*casting is a simple one: that people who know what they want and are sufficiently motivated can be asked or persuaded to watch at less accessible times of day, ie effectively through narrowcasting on broadcast television. We already accept for example that some 'closed' target group programming both for radio and television can be downloaded at night: radio for schools and television for doctors. A lot of Open University (OU) programming is already transmitted in anti-social hours.

The strength of broadcast television is that it reaches virtually everywhere and is free at the point of use. It reduces at a stroke two of the main barriers to access faced by all other forms of education: geography and finance. The educational access argument for keeping such narrowcasting as the Open University and the Open College on broadcast television is therefore a powerful one. While space remains available on broadcast channels, and I include in this the possibility that space is protected by regulation, then clearly broadcasting is the most accessible option for both types of programming.

If space becomes unavailable, or programming is moved to extremely anti-social hours and even to down time, then it is necessary to consider whether or not the time has come to choose other narrowcast options.

The breakdown of monopolies

The breakdown of the duopoly of broadcasting has been much discussed. First the BBC's monopoly was broken to introduce the Independent Television system, then Channel Four was set up which further disaggregated the component parts of what had until then been effectively a vertically integrated production system. With Channel Four, the production function has been separated from the commissioning and editorial functions with the channel acting essentially as a publishing house, and this model is very likely to be used increasingly for new channels. The structure of Channel Four is value free. It can be used as an unregulated commercial structure or it can be used as in the past as an integral part of a regulated public broadcasting system.

Disaggregation has now been taken some steps further with the demand for a higher proportion of independent production across all parts of the industry, and with the probability of the privatising of transmitters.

We tend to think of the breaking down of the duopoly as politically motivated, and as an attack on public service broadcasting. This is not strictly the case. New technologies which are bringing new choices to consumers are the engine of the breakdown and we cannot be Luddite in keeping these technologies back. Ultimately, adding more choice removes power from producers whether paternalistic or not and places it in the hands of consumers. We then need to make sure as in other areas of our life that consumers have proper protection.

Michael Young, and I have been grateful to him for the power of his observation, has come to the same issue from a different perspective. He pointed, in a speech to the Fabian Centenary New Year School in 1984, to a related set of changes that had already taken place. There has already been a shift of scale of people's lives outside work. The small (and private) has increasingly replaced the big (and public). The watch has replaced the public clock. The fridge has replaced the ice factory, the washing machine the public laundry. The private bathroom the municipal baths, television the cinema. The car, the bus or train. And even so, he suggested, the new home computer and teletext replace the newspaper. He did not add, at that stage, the video replacing the cinema, and video ownership has increased dramatically over this decade. The most important thing is that all these changes have to do with accessibility, freedom and choice. Evidently the small (and private) are more accessible to the individuals who *possess* them than the large (and public). That is the nub of the matter.

Of course the better-off had access to their own bath houses and ice houses several centuries earlier than they were made available to the community. Victorian philanthropy and enlightened self-interest coinciding with the industrial revolution led to the development of much of municipal provision in the nineteenth century, including the foundation of many universities.

The provision of these services developed into monopolies or near monopolies of supply, more because of their scale and nature than for any philosophical reason. The Victorians, indeed, would not have agreed with Mrs Thatcher when she said there is no such thing as society. A side benefit was the universality of provision, and a major characteristic was the fact that the user did not normally pay at the point of use. A negative was that these structures did not allow much flexibility and individuality in use, particularly in relation to geographical location.

The point of this discussion is that there are parallels between the provision of education and broadcasting. With both of these we have taken for granted the principle of universality of access, and indeed endeavour with education to ensure equality of access. Though of course nobody can guarantee equality of outcomes.

What changes, in Michael Young's scenario, is that those who can afford the small and private maintain their access while those who cannot are increasingly denied it or may only be provided with a lower standard of service; the obvious example of this is the increase in car ownership which has led inevitably to a reduction in demand for public transport such that the standard of service of trains, tubes and buses is now lower. Increasingly its main users are those who have little choice: the old, the young and the poor.

Just as the broadcasting institutions have held a monopoly of the power to broadcast moving visual images, so educational institutions have had a monopoly of the provision of education. Originally provided to the élite on a one-to-one basis or for select small groups, and then made available mainly to children in larger groups, it was provided only in given locations and in predetermined ways surrounded by rules and conventions which often had little to do with the nature of the learning to be achieved and a lot to do with maintaining closed professions and privilege. The most important contribution of the Open University may well turn out to be the demystifying of knowledge and making it open and accessible to the ordinary person in bookshops and on television. It broke the monopoly power of conventional educational institutions.

The Open University's role at its inception

The Open University did not at its inception twenty years ago set out to re-write the curriculum of higher education. As Birnbaum said:

> The Open University has begun with a fairly straightforward notion of subject matter which assumes that students have much to learn from an intact cultural tradition (Birnbaum 1974: 43).

What it did was to bring education out of its cloisters and place it in the public domain. The Open University was to make active use of the full range of the media for instruction in order to reach many more people without requiring vast capital sums to be spent on bricks and mortar. It was to do it for a purpose, spelled out clearly by the Planning Committee and the University's founding parents.

> For long regarded as a privilege of the few, the opportunity to engage in higher education is at last becoming widely accepted as a basic individual right (DES 1969: 2).

The objects of the Open University were laid down as:

> To provide opportunities, at both undergraduate and postgraduate level, of higher education to all those who, for any reason, have been or are being precluded from achieving their aims through an existing institution of higher education (ibid.: 5).

Lord Crowther in his inaugural address at the Open University's Charter Ceremony on 23 July 1969 restated its mission clearly.

> The first and most urgent task before us is to cater for the many thousands of people, fully capable of a higher education, who, for one reason or another, do not get it or do not get as much of it as they can turn to advantage, or as they can discover, sometimes too late, that they need (Open University 1970: 17).

The Open University was expected to press into the service of this cause all the existing teaching media and over the years to develop others. They and institutions like them world-wide have extended access to hundreds of thousands more learners through the intelligent use of technologies of delivery.

The point, and it is a threatening one, is that the development of open and distance learning breaks down the monopoly power of conventional educational institutions. For learners, it removes the barriers to access of time as well as place. Open learning packages can be delivered to or bought by people for use in their own homes. That is why it is so important in providing opportunities for adults and why open and distance learning have been encouraged by the Training Agency and embraced so readily by employers for training. This brings us back to money, and to who pays at what point in the process.

Broadcasting has heretofore been free at the point of use. So has higher education in the United Kingdom. The community, as with broadcasting, has paid through varying forms of taxation and the user has not had to pay directly. As with schooling, we expect full-time initial education to be provided free by the community. This assumption is not carried over to part-time study. Though the fees in the early years of the Open University felt really quite low, this is not the case now. Open learning packages will be paid for by individuals or their employers, and most new technologies will not be free, though some satellite channels look like being so for the foreseeable future.

Education and/or training?

For most learners, the difference between education and training is not a helpful or relevant one. The fact that vocational is a good word and non-vocational is currently seen as less good is also unhelpful. The same subject of study and indeed the same course may be vocational for some students and of general interest to others. A course in Portuguese, for example, recently put on to interest future holidaymakers on the Algarve has been completely subscribed to by twenty-four business people!

However, the structural changes which are emerging do affect access to education and training in different ways and it is worth looking at these differences. The government has now for many years given priority to training rather than education. Indeed, it is clear that governments of both complexions have worked on too short time-scales to give a proper priority to the longer term educational needs of the whole community. Initiatives in recent years from the Department of Employment and the Training Agency and its predecessor bodies have focused not just on 'education for work' but effectively on 'education for the first job', replacing the fundamental task of 'education for life'. Moves by the National Economic Development Office (NEDO) and some of the major industrial companies to refocus on the country's need for more and better general education are much to be welcomed. It is understandable for government and the Training Agency to be interested in the quicker payoff from training but it is a short-sighted view.

In the educational area, we expect universality of provision or, at higher levels, selection according to ability to benefit rather than other criteria. Training is provided more selectively according to professional or labour market needs. Education is seen more generally as feeding into public and community capital while training feeds into private or personal capital. Education can be seen as investment in the whole community whereas training is a personal or private good. Education has typically been made available free to people at the point of use and paid for by the community whereas training is increasingly to be paid for by the individual or the employer. If these assumptions continue to hold, we are likely to see the continuation of conventional provision of education through existing 'large and public' institutions, but a major switch to the 'small and private' use of new technologies and open and distance learning packages in training.

Structural characteristics of education and training

Education	Training
Longer time scales	Shorter time scales/quicker pay off
Universality	Selectivity
Investment in the community	A personal or private good
Feeding into public capital	Feeds into private or personal capital
Free at the point of use/paid for by the community	Paid for by the individual or the employer
Public provision	Private provision
Broadcasting	Narrowcasting
'Large and public'	'Small and private'
Conventional provision	Open and distance learning packages

Broadcasting has been able to deliver educational programming without financial and geographical barriers, whether it be at the level of the Open University or to the Open College, unemployed, elderly, illiterate or handicapped groups. Such important, and often large, groups will need to continue to be served by broadcasting. Access series and taster or 'call-bird programmes' will similarly need to be broadcast rather than narrowcast. Provided these functions are protected and maintained, it will be equally important to add to the array of provision and people's choice by using new technologies and new narrowcast options as effectively as possible.

If, however, the large and public provision of education ceases to be paid for by the community, then we risk having an even more educationally divided society, with only those able to pay up-front having access to new opportunities and the poorer and unemployed as the educational have-nots. That would not be an acceptable outcome either in democratic or economic terms.

Market forces in education

At the same time, it is current government policy to encourage the development of market forces in the provision of education and training. They wish to disaggregate the services which they, the government, pay for from higher education. They also wish to establish the principle of individuals purchasing services from providers, as Robert Jackson made clear at Chevening:

> . . . we have to make a basic conceptual shift from the idea of the Government providing higher education through institutions . . . to an alternative paradigm, of the Government enabling individuals to purchase services from providers who are independent of Government, but which are obliged to be more responsive to the customers thus enabled (Jackson 1988c: 428).

The cost of different functions of higher education will be considered by government and their funders separately. Higher education will be encouraged to look for other customers, and cross subsidy inside institutions may be more difficult.

The structure of higher education

The boundaries of what constitutes higher education are in themselves becoming more blurred. The Education Reform Act of 1988 merely defines higher education in terms of descriptions of courses which are deemed to be above the level of courses normally taken at school or in further education. It is seen to be at a 'higher' academic or intellectual level than what precedes it. Its normal form of delivery in this country, the three-year first degree studied normally in one go, normally in one place and normally in one subject or in an integrated group of subjects, is still the dominant form in the polytechnics, colleges and universities of England, Wales and Northern Ireland. Access has not until recently had to be an issue of much concern to such institutions. The task of reaching mature students in large numbers has been left to the Open University. Indeed, the Department of Education and Science, as late as 1978 and in the face of continued high demand for the Open University, went on record as saying that there was little evidence of unsatisfied demand for part-time degrees (DES 1978). Inside higher education, academics and learners continued to teach and learn in conventional ways, relying heavily on print. Though many institutions were increasingly equipped with an array of new technological resources, their use has not been very encouraging nor have they been used, particularly, to assist access.

Over this time, however, the structures of the tidy three-year degree course have been changing. The credit structure adopted by the Open University is now paralleled by an increasing number of degrees based on modular or unit structures both in universities and polytechnics. The agreement on transferability of credit between the Open University and the Council for National Academic Awards (CNAA) in 1977 was an important step in opening up opportunities for learners and also provided conventional institutions with welcome extra students. At the same time academics had to rethink the assumptions on which the three-year integrated course had been structured. Could the academic content also be disaggregated into smaller component parts? The answer of course was frequently in the affirmative, and there is no question that the public availability of the Open University course materials and their use, publicly or privately, by academics in other institutions must have assisted in this. Increasingly the tidy, vertically integrated structures of the past are changing into modular and more flexible patterns and movement is possibly within systems and between systems.

This renders more transparent the intellectual links between what has been traditionally taught in higher education, what was being taught or demanded by the adults entering higher education through the Open University, frequently while they were also engaged in employment, and what was starting to be called post-experience or continuing education. Whereas much traditional adult education has not been tied to any particular level or indeed to qualifications at all, many post-experience or continuing education courses are at intellectual levels which are indistinguishable from those of degree level work. As the Open University has demonstrated, while not ideal for the educationally disadvantaged, distance and open learning techniques prove particularly suitable for busy, mature and motivated adults. The Manpower Services Commission (MSC) recognised this early on in its decision to fund the Open Tech initiative. Indeed the Training Agency has deliberately continued the MSC's policy of promoting open learning as a valuable, accessible and economic means of providing training for adults.

So the move away from tightly integrated degree structures delivered face-to-face at individual institutions, dependent on the expertise of local academics, has opened up the possibility of an increased use of a wider variety of media and in its turn more flexible access. Adults can use a variety of media in their own time and in their own place to continue their learning. They may study only one course module, or add them up in different ways. The other major barrier that has prevented this until now, that of accreditation, is also being increasingly eroded. With transferability of credit, the addition of open and distance learning routes to many qualifications, the Open Polytechnic following upon the heels of the Open University, together with the CNAA's credit accumulation and transfer scheme, the accreditation of experiential learning and competency-based assessment as with the National Vocational Qualification, many adults may well prefer to study through these routes rather than through the conventional even old-fashioned system! Many may well of course not have the choice, as the cost of full-time study will be beyond their means.

Of course, as noted earlier, these disaggregated systems also have their costs and each element will have to be separately paid or accounted for. One of the new barriers to access to accreditation will be the charges levied to individuals by the National Council for Vocational Qualifications (NCVQ) for individual qualifications, since it is required by the government to be self-funding.

Using the media for the delivery of education

The media are in themselves value free. They are merely delivery systems to be used for appropriate purposes. In far too many projects people have mistaken the medium for the message and planned totally inappropriate purposes and content for particular delivery systems. The current example of this looks like being Olympus, the European Space Agency's newly launched high-power communications satellite. A recent example closer to home was the Open College which, despite clear warnings, expected at its inception to be broadcast-led. It is one thing to have access to the medium of broadcasting and to use it intelligently and effectively, it is quite another for an *educational* institution to be broadcast-led. The Open College was first named 'The College of the Air' just as previously the Open University had originally been named 'The University of the Air'. Of course, they both use television, but it forms only a small part of the learning process.

Neither are the media necessarily cheap or expensive to use. Print still remains an invaluable, cheap and flexible medium as does the delivery system of the postal service. Of course, some media are more expensive than others. However, while the cost of face-to-face teaching tends to increase in proportion to the number of learners being taught, the cost of using the media for distance teaching is capital intensive at the front of the system. Once the up-front investment has been made, the marginal cost of extra students is low in relation to the fixed cost. There is every incentive to expand the number of students studying each course, and indeed to sell the course materials to other institutions and to other countries. Open University materials are widely used in many countries, not just English-speaking ones. Other initiatives such as the Commonwealth of Learning and the American National Technological University expect to use materials across national boundaries. Satellite communications will make the academic village smaller, encouraging links between learning projects on different continents.

What new options are likely to benefit higher education?

Cable is clearly not, and never will be, a major player in the educational field, except perhaps locally. In terms of access, cable will only ever cover perhaps a half of urban areas and the level of take-up is not so far encouraging. The developing model for general viewing which is probably more realistic looks like this, though it obviously depends on cost, marketing and programming:

Urban *Rich*	Satellite/ some cable	*Rural* *Rich*	Satellite
Urban *Poor*	Broadcast/ some cable	*Rural* *Poor*	Broadcast only

Murdoch's current satellite strategy is however extremely practical, low-cost and overcomes geographical barriers. Its take-up curve is likely to rise faster than the pessimists suggest if it provides enough different programming of the sort people want: golf, cinema films, 'soft' pornography are all good examples.

It is a pity that most recent discussions of the possibility and desirability of a dedicated education and training channel on satellite were so closely related to the future of Independent Television schools programming and were therefore not given a proper airing, except in *The Times Educational Supplement.* The proposition is that while much educational broadcasting is properly aimed at everybody at home and needs to stay on broadcast channels (access to the arts and sciences and consumer education are examples), much of it is effectively narrowcasting, targeted to closed groups. Schools Television and the Open University are both of this kind, curriculum-led and often designed to be mediated by teachers or tutors. Closed audience groups, who know what they want, can be asked and will indeed want to organise their viewing and recording off air in advance and not leave it to chance. A recent estimate (Sargant 1988) showed nearly 60 hours of educational programming for closed audience groups being broadcast each week in term time. The cost of dishes is not high in relation to other costs, particularly given the flexibility and extra resource that will accrue.

There is no reason why a single channel cannot carry programming from a variety of sources. If the channel is operated as an open carrier for education and training anyone who wishes to deliver narrowcast or targeted learning could buy the requisite number of slots on it as though they were buying advertising time. Good, or more accessible, time slots could command premium prices. Less accessible time slots can be cheaper and be used for specific and highly motivated target groups, particularly those that are geographically scattered but homogeneous in interest.

It is possible to plan a structure which can accommodate both private interests and the community at large. For example, employers wishing to update employees in a number of scattered sites could buy the time they need and encrypt the material if it was confidential. One television guide for educators and trainers would be a bonus, and make the organisation of recording by institutions easier. The programming is likely to acquire more status when it is promoted on the 'Learning Channel' and not hidden away in the corners of other channels. Schools, the Open University and the Open College all work on a high proportion of repeat programming which with agreement could be carried over. Such a channel could also systematically provide more programming accessible to the deaf and hard-of-hearing. Two educational experiments using satellite channels will start to transmit in Europe in 1990. It is significant that the first of these, the EEC-funded experimental Channel E, the Knowledge channel, will transmit on an Astra satellite transponder number 9 sharing it with TV10, a Dutch commercial company. Due to start transmitting on 7 December 1989, it will have three regular time slots each weekday: 6.30–7.00 am, 10.00–10.30 am and 3.00–3.30 pm, and probably a mid-day slot at the weekends. In the experimental phase Channel E is planning to use existing education or training programmes and learning materials from any source, provided they meet educational standards and the rights have been cleared. The programmes may have originated in any European language and will then be sub-titled into one other. The experiment will be closely monitored to provide information on costs, structure and programme availability since the aim is to put in place a European Open Learning Channel. In the short term Channel E, which uses existing sets, Astra dishes and also links into cable, represents a financially cheaper and more practical proposition than Olympus.

The other major development is the launch of Olympus, the European Space Agency's satellite, which started test transmissions in autumn 1989 and begins regular transmission in 1990. Described as the most powerful communications satellite in the world, it will carry nine hours a day of education and training programmes on its high-power European direct broadcast beam. They are planned to be originated through Eurostep, a user's association of 300 organisations from 16 countries. The BBC has of course in the shape of BBC Enterprises a major role in the provision of peak-time programming on Olympus and will undoubtedly include in its scheduling some of the BBC's continuing education output.

What is interesting is the fact that neither Channel E on Astra nor Eurostep, the grouping of European Olympus users, has included the possibility of using conventional *broadcast educational* programmes in their plans. On Olympus, control of allocation of hours, scheduling, content and production is in the hands of education and trainers. Programmes will come out of television studios and audio-visual centres in schools and colleges and higher education. The schools network is already very active and the Training Agency is a major player in this ambitious and exciting project; but, while they have maintained their virginity at this point, it is quite clear that they are having to learn many lessons from scratch and reinvent some wheels already invented and broken on previous satellite demonstrations. Some of this should have been preventable in a proper partnership and will have a cost.

The importance of Olympus, apart from its European dimension, is that it is the beginning of a new generation of larger satellites with the possibility of interactivity through two-way audio. On the negative side, it will require a different and probably more expensive dish only likely to be affordable by institutional users, and it will transmit in DMAC or D2MAC rather than in PAL, so it faces an immediate difficulty in the current lack of availability of DMAC receivers. A further negative aspect is that one of its two tubes has already burnt out, and it therefore has no back-up.

Learners will need to view at centres rather than at home, though of course centres can be in hotels, medical schools, clubs or workplaces as well as on educational and training establishments. Much of the programming, in order to obtain the benefit of interactivity, is expected to be live from studios with conference call bridging. Most of the participants from post-school education have quite specialist, ie narrowcast, educational goals and target groups.

It is interesting that these plans are almost diametrically the opposite of the way in which programming is increasingly being planned by the Open University, for instance. The most recent analysis of viewing rates and VCR access from the Open University shows the continued maintenance of an encouragingly high viewing rate for programmes in spite of, the authors note, a deterioration in the quality of broadcast transmission times (Crooks and Kirkwood 1989). The maintenance of these high rates is attributable to a compensatory increase in video viewing at more convenient times. The volume of home recording now accounts for all but 9 per cent of the total viewing figure for post-foundation course programmes and all but 7 per cent of foundation course programmes. Overall access to video equipment among Open University students had already reached 86 per cent in 1988, and will continue to increase. The Open University, of course, already chooses video cassette as the appropriate medium for some courses and also has had a broadcast loan scheme to back up broadcasting. However, it is still more economic for them to transmit programmes for home recording for large population courses than to distribute programmes on video.

An associated Open University recommendation notes the substantial educational advantages of video format programmes, ie programmes designed for video cassettes from the start, over those designed for transmission only. An obvious policy issue for the BBC (rather than the Open University) will be to determine for how long it will be prepared to make air time available even for high population courses simply as a method of distribution, particularly when they are increasingly made in a video rather than in a broadcast format.

Funding is as yet only a partial problem for Eurostep users on Olympus as the European Space Agency is providing time on the satellite free for three years, and is also providing a professionally staffed play-out centre. Participating organisations will obviously need to fund programme production and delivery to the play-out centre, but do not have to fund transmission costs. The project is, as noted earlier, another example of a technology-led rather than a needs-led enterprise. The ESA's philanthropy is much to be welcomed and it behoves us all to make the best of this experimental period, as it does to make the best of Channel E's experimental time. They are not in competition with each other. At the same time it raises again the issue of the feasibility of a more broadly based United Kingdom education and training channel on which a wide variety of users, both publicly and privately funded, could buy time for a wide variety of programming. A second Astra satellite is due to be launched soon providing more spare channels. A transponder on Astra, unlike

Olympus, only costs around £5–6 million and the cost of the dishes is well within the competence of most schools' and colleges' local management arrangements, let alone individuals'. Obviously BSB's higher picture and sound quality and telesoftware/digital data capacity would have been of greater benefit particularly to schools, but the price would have been higher and might only have got off the ground with the sort of injection of government stimulus support and subsidy which Kenneth Baker put into the micro revolution in schools when at the Department of Trade and Industry. Obvious candidates for such a channel already exist, even apart from schools: the Open College, the Open University, the Training Agency, the Open Polytechnic and any business or industry grouping with education and training needs where learners and/or sites are scattered. It would be important to ensure that all the provision was not in the vocational area. For many people, non-vocational programmes are just as important. Indeed the Open College of the Arts would be an appropriate participant. Large numbers of older people, people taking early retirement or changing stream are interested in arts, culture and social studies and not just in vocational areas. The Open University is a candidate since, as we have seen, it has been moved to less favourable transmission hours and is mainly recorded at home. The Open College is a candidate since the transmission time it was offered by Channel Four was predicated on the unemployed being a main target group, which they are now certainly not. The Open College of the Arts has a particular need for the delivery of visual content.

It will however be ironic if the educators and trainers get their hands on a channel just at the time when broadcast education is being forced off the important Independent Television channel. We need to fight to keep space for the educationally and socially disadvantaged (the wantless) on the broadcast channels, but we must also fight to gain new appropriate space on the new channels.

Access to education via broadcasting

Questions of access arise at a variety of levels. In broadcasting terms they usually include questions such as these:

1 Do people have access to sets and control of them?

2 Are they around at the time of transmission, or can they record on video?

3 Are there psychological barriers to watching? Should programmes be labelled educational or not?

4 Do the programmes lead people on to other things 'educational'?

5 Are the broadcasters making proper links with 'the field' to ensure that people's interests can be followed through?

6 Are the back-up and help lines providing the further access and help needed?

Most of these questions are more appropriate for stand-alone educational broadcasting for open audiences than for institutions using broadcasting as part of a learning package. There are three issues which it seems most relevant to focus on here.

Firstly, the media are extremely powerful in informing people about opportunities and therefore in making the opportunities more accessible.

Secondly, the media cannot only take people to places, allow people to eavesdrop and meet people they could never meet in person, but they can also enable them to see things with the help of a camera they could not see with their naked eye.

Thirdly, different media may be used as elements in a complete learning package, planned from the outset to provide a systematic learning opportunity, each element being carefully chosen to make its own distinct contribution. Such a learning package can be used by a learner at home, overcoming other barriers to access.

The function of providing information about opportunities to people was extremely important at the start of the Open University, as it was nearly twenty years later to the Open College. A survey among the general public before the Open University went on air showed that one in three of the population knew about it, and of those, one in five knew that it was to use television and radio. Two years later, in 1973, the proportion knowing of the Open University had increased to 44 per cent with one in three knowing it used television and radio.

The Open College was launched in autumn 1987 with its broadcasting on Channel Four. Research carried out in the summer of 1988 showed over a third of the population claiming to have heard of the Open College. More surprisingly, television was recorded as the source of that information for 73 per cent of those who had heard of it.

The second point can be made briefly by example: the film or television camera is a better eye for much of the visual arts than our own. The stained glass in Chartres Cathedral can be seen much closer to. The macro-camera describes the detail of Tudor miniatures better than one's own eye. The camera can now go inside the body. A planned series on world geography will use satellite photography to show us the world and its elements from quite different perspectives. Even if we could all go on a 'Grand Tour', we are unlikely to see all the sites of artistic work covered in 'Art of the Western World'. An important point about the use of television for science at the Open University was that it enabled the replacement of some part of the laboratory experience which was in fact observation rather than actual hands-on manipulation. Thus we again return to the note of disaggregation, this time of what one is teaching, in order to be able to use the most effective medium to teach each of its component parts.

The third issue returns us to our original argument that we use the medium to get to people who cannot be reached in other ways. Many conventional institutions have not reached out widely enough and have hedged themselves around with barriers to access, some more justified than others.

Wider access for different groups

Developing Access (Unit for the Development of Adult Continuing Education 1988), a discussion paper on guidance and access, endeavours to take a more positive line and asks what a systen would need to be in order to be perceived 'as an accessible system' by its users. In a useful analysis, they consider requirements for appropriate entry mechanisms, for the curriculum, for quality, for support to individuals, for evaluation and monitoring, and so on. At the end of the day what they are requiring is a thoroughly good and effective system. By definition such a system would have to be accessible! Indeed there are individual examples of such good institutions, but not yet enough of them. Some institutions are good in some respects but not others. Some have crêches, while some only have car parks. Some have strong records of admitting mature students without standard qualifications, others do not. Few universities have significant numbers of black or other ethnic minority students. A number of polytechnics have developed very effective access policies and are putting the right of higher education to shame. An example is the Polytechnic of North London where in 1988 over half the graduates were women and 30 per cent were from ethnic minorities.

The Open University has reached a wider array of people than virtually any other institution of higher education in this country. People can study at home and do not need a prior qualification. In its early years it was much criticised for its failure to reach the working class in any large numbers, and is now being criticised for failing to reach ethnic minorities. In the first few years the middle-class image was particularly enhanced by the high proportion of teachers, most of whom only held teaching certificates and had a major incentive to study with the move to a graduate teaching profession. A recent study (Woodley 1987) considered what the Open University has done for those with lower qualifications. Woodley notes that the proportion of those with no qualifications has remained remarkably constant between 1971 and 1987 at the one-in-ten level. By 1985, four out of ten did not hold the normal higher education entry requirements. The proportion of applicants with teaching certificates has dropped from just over one third to 7 per cent during this period and it is those with 'A levels or less' who have increased. The difference in performance shows up immediately with only four out of ten with low qualifications gaining a credit in their first year compared with around seven out of ten of the highly qualified gaining a credit in each of the seven years from 1980 to 1986. However, their performance year by year has been, he notes, remarkably constant, ie there are a number, albeit a low number, who *can* survive and for whom the Open University provides a new point of access.

Students may take several years to graduate and it is necessary to look at cumulative graduation rates over a number of years. While each of the first seven intakes of teachers graduated at virtually identical rates over a ten-year period, the graduation rates for those with no qualifications have tended to decline, and it is clear that even allowing for them taking a longer time to study they are never going to catch up. All of this sounds very negative, until we remember that we need to look at these trends not just in comparative terms, but in terms of absolute numbers. Woodley notes that there were some 4,000 undergraduates with no previous qualifications in the Open University at that point, and 20,000 who did not possess the entry requirement for conventional degree programmes. Compared with other institutions of higher education, these are very large numbers.

The irony is that while the Open University, by opening up entry qualifications and using the media to overcome geographical barriers, can open up access for some, the nature of the educational experience it can provide is not the most helpful for the less well educated and socially disadvantaged. It puts a heavy premium on a high level of literacy, on personal motivation and confidence and on the ability to independently structure one's life and studies. It is the disadvantaged who should be offered the advantage of the 'face-to-face dialectic', rather than those who are manifestly advantaged. While the Open University itself can do more to provide advice, support and preparation for the intending students in order to prevent its open door becoming a revolving door for too many people, the media and distance learning are not intrinsically useful in this respect.

> The OU might be put in the position of *apparently* providing opportunities which, for many, were not genuine or continuing, or might effectively be only second best for those who were forced to utilize them (McIntosh 1975: 180).

It is face-to-face institutions who need to change their ways and open their doors more widely. The universities also need to copy the polytechnics and colleges which, with the support and approval of the CNAA, allow and indeed encourage much more movement between institutions. These issues have been discussed and understood for many years now. The Leverhulme-funded study on *Access to Higher Education* (Fulton 1981) made nine recommendations to improve access: movement on most of them has been minimal. They include the following:

> The sharp administrative and academic distinction between advanced and non-advanced courses should be abandoned.

> Courses of higher and further education should be available to all those who can benefit from them and wish to do so. All admitting units should admit at least 25 per cent of students using criteria other than A levels.
>
> The universities and the CNAA should devise certificates of partial completion of degree courses, to be awarded after appropriate assessment.
>
> The present grant system should be replaced with a system of 'educational entitlement' whereby every citizen is entitled to support for his or her education or training, regardless of its level.
>
> All institutions, and especially those with highly competitive entry requirements, should undertake significant experiments with positive discrimination . . . When admitted, such students will need special support . . .
>
> It should be the policy of government and of higher education institutions to encourage the participation of *adults* in courses of further and higher education at all levels, and to make appropriate provision for their special needs (Fulton 1981).

I have quoted these recommendations at length since this and other important and informative work in the area has sunk virtually without trace intellectually and politically. It is not necessary to start from scratch and reinvent the wheel each decade. It is necessary for there to be enough political will and re-allocation of resources towards supporting increased access. What is sad, for a whole generation of potential learners, is that conventional institutions were not prepared to shift until the joint pressures of demography and economics forced them to. Richard Hoggart speaking as Chairman of the Advisory Committee for Adult and Continuing Education (ACACE) said that he would welcome their deathbed repentance when it came!

Of course the world has not stood entirely still and many individual institutions have made important changes, but the system as a whole, particularly in universities, has moved slowly.

The provision of access courses

Perhaps the most important development has been the increase in the provision of access courses, particularly through colleges of further and higher education. The growth in numbers is phenomenal: the Educational Counselling and Credit Transfer Information Service (ECCTIS) now lists 570 courses (ECCTIS 1989). Responding to this growth, the Department of Education and Science initiative in bringing people together across the binary line and setting up the Access Courses Recognition Group (ACRG) jointly staffed by the Council for National Academic Awards and the Committee of Vice-

Chancellors and Principals is significant. Validation of access courses is a problem. What level should they be at? Do they need validation? Should there be national standards with an agreed currency? There is concern that they should not become an alternative barrier. One of their strengths has been the ability to develop in response to the needs of particular groups and localities, and to be matched to particular course and institutional needs. Educators working locally tend to dismiss the need for a nationally agreed currency for access courses. The ACRG is currently planning to franchise agencies to validate access courses which may have varied content to meet local needs though reaching an agreed national level. A major limitation on broadcasters for their telecourse initiatives is the lack of any nationally agreed framework of content to work to. If national broadcasters were again to provide access courses they would wish to work to a nationally agreed rubric, but offer an open or distance-learning study route. Perhaps the National Extension College or the planned Open Polytechnic could be franchised to agree distance-learning access courses.

In the context of this chapter, it is worth noting that the first major set of what were effectively 'access' courses was provided by BBC Further Education together with the National Extension College as a preparation for the Open University. These preparatory, or 'Gateway' courses as they became known, were aimed at the open audience at home. Programmes were broadcast on radio and television, textbooks could be bought by post or in the bookshops, many colleges ran associated face-to-face courses and the National Extension College developed a correspondence course for each of the three series. We never knew exactly how many people followed those courses from the 'open audience', but some 7,000 returned the reply-paid questionnaire card inserted in the independent learning textbooks (McIntosh 1970). Around one half were found to be 'highly likely' to enrol for the Open University. The Associated Examining Board provided an optional assessment for those who wanted pieces of paper. Those who had completed preparatory courses then went on to complete and pass their Open University foundation courses at significantly higher rates than other students.

The 'Gateway' courses were only broadcast for two years, although the materials continued in demand for a long time and the courses undoubtedly would have continued to interest potential students for many years. The BBC would not, understandably, commit schedule time for more than two years out of its Further Education slots. The Open University would not commit its own broadcast time either, though the argument for the Open University was a more complex one and one which is relevant to the whole of the development of access provision.

The Open University was and still is committed to open admission as far as prior educational qualifications are concerned. The intellectual entry to foundation courses is accessible to people without prior knowledge in the field, though obviously not to people without any ability. The setting up or approval of any course as a 'preparation' for the Open University immediately questions this openness and indeed allows the course writers not to have to work so hard to maintain this 'open' entry, since responsibility can be passed down the line to the access course.

The gateway instead of being open has to be climbed over and becomes just another barrier to access. The over-organisation and accreditation of access courses over the country as a whole holds just such a danger, that it merely becomes another rung on the ladder to be completed by everybody without conventional qualifications. This is a particular problem financially since access courses are not eligible for mandatory grants, and discretionary grants in many areas are virtually nonexistent.

The Gateway courses were, of course, designed for part-time study, as is the Open University, and grants, therefore, although desirable for part-time study, are not essential. Although broadcasters are not likely to wish to develop programme series which are specifically designed for access to particular institutions or for particular localities – these would be more suitable for narrowcasting – there are some programme areas which are likely to interest a broad adult audience as well as being appropriate as a foundation for more systematic study. The strength of broadcasting is that it can reach out to people in their own homes, who may not yet know what they want, and engage their interest.

What is more difficult is to convert this interest into more systematic learning so that people who want to may use it as a stepping-stone into other parts of the educational system. This is not a fanciful idea. At least one student of the Open University course 'War and Society' confided to Jeremy Isaacs at the Open University Summer School that her interest in history had been first kindled through viewing 'The World at War' on television.

Types of telecourses

Channel Four has, over the years, (as also has the BBC) experimented in a variety of ways to provide more systematic learning opportunities to people. Since it did not have an educational infrastructure in the way that the BBC and Independent Television have, we concentrated on opportunities for individuals through distance learning rather than working on projects which would have to rely on other mediators, and within this tried to develop a range of possible exemplars. My goal as I arrived at Channel Four was to further disaggregate the functions of educational institutions to make their output more accessible to people, just as television was being disaggregated!

With numeracy, the key extension of opportunity was through the National Extension College (NEC) which provided sets of computer-marked diagnostic tests with individualised letters sent back to the students at home.

They had the benefit of the new technology, but only had to pay the cost of a postage stamp. With 'Write On', we again contracted with the NEC to provide a tutor marking service for five written assignments through the course.

Another improvement in disaggregation that I hoped to achieve was to make textbooks available as part-work from bookshops and newsagents. This would have removed the onus of registration from students and therefore the necessity to pay money up-front, which might not be refundable if the course turned out unsuitable. Most commercial correspondence colleges make their money on the Colman's principle (the mustard left on the side of the plate). We never achieved this, though we discussed it tentatively with different publishers.

We evolved a different strategy with 'Looking Into Paintings', where we worked with the Open University; we developed a study pack of textbook, tapes, postcards, study guide and the possibility of joining self-help groups. 3,300 full packs were sold at £17.50 on the first run of the series, and 6,000 of the textbook at £9.95. None of these projects though had the possibility of any assessment. This leads back to our earlier discussion.

In America the concept of telecourses is well known and accepted, as is their credit structure of qualifications post-school. Apart from Annenberg telecourses, many Public Broadcasting Service (PBS) stations and colleges and universities have registered students studying telecourses for credit, usually as part of associate or bachelor degrees. We have no real equivalent here, and certainly not at degree level. Indeed it was interesting though ironic that one of Channel Four's own series, 'The World – A Television History', had a telecourse designed to clamp on to it by South Carolina's PBS station.

In the vocational area we and Yorkshire Television did manage to develop what were in effect telecourses in the areas of economics and marketing, by working closely with the Business and Technician Education Council (BTEC) who designed appropriate syllabuses and included them as part of their planned Certificate of Business Administration. An array of courses are now on offer for this qualification. It is a modular structure. The National Council for Vocational Qualifications (NCVQ) is currently endeavouring to put in place a rational, national, transferable, framework for vocational qualifications, but there is no such planning on the non-vocational side. It is difficult to know, in the absence of any appropriate qualifications, at what level to pitch the learning materials for such major broadcast enterprises as last year's London Weekend Television/Channel Four 'Ten Great Writers' telecourse or this autumn's Annenberg funded 'Art of the Western World'. In the United States such courses can clearly be utilised to study for credits towards a degree. Arguably in the United Kingdom they could be located at the level of access courses, but access to what, and who would validate them? A levels have never been a very helpful gate of entry for adults into higher education. We have argued for proper alternatives to A levels for adults for many years; clearly now that GCSE is in place, A and AS levels must be re-thought. As Peter Newsam would remind us, the education industry is dominated by those with a background in schools. They think about adults only as an after-thought. Adults deserve a before-thought as new structures to replace A levels are planned.

The need for non-vocational qualifications post-school

Many people have left and still leave school at 16 and wish to return to education later. They need a pattern of relevant qualifications which have currency both for educators and for employers. Current work on the recognition of access courses is a start but it does not provide a linking or broad enough framework. It is usually thought of as access to somewhere else rather than as a step on a ladder in its own right. Can the Department of Education and Science not follow the example of the Department of Employment in the vocational area and plan a proper broad array of qualifications suitable for adults? Broadcasters would then have a framework to gear their more systematic offerings to and broadcast resources could be put to increased use. This would genuinely provide a new point of access for many adults and probably help many colleges and sixth forms with revenue materials as well.

Charging and protecting the consumer

We now return to the most significant barrier to access: money, and the proposed shifting of payment from the community as a whole to individuals.

Once we move away from universality of provision and close regulation and people are expected to pay at the point of use, then we need to return to the issue of consumer protection. It was matching the HUNT plans for cable against the National Consumer Council's set of basic consumer principles which made it clear that cable as it was then being planned could not be expected to meet consumers' needs let alone educators' needs (McIntosh 1983). The basic principles the NCC has identified if peoples' needs are to be met are

(a) access and availability;

(b) information;

(c) choice;

(d) value for money;

(e) redress for consumers;

(f) representation.

All of these requirements apply to broadcasting and indeed to education: adequate and clear information that is user-friendly, alternative forms of supply, reasonable transmission or class times, avoidance of geographical barriers, clear information about value for money, complaints and redress machinery. Unlike most nationalised and some newly privatised industries there is no adequate complaints machinery for broadcasting or for education. Neither is there effective consumer representation in broadcasting, and such as there is in education is patchy.

It is not easy to see how it will be possible for the country to double the number of students in higher education within 25 years and at the same time expect to move to students paying a significant proportion of the fees themselves. By definition, an expansion of numbers on such a scale means widening access to different groups of students, many of whom will be less financially advantaged as well as less educationally advantaged. Nor do we have a tradition in this country of paying directly for higher education in the way that people in the United States pay for their tuition. Education is not the taken-for-granted 'good' here that it is there, where competitiveness and upward social mobility are accepted goals and to deny access to education is effectively to deny equal opportunity and therefore the opportunity of equal participation in the democracy.

We have until recently been content with a higher education system that selects only a small proportion of the age-group which the schools have already predetermined as highly likely to succeed. Schools have until now been content to be the system's selection device. With the introduction of GCSE and now the National Curriculum, the place of A levels as the gate to a degree course must come under scrutiny. Even though the Prime Minister has currently rejected the Higginson proposals (DES 1988b), there is increasing dissatisfaction with the narrowness of the current sixth-form curriculum. It has of course been matched to a more narrow intellectual view of scholarship than is current in higher education in many other countries with higher participation rates. If participation is to increase and we are to move further towards a system of mass higher education then the content of the curriculum and its scope will also need to change.

A levels act as the educational filter, but do not in themselves provide a guarantee of a place as the passing of the equivalent examinations do in some other countries. Selection according to grade, though, is widely used to determine entry and hence to control numbers and costs both to the institution and the community. Once a student has been selected, the system is essentially free, though maintenance is means tested. What this means in terms of the country's overall education needs is that a small number of the intellectual élite get a very large share of the post-school education budget cake. It is this issue that is attracting increasing attention.

The Manpower Services Commission in 1983 attempted to focus employers' attention on adult training needs with the publication of its discussion paper *Towards an Adult Training Strategy* (MSC 1983a) and its subsequent *Proposals for Action* (MSC 1983b). The Royal Society of Arts' Industry Matters initiative has also focused on the need to widen access:

> A level dominance has served its purpose for what must now be seen as the anachronism of a higher education system that nurtures a thin stream of excellence . . . Unless access is widened, employers and the country as a whole, will be denied the supply skills and competence necessary for survival in a competitive world . . . The nation now needs a broad highway of competence in which excellence will have its part, but not as the best being the enemy of the good (RSA 1988: 4–5).

Educational entitlements

The argument put forward by the Advisory Council for Adult and Continuing Education (ACACE 1982) for educational entitlements for adults was designed to give to those adults who had left school early the equivalent educational and financial opportunities that are already made available to those who take the élite escalator through A levels to a degree. In support, it was suggested that giving people who were educationally 'wantless' or disadvantaged a 'good' in this way would assist in their motivation and encouragement. The use of the term 'entitlement' was deliberate and necessary to distinguish it from the more political concept of an educational voucher. It is one thing to give a cash voucher to encourage people to shop around for a service to which their children are already universally entitled. It is quite another to provide people with an additional educational entitlement for themselves.

The idea of an entitlement is not new in itself. The mandatory grant is effectively an entitlement, but limited to particular courses and to particular groups of people. Paid educational leave provides entitlements for some employees, but it is limited as a national strategy since many people have no employers to grant it them. A recent suggestion (Schuller 1989) argues for an entitlement for the over-fifties, and this idea has been picked up by the Labour Party in its policy review. ACACE had suggested a two-tier system of entitlements. The first tier might consist of a one-off entitlement to a given number of years of full-time study or its equivalent. Those who completed their post-school education without a break in youth would have spent most or all of their first-tier entitlement. Those who had not could return and use their entitlement later on in life. Sir Christopher Ball has recently usefully suggested that we learn to recognise '*deferred* progression into further and higher education as normal and sensible' (Ball 1989b: 7). The second-tier entitlement might consist of a lighter set of credit units which could be accumulated throughout life; perhaps, it was suggested, at the rate of one week's entitlement for every year beyond the minimum school-leaving age.

This could be used for any form of education, either year-by-year or accumulated for a longer period of study. It would certainly be available for part-time study. Of course not everybody would take up their entitlements. In an ideal world, an entitlement would be universal in its application and learners would be free to choose what to study. However, it is of course possible for governments to continue to use entitlements selectively for particular types of courses, or for particular groups of people, for example. Turned on its head, the agreement that adults following the Employment Training Programme are supported to the tune of their dole money, plus £10 and expenses, is in fact a form of entitlement. It is limited to those who have been unemployed for over six months and is also limited to those training through the Employment Training Programme.

It is a small step in policy terms to suggest that some unemployed people might do better on other courses of study, many of which are already available through further and higher education, rather than through the Training Agency. Some of these courses might even be access courses for higher education! Such arguments gain further impetus from the Confederation of British Industry's task force which has been reported as working closely with the Department of Education and Science and the Department of Employment on a proposal to move from funding the Youth Training Scheme to providing every 16-year-old with an individual credit to cover the cost of the education and/or training required to reach their target qualifications (Confederation of British Industry 1989). The initial objective is described as obtaining either five GCSEs or a corresponding vocational qualification. A further target, however, is that at least half the age-group should reach A levels or its equivalent. It is not clear whether these credits are to be bankable or may only be used at a particular age. Clearly they may be used in education as well as training and therefore for existing courses in further education. This proposal should clearly assist in increasing access.

It could be reasonably argued that educational entitlements are tangential to a discussion of access and the media. The link comes through the need and desire to increase adult participation in education and training, much of which will be part-time and as we have argued will use open and distance media-based learning routes. Policy makers appear to consider full-time study with one side of their brain and fail to make any connection with part-time study. The White Paper on student loans (DES 1988e), for example, concentrated entirely on loans for full-time study. Yet the Department of Employment set up a loans scheme for adult training *several* years ago, and there is a flourishing loans scheme in operation for Master in Business Administration (MBA) programmes (Department of Employment 1984; Planning Exchange 1987).

Most adults do not wish to study full-time, and certainly do not want to do it in a residential setting. Part-time study in that sense is already more economical for the country as most students studying part-time maintain themselves. It has never been seen to be equitable for part-time students to have to pay their own fees while full-time students get them free. While full-time tuition remains free, we must continue to argue for the same rights for part-time study. A modest compromise would be to allow part-time tuition fees to be set against income tax.

However, if the government moves towards a system of means-testing for full-time tuition fees, or a mixed system of loans and scholarships, then it would be equitable for means-tested fees also to be a possibility for part-time study. This would redress somewhat the historical imbalance of advantage to full-time study. Of course some people on very low incomes get their fees waived or reduced or are already eligible for hardship funds. People studying part-time on the dole under the 21 hour rule are also effectively given financial support to study.

These inconsistencies in current policies and funding practices need thinking through and resolving if we are to maintain and increase access not just to initial higher education but also to continuing opportunities for education and training for adults. A planned system of entitlements would assist these goals and enable learners to make proper choices from the array of provision open to them, choosing media delivered studies when they offered a personal or educational advantage or conventional opportunities if they needed or preferred them.

There is finally another danger in this brave new dawn. It is not just that open-learning packages will be commercially produced but that access to information itself may be further controlled. To return to Murdoch. He talks of moving from an industrial society to an information society, in which wealth creation will depend on the processing of information. Information used to be made available in print, a cheap flexible and portable medium and easy to store. It is increasingly held in electronic form requiring access to electricity and electronic gadgetry and often requiring payment for access not once only but each time a search is made. Ironically, just as librarians are endeavouring to open up to a wider clientele, so the equipment of their trade has become more expensive, requires more guarding and is therefore likely to be less accessible.

Basic access to information is likely to become more costly and new barriers to access will be set up just as we are reducing the old ones. These trends caused by technology are being aided and abetted by the current encouragement of privatisation and by commercial interest in the ownership of databases and other stores of knowledge. Access to information will be restricted by those who control the databanks. For example, several publishers have shown an interest in acquiring the commercial right to exploit the store of knowledge built up in the public sector of higher education which would be the intellectual base of the open-learning material for an Open Polytechnic. The government's proposal to move training into the private sector through Training Enterprise Councils (TECs) will similarly move developments in training expertise out of the common domain of education and into private commercial hands. Not only are these local rather than national but they are led by employers' short-term needs. While some providers and sponsors of training packages and programmes may be happy to have their learning materials and programmes freely available, others may not. These trends are not encouraging from the point of view of educational access.

There is increasing pressure on higher education to seek funds from private industry. Private funders are, of course, likely to be interested in funding research relevant to themselves, and may wish it to remain private. When research was publicly funded the resultant knowledge was clearly placed in the public domain. With the quite proper increased acceptance of the concept of intellectual property and an understanding of its commercial value, these issues become more complex. Does the intellectual property right belong to the academic who prosecuted the work, the funder who funded it (whether government or private) or to the higher education institution where the work was carried out? When that information was produced in reasonably cheap accessible book form, it could be made available easily. Now, even in the public sector, the information will not be held in individual libraries, which will only keep indexes, scan keywords and provide individual copies on payment of a fee. The new technological methods of holding and delivering knowledge impose new barriers even without the increase of commercial control.

Freedom of access to information for higher education becomes a major issue in maintaining access to scholarship and research at a cost that individuals and individual organisations can afford. Indeed these are issues that already urgently affect developing countries making them increasingly 'information poor' and therefore implicitly the academic community internationally.

Paradoxically, therefore, we are now at a time when the media can assist in providing wider access to educational opportunities and in making knowledge more widely available. At the same time, the shift to an entrepreneurial view of society, with priority being given to market forces and to the notion of people paying for individual services, erects increased financial barriers to access. The very structures now used to hold and deliver knowledge and information place further controls on its availability, and therefore also erect new, and perhaps more serious, barriers to access.

Note

1 Some of this chapter is taken from the Barry Taylor Memorial Lecture given by the author to the BBC's Educational Broadcasting Council on 29 September 1989.

References

Acker, S. (1984) 'Women in higher education; what is the problem?' in Acker, S. and Warren Piper, D. (eds.) *Is Higher Education Fair to Women?* Guildford: SRHE and NFER-Nelson.

ACTION (1978) *Evaluating service-learning programs: a guide for program co-ordinators*. Washington DC: National Center for Service-Learning.

ACTION (1979) *The service-learning educator: a guide for program management*. Washington DC: National Center for Service-Learning.

Advisory Board for the Research Councils (1987) *A Strategy for the Science Base*. London: HMSO.

Advisory Council for Adult and Continuing Education (1982) *Continuing Education: From Policies to Practice*. Leicester: ACACE.

Aiello, N. C. and Wolfe, L. M. (1980) *A Meta-analysis of Individualized Instruction in Science*. Paper presented at the annual meeting of the American Educational Research Association. Boston MA 7–11 April 1980.

Anderson, J. (1985) *Research Bibliography in Experiential Education*. Panel resource paper 10. Raleigh NC: National Society for Internships and Experiential Education.

Arnold, M. (1985) *Arnold: poems selected by Kenneth Allott*. Harmondsworth: Penguin.

Ashby, E. (1971) *Any Person, Any Study*. New York: McGraw-Hill.

Ashworth, J. (1989) 'Graduates – for better, for worse'. *Nature*, **337**, 19 January 1989.

Association of Graduate Careers Advisory Services (1989) *What do Graduates do? 1989*. Manchester: Hobson.

Baker, K. (1989a) 'Higher Education – 25 Years On'. Secretary of State's speech at Lancaster University: 5 January 1989. London: DES.

Baker, K. (1989b) *Further Education: A new strategy*. Speech by the Rt Hon Kenneth Baker MP, Secretary of State for Education and Science, at the annual conference of the Association of Colleges of Further and Higher Education in London on 15 February 1989. London: DES.

Ball, Sir C. (1989a) 'Should Education Continue?' *Adults Learning*, **1**, 1.

Ball, Sir C. (1989b) *Aim Higher. Widening Access to Higher Education*. Interim Report for the Education/Industry Forum's Higher Education Steering Group. London: RSA.

Ball, Sir C. (1990) *More Means Different. Widening Access to Higher Education.* London: RSA/Industry Matters.

Barnett, C. (1986) *The Audit of War*. London: Macmillan.

Barrows, H. and Tamblyn, R. (1980) *Problem-Based Learning: An Approach to Medical Education*. New York: Springer.
Bell, D. (1973) *The Coming of Post-Industrial Society*. New York: Basic.
Berdahl, R. (1959) *British Universities and the State*. London: Cambridge University Press.
Birnbaum, N. (1974) 'A View from New England' in Tunstall, J. (ed.) *The Open University Opens*. London: Routledge and Kegan Paul.
Bloom, A. (1988) *The Closing of the American Mind*. Harmondsworth: Penguin.
Boot, R. and Reynolds, M. (1983) *Learning and Experience in Formal Education*. Manchester: Manchester University Department of Adult Education.
Boud, D. (ed.) (1985) *Problem-based Learning in Education for the Professions*. Kensington, Australia: Higher Education Research and Development Association of Australasia.
Boud, D., Keogh, R. and Walker, D. (eds.) (1985) *Reflection: Turning Experience into Learning*. London: Kogan Page.
Bourner, T. with Hamed, M. (1987) *Entry Qualifications and Degree Performance*. CNAA Development Services Publication 10. London: CNAA.
Boydell, T. (1976) *Experiential Learning*. Manchester: University of Manchester Department of Adult Education.
Brennan, J. and McGeevor, P. (1988) *Graduates at Work: Degree Courses and the Labour Market*. London: Jessica Kingsley.
Bridge, W. and Elton, L. R. B. (1977) *Higher Education Learning Project (Physics)*. London: Nuffield Foundation.
Bridger, S. (1988) *Women Learning: A Consumer View of Access Provision*. Bradford: Bradford Women's Employment Group.
Brooks, S. E. and Althof, J. E. (1979) *Enriching the Liberal Arts through Experiential Learning*. New Directions for Experiential Learning, **6**. London: Jossey-Bass.
Bryant, R. and Noble, M. (1989) *Education on a Shoestring*. Oxford: Ruskin College.
Burgess, T. and Pratt, J. (1974) *Polytechnics: A Report*. London: Pitman.
Burton, L. (1987) 'From failure to success: changing the experience of adult learners of mathematics'. *Educational Studies in Mathematics*, **18**.
Button, B. L., Sims, R. and White, L. (1990) 'Experience of proctoring over three years', in Goodlad, S. and Hirst, B. (eds.) *Explorations in Peer Tutoring*. Oxford: Basil Blackwell (1990 forthcoming).
CAEL (1975a) *The Learning and Assessment of Personal Skills: Guidelines for Administrators and Faculty*. CAEL Working Paper 4. Princeton NJ: Cooperative Assessment of Experiential Learning.
CAEL (1975b) *The Learning and Assessment of Interpersonal Skills: Guidelines for Students*. CAEL Working Paper 5. Princeton NJ: Cooperative Assessment of Experiential Learning.
CAEL (1975c) *A Guide for Assessing Prior Experience through Portfolios*. CAEL Working Paper 6. Princeton NJ: Cooperative Assessment of Experiential Learning.
CAEL (1975d) *A Student Handbook on Preparing a Portfolio for the Assessment of Prior Experiential Learning*. CAEL Working Paper 7. Princeton NJ: Cooperative Assessment of Experiential Learning.

CAEL (1975e) *A Task-based Model for Assessing Work Experience.* CAEL Working Paper 8. Princeton NJ: Cooperative Assessment of Experiential Learning.

CAEL (1975f) *A Student Guide to Learning through College-sponsored Work Experience.* CAEL Working Paper 9. Princeton NJ: Cooperative Assessment of Experiential Learning.

Cantor, L. M. and Roberts, I. F. (1986) *Further education today: A critical review.* London: Routledge and Kegan Paul.

Carswell, J. (1986) *Government and the Universities in Britain: Programme and Performance 1960–1980.* Cambridge: Cambridge University Press.

Cawley, P. (1989) 'The introduction of a problem-based option into a conventional engineering degree course'. *Studies in Higher Education,* **14,** 1.

Chickering, A. (1977) *Experience and Learning: An Introduction to Experiential Learning.* New Rochel NY: Change Magazine Press.

Clarke, S. (1988) 'Another look at the degree results of men and women'. *Studies in Higher Education,* **13,** 3.

Committee of Inquiry into Higher Education for Newham (nd) *Higher Education for Newham: Report of the Committee of Inquiry chaired by Professor P. Toyne.* London: Newham Council.

Committee of Vice-Chancellors and Principals (1985) *Report of the Steering Committee for Efficiency Studies in Universities.* London: CVCP.

Committee of Vice-Chancellors and Principals (1987) *Academic Standards in Universities. A report on universities' methods and procedures for maintaining and monitoring academic standards, in the light of advice given in the document on 'Academic standards in universities' prepared by the Committee's academic standards group under the chairmanship of Professor P. A. Reynolds which was published in July 1986.* London: CVCP.

Committee of Vice-Chancellors and Principals (1989) *The Teaching Function. Quality Assurance. Detailed proposal for a CVCP academic audit unit to monitor universities' own quality assurance mechanisms.* London: CVCP.

Committee of Vice-Chancellors and Principals and Council for National Academic Awards (1989) *Access Courses to Higher Education: A Framework of National Arrangements for Recognition.* London: CVCP/CNAA.

Committee of Vice-Chancellors and Principals and Standing Conference on University Entrance (1985) *Choosing A Levels for University Entrance.* London: CVCP/SCUE.

Committee of Vice-Chancellors and Principals and Standing Conference on University Entrance (1988) *Universities' Review of Degree Courses and of Entrance Policies in Response to Secondary Curriculum Change and Wider Access. A Progress Report from the CVCP and SCUE.* London: CVCP/SCUE.

Committee on Higher Education (1963) *Higher Education: Report of the Committee appointed by the Prime Minister under the Chairmanship of Lord Robbins 1961–63* Cmnd. 2154. London: HMSO.

Committee on the Curriculum and Organisation of Secondary Schools (1984) *Improving secondary schools.* Report of the Committee on the Curriculum and Organisation of Secondary Schools chaired by Dr David H. Hargreaves.

London: Inner London Education Authority.
Committee to Review Assessment in the Third and Fourth Years of Secondary Education in Scotland (1977) *Assessment for all*. Edinburgh: HMSO.
Confederation of British Industry (1989) *Towards a skills revolution – a youth charter*. London: CBI.
Conrad, D. and Hedin, D. (eds.) (1982a) *Youth Participation and Experiential Education*. New York: The Haworth Press.
Conrad, D. and Hedin, D. (1982b) *Experiential Education Evaluation Project*. St Paul, Minnesota: University of Minnesota.
Consultative Committee on the Curriculum (1977) *The Structure of the Curriculum in the Third and Fourth Years of the Scottish Secondary School*. Edinburgh: HMSO.
Council for Industry and Higher Education (1987) *Towards a Partnership. Higher Education – Government – Industry*. London: CIHE.
Council for National Academic Awards (1984) *Access/Preparatory Courses*. London: CNAA.
Council for National Academic Awards (1989a) *Going Modular*. Information Services Discussion Paper 2. London: CNAA.
Council for National Academic Awards (1989b) *Engineering Courses and Credits: A CNAA/Training Agency Project*. Development Services Project Report. London: CNAA.
Crooks, B. and Kirkwood, A. (1989) *VCR Access and Television Viewing Rates – undergraduate students in 1988*. Report No 26, Student Research Centre, Institute of Educational Technology, Open University (mimeo).
Crowther, Lord (1969) Inaugural address on the occasion of the Charter ceremony, 23 July 1969, reproduced in the Open University Prospectus 1971. Milton Keynes: Open University.
Daly, D. W. and Robertson, S. M. (eds.) (1978) *Keller Plan in the Classroom*. Glasgow: Scottish Council for Educational Technology.
Davie, G. (1961) *The Democratic Intellect*. Edinburgh: Edinburgh University Press.
Davie, G. (1986) *The Crisis of the Democratic Intellect*. Edinburgh: Polygon.
Davis, R. H., Duley, J. S. and Alexander, L. T. (1977) *Field Experience. Guides for the Improvement of Instruction in Higher Education*. East Lansing: Michigan State University Instructional Media Center.
Department of Education and Science (1969) *The Open University: Report of the Planning Committee to the Secretary of State for Education and Science*. London: HMSO.
Department of Education and Science (1978) *Higher Education into the 1990s: A Discussion Document*. London: DES.
Department of Education and Science (1982a) *Mathematics counts. Report of the Committee of Inquiry into the Teaching of Mathematics in Schools under the chairmanship of Dr W. H. Cockcroft*. London: HMSO.
Department of Education and Science (1982b) *17+: A New Qualification*. London: HMSO.
Department of Education and Science (1985a) *The Development of Higher*

Education into the 1990s Cmnd 9524. London: HMSO.
Department of Education and Science (1985b) *Inter-sectoral Cost Comparisons* (mimeo).
Department of Education and Science (1985c) *International Statistical Comparisons of the Education and Training of 16 to 18 Year Olds*, Statistical Bulletin 10/85. London: DES.
Department of Education and Science (1987) *Higher Education: Meeting the Challenge* Cmnd 114. London: HMSO.
Department of Education and Science (1988a) *Survey of Adult Education Centres in England 1985–86: Enrolments, Courses, Hours of Tuition and Subjects of Study*. Statistical Bulletin 10/88. London: DES.
Department of Education and Science (1988b) *Advancing A Levels: Report of a Committee appointed by the Secretary of State for Education and Science and the Secretary of State for Wales*. (The Higginson Committee Report.) London: HMSO.
Department of Education and Science (1988c) *Report by H.M. Inspectors on the Contribution of Further and Higher Education to Professional, Commercial and Industrial Updating carried out Spring and Summer 1987*. London: DES.
Department of Education and Science (1988d) *Education Statistics for the United Kingdom 1988 Edition*. London: HMSO.
Department of Education and Science (1988e) *Top-up Loans for Students*. London: HMSO.
Department of Education and Science (1989a) *Statistics of Schools in England – January 1988*. Statistical Bulletin 8/89. London: DES.
Department of Education and Science (1989b) 'John MacGregor welcomes SEAC advice on Advanced and Advanced Supplementary Examinations'. Press Release 268/89, 22 August.
Department of Employment (1984) *Training Loans: A Proposal by the Secretary of State for Employment for an Experimental Training Loans Scheme for Adults*. London: Department of Employment.
Department of Employment (1988) *Employment for the 1990s* Cmnd 540. London: HMSO.
Department of Employment and Department of Education and Science (1986) *Working Together – Education and Training* Cmnd 9823. London: HMSO.
Dewey, J. (1963) *Experience and Education*. New York: Collier.
Donaldson, L. (1975) *Policy and the Polytechnics*. Farnborough: Saxon House.
Duley, J. (1978) *Basic Skills for Experiential Learning: What skills do students need to make the most of experiential learning opportunities?* Paper 75. East Lansing: Michigan State University Instructional Media Center.
Duley, J. (1982) *Learning Outcomes: Measuring and Evaluating Experiential Learning*. PANEL Resource paper 6. Raleigh NC: NSIEE.
Educational Counselling and Credit Transfer Information Service (1989) *Access to Higher Education: Courses Directory*. Milton Keynes: ECCTIS.
Engineering Professors' Conference (1989) *EPC/Training Agency Project: Survey Report*. Liverpool: EPC Research Unit, University of Liverpool.
Education for Capability (nd) *Education for Capability*. Publicity leaflet. London: Royal Society of Arts.
Evans, N. (1981) *The Knowledge Revolution: Making the Link between Learning*

and Work. London: Grant McIntyre.
Evans, N. (1984a) *Exploiting Experience*. FEU/PICKUP Project Report. London: Further Education Unit.
Evans, N. (1984b) *Access to higher education: non-standard entry to CNAA first degree and DipHE courses*. Development Services Publication 6. London: CNAA.
Evans, N. (1987) *Assessing Experiential Learning: A Review of Progress and Practice*. London: Longman for FEU Publications.
Evans, N. (1988) *The Assessment of Prior Experiential Learning*. Development Services Publication 17. London: CNAA Development Services Publications.
Fleetwood-Walker, P. and Toyne, P. (1985) 'Jam Today? The UGC and NAB Reports' in Titmus, C. (ed.) *Widening the Field: Continuing Education in Higher Education*. Guildford: SRHE & NFER-Nelson.
Fulton, O. (ed.) (1981) *Access to Higher Education*. Guildford: SHRE.
Fulton, O. and Ellwood, S. (1989) *Admissions to Higher Education: Policy and Practice*. Sheffield: Training Agency.
Further Education Unit (1979) *A Basis for Choice*. London: FEU.
Further Education Unit (1987) *Access to Further and Higher Education: A Discussion Document*. London: FEU.
Further Education Unit (nd) *Aspects of Assessing Experiential Learning – Case Studies*. London: DES/FEU.
Gallie, D. (1989) *Technological Change, Gender and Skill. Social Change Economic Life Initiative*. ESRC Working Paper 4.
GCE Examining Boards (1983) *Common Cores at Advanced Level*. Np: GCE Examining Boards.
GCE Examining Boards (1987) *Common Cores at Advanced Level. First Supplement*. Np: GCE Examining Boards.
Goodlad, S. (1977) *Socio-technical Projects in Engineering Education*. General Education in Engineering (GEE) Project. Stirling: The University of Stirling.
Goodlad, S. and Hirst, B. (1989) *Peer Tutoring*. London: Kogan Page.
Goodlad, S. and Hirst, B. (eds.) (1990) *Explorations in Peer Tutoring*. Oxford: Basil Blackwell.
Griffin, C. (1983) *Curriculum Theory in Adult and Lifelong Education*. Beckenham: Croom Helm.
Harvey Jones, Sir J. (1987) *Management and Education*. The Smallpeice Lecture 1987. Leamington Spa: The Smallpeice Trust.
Hendel, D. D. and Enright, R. (1978) 'An evaluation of a full-time work study programme for undergraduates'. *Alternative Higher Education*, **3**.
Her Majesty's Government (1988) *The Education Reform Act*. London: HMSO.
Her Majesty's Inspectorate (1989a) *The English Polytechnics*. An HMI commentary. London: HMSO.
Her Majesty's Inspectorate (1989b) *Higher Education in the Polytechnics and Colleges: Engineering*. London: HMSO.
Her Majesty's Treasury (1989) *The Government's Expenditure Plans 1989–90 to 1991–92*. Ch. 12 – Department of Education and Science Cmnd 612. London: HMSO.
Hursh, D. E. (1976) 'Personalized systems of instruction: what do the data indicate? *Journal of Personalized Instruction*, **1**.

Inner London Education Authority (1983) *Review of Advanced Further Education in Inner London*. London: ILEA.

Institute of Manpower Studies (1988) 'Issues in UK Employment and Training'. Report of a speech by Geoffrey Holland at the IMS Senior Executives Conference in April 1988. *IMS News*, Supplement No 83, June 1988.

Jackson, R. (1988a) 'The Funding of Higher Education'. Chevening discussion paper, 25 July 1988.

Jackson, R. (1988b) Opening address to a Royal Society conference on Access to Higher Education on 14 June 1988. London: DES.

Jackson, R. (1988c) 'Chevening discussion papers'. *Education* 4 November 1988.

James, H. (1986) *The Princess Casamassima*. Harmondsworth: Penguin.

Johnston, J. M. (ed.) (1975) *Behavior Research and Technology in Higher Education*. Springfield, Illinois: Charles C. Thomas Publisher.

Joseph, Sir K. (1984) Speech by the Rt Hon Sir Keith Joseph, Secretary of State for Education and Science, at the North of England Education Conference, Sheffield, on Friday 6 January 1984. London: DES.

Keeton, M. and Associates (1977) *Experiential Learning: Rationale, Characteristics and Assessment*. London: Jossey-Bass.

Keller, F. S. (1968) 'Good-bye teacher'. *Journal of Applied Behavior Analysis*, **1**.

Keller, F. S. and Sherman, J. (1974) *The Keller-Plan Handbook*. Menlo Park, California: W. A. Benjamin Inc.

Kelly, A. (ed.) (1981) *The Missing Half: Girls and Science Education*. Manchester: Manchester University Press.

Knowles, M. (1975) *Self-directed Learning: A Guide for Teachers and Learners*. Chicago: Follett Publishing.

Kolb, D. A. (1984) *Experiential Learning: Experience as the Source of Learning and Development*. Englewood Cliffs: Prentice-Hall.

Kulik, J. A. and Kulik, C.-L. C. (1976) 'Research on the personalized system of instruction'. *Journal of Programmed Learning and Educational Technology*, **13**, 1.

Kulik, J., Kulik, C.-L. C. and Carmichael, K. (1974) 'The Keller Plan in science teaching: an individually paced, student-tutored, and mastery-oriented instructional method is evaluated'. *Science*, **183**, 4123.

Kulik, J., Kulik, C.-L. C. and Cohen, P. A. (1979) 'A meta-analysis of outcome studies of Keller's Personalized System of Instruction'. *American Psychologist*, **34**, 4.

Lepenies, W. (1989) 'A Home of Lost Causes and Impossible Loyalties', *Universiteit en Hogeschool*, September 1989.

Locke, M., Pratt, J., and Burgess, T. (1985) *The Colleges of Higher Education 1972 to 1982*. London: Critical.

Lucas, S. and Ward, P. (eds.) (1985) *A Survey of 'Access' Courses in England*. Lancaster: University of Lancaster School of Education.

McIntosh, N. (1970) 'An integrated multi-media educational experience . . .?'. *Educational Television International*, **4**, 2.

McIntosh, N. (1975) 'Open admission – an open or revolving door?'. *Universities Quarterly*, **29**, 2.

McIntosh, N. (1983) 'How will information technology serve the community?'. *PITCOM*, **1**, 2.

McNair, S. (forthcoming) 'Mass Higher Education: The adult agenda'. *Adults Learning*.

MacVicar, M. and McGavern, N. (1984) 'Not only Engineering: the MIT Undergraduate Research Opportunities Program', in Goodlad, S. (ed.) *Education for the professions: quis custodiet . . . ?* Guildford: SHRE and NFER-Nelson.

Manpower Services Commission (1983a) *Towards an adult training strategy: a discussion paper*. Sheffield: MSC.

Manpower Services Commission (1983b) *Adult Training Strategy. Proposals for Action*. Sheffield: MSC.

Manpower Services Commission and Department of Education and Science (1986) *Review of Vocational Qualifications in England and Wales*. London: HMSO.

Ministry of Education (1956) *Technical Education* Cmnd 9703. London: HMSO.

Moore, D. (1981) 'Discovering the pedagogy of experience'. *Harvard Educational Review*, May, **51**, 2.

Mortimore, P. and Mortimore, J. (1989) 'Changes in Schooling: The Impact on Higher Education'. *Higher Education Quarterly*, **43**, 1.

Murdoch, R. (1989) *Freedom in Broadcasting*. Text of the MacTaggart Lecture delivered by Rupert Murdoch at the Edinburgh International Television Festival on 25 August 1989. Np: News Corporation Ltd.

National Advisory Body for Local Authority Higher Education (1984a) *Report of the Continuing Education Group*. London: NAB.

National Advisory Body for Local Authority Higher Education (1984b) *A Strategy for Higher Education in the Late 1980s and Beyond*. London: NAB.

National Advisory Body for Public Sector Higher Education (1988) *Action for Access: Widening Opportunities in Higher Education*. London: NAB.

National Advisory Body for Public Sector Higher Education and University Grants Committee (1984) *Higher Education and the Needs of Society*. Joint Statement. London: NAB/UGC.

National Advisory Body for Public Sector Higher Education and University Grants Committee Continuing Education Standing Committee (1987) *Report of the Study of Credit Transfer/Accumulation and Qualifications Structures*. London: NAB/UGC.

National Council for Vocational Qualifications (1987) *The National Vocational Qualification Framework*. London: NCVQ.

National Council for Vocational Qualifications (1989) *National Vocational Qualifications. Criteria and Procedures*. London: NCVQ.

National Institute for Adult Continuing Education (1989) *Adults in Higher Education: A Policy Discussion Paper*. Leicester: NIACE.

Network of Australian Women in Adult Education (1986) *Feminist Learning Principles* (mimeo).

Neufeld, V. and Chong, J. (1984) 'Problem-based Professional Education in Medicine' in Goodlad, S. (ed.) *Education for the Professions: quis custodiet . . . ?* Guildford: SRHE and NFER-Nelson.

Open University (1970) *Open University Prospectus 1971*. Milton Keynes: Open University.

Osborne, M. (1988) 'Access courses in mathematics, science and technology: current and planned provision'. *Journal of Access Studies*, **3**, 1.

Osborne, M. and Woodrow, M. (1989) *Access to Mathematics, Science and Technology*. London: FEU.

Otter, S. (1988) *Student Potential in Britain*. Leicester: UDACE.

Parker, P. (1986) *Design for Learning*. The Smallpeice Lecture 1986. Leamington Spa: The Smallpeice Trust.

Parry, G. (1986) 'From patronage to partnership'. *Journal of Access Studies*, **1**, 1.

Parry, G. (1989a) *Access and Preparatory Courses offered by or in association with the universities*. A report on a survey undertaken by the Standing Conference on University Entrance. London: CVCP.

Parry, G. (1989b) 'Marking and Mediating the Higher-Education Boundary' in Fulton O. (ed.) *Access and Institutional Change*. Milton Keynes: SRHE and Open University Press.

Parry, G. (ed.) (1990) *Wider Entry to Engineering Higher Education*. Precedings for a Conference on Higher Education held at the Royal Society of Arts on 17 January 1990. London: Engineering Council, Royal Society of Arts and Training Agency.

Parry, G. and Davies, P. (1990) *Wider access and the professional engineering institutions*. London: British Petroleum and CNAA.

Pearson, R., Pike, G., Gordon, A. and Weyman, C. (1989) *How Many Graduates in the Twenty-first Century? The Choice is Yours*. Brighton: Council for Industry and Higher Education and Institute of Manpower Studies.

Percy, K. and Ramsden, P. (1980) *Independent Study: Two Examples from English Higher Education*. Guildford: SRHE.

Planning Exchange (1987) *Paying for Training: A Comprehensive Guide to Sources of Finance for Adult Training*. London: DES Adult Training Promotion Unit.

Rae, J. (1989) *Too little too late? The challenges that still face British education*. London: Fontana.

Robbins, D. (1988) *The Rise of Independent Study*. Milton Keynes: SRHE and Open University Press.

Robin, A. R. (1976) 'Behavioral instruction in the college classroom'. *Review of Educational Research*, **46**, 3.

Robinson, E. (1968) *The New Polytechnics*. Harmondsworth: Penguin.

Royal Society (1983) *Demographic Trends and Future University Candidates*. A Working Paper. London: Royal Society.

Royal Society (1988) *Access to Higher Education*. Papers presented to the Conference on Access to Higher Education held at the Royal Society on 14 June 1988.

Royal Society and Engineering Council (1989) *Science Education 16–19: a conference report*. London: Royal Society.

Royal Society of Arts (1988) *Raising the Standard. Wider Access to Higher Education*. London: RSA (Industry Matters).

Rudd, E. (1988) 'Reply to Clarke'. *Studies in Higher Education*, **13**, 3.

Russell, R. (1989) *Further Education and Industrial Training in England and Wales*. Weston-super-Mare: Elmsleigh Education Training and Advisory Services.

Ryan, B. A. (1974) *Keller's Personalized System of Instruction: An Appraisal*. Washington DC: American Psychological Association.

Sargant, N. (1988) 'Education and Broadcasting' in Paine, N. (ed.) *Open Learning in Transition*. Cambridge: National Extension College.

Schein, E. H. (1972) *Professional Education*. New York: Carnegie Commission on Higher Education, McGraw-Hill.

Schon, D. (1983) *The Reflective Practitioner*. New York: Basic Books.

Schon, D. (1987) *Educating the Reflective Practitioner*. London: Jossey-Bass.

School Examinations and Assessment Council (1989) *Consultation on the Secretaries of State's Remit to the School Examinations and Assessment Council on the Promotion of AS Examinations and the Rationalisation of A Level Syllabuses: Report of the Findings*, with supplementary paper 'Advanced and Advanced Supplementary Examinations'. London: SEAC.

Schools Council (1966) *Sixth form curriculum and examinations*. Schools Council Working Paper 5. London: HMSO.

Schools Council (1973) *16–19: Growth and response. Examination structure*. Schools Council Working Paper 46. London: Evans/Methuen Educational.

Schuller, T. (1989) *Education and the Third Age*. London: Education Reform Group.

Secondary Heads Association (1983) *A View from the Bridge*. A SHA Discussion Document. London: SHA.

Secondary Heads Association (1984) *Response to the DES Consultative Document on AS Levels*. London: SHA.

Shinn, C. (1986) *Paying the Piper: The Development of the University Grants Committee 1919–1946*. Lewes: Falmer.

Smithers, A. and Griffin, A. (1986) 'Mature students at university: entry, experience, and outcomes'. *Studies in Higher Education*, **11**, 3.

Smithers, A. and Robinson, P. (1988) *The Growth of Mixed A Levels*. Manchester: Carmichael Press.

Smithers, A. and Robinson, P. (1989) *Increasing Participation in Higher Education*. London: British Petroleum Educational Service.

Spender, D. (1981) 'Sex bias' in Warren Piper, D. (ed.) *Is Higher Education Fair?* Guildford: SHRE.

Standing Conference on University Entrance (1984) *School Examinations: 'AS' Levels. Universities' response to the proposals by the Secretaries of State on 'AS' Levels*. London: SCUE.

Standing Conference on University Entrance and Schools Council (1969) *Proposals for the curriculum and examinations in the sixth form*. London: SCUE and Schools Council.

Stanton, T. and Ali, K. (1987) *The Experienced Hand: A Student Manual for making the most of internships*. Cranston RI: Carroll Press.

Statistical Office of the European Communities (1988) *EUROSTAT: Demographic Statistics*. Luxembourg: Statistical Office of the European Communities.

Steiner, G. (1989) *Real Presences*. London: Faber.

Stephenson, J. (1983) 'Higher Education: School for Independent Study' in Tight, M. (ed.) *Adult Learning and Education*. Beckenham: Croom Helm.

Stewart. W. A. C. (1989) *Higher Education in Postwar Britain*. London: Macmillan.

Strachan, R., Brown, J. and Schuller, T. C. (1989) 'Raising interest in science through novel adult education courses – a stepping stone to access'. *Journal of Access Studies*, **4**, 1.

Taveggia, T. C. (1976) 'Personalized instruction: a summary of comparative research 1967–1974'. *American Journal of Physics*, **44**, 11.

Tight, M. (1989) 'The Ideology of Higher Education' in Fulton, O. (ed.) *Access and Institutional Change*. Milton Keynes: SRHE and Open University Press.

Times Higher Education Supplement (1988) 'The Chilver principle', THES 25 July 1988.

Trow, M. (1989) 'American Higher Education – past, present and future'. *Studies in Higher Education*, **14**, 1.

Unit for the Development of Adult Continuing Education (1988) *Developing Access: The Discussion Paper*. Leicester: UDACE.

Unit for the Development of Adult Continuing Education (1989a) *Open College Networks: Current Developments and Practice*. Leicester: UDACE.

Unit for the Development of Adult Continuing Education (1989b) *Understanding Competence*. Leicester: UDACE.

Unit for the Development of Adult Continuing Education (1989c) *Understanding Learning Outcomes*. Leicester: UDACE.

United Nations Educational, Scientific and Cultural Organization (1988) *Statistical Yearbook 1988*. Paris: UNESCO.

Universities Central Council on Admissions (1989) *Statistical Supplement to the Twenty-sixth Report 1987–88*. Cheltenham: UCCA.

University Grants Committee (1984a) *Report of the Continuing Education Working Party*. London: UGC.

University Grants Committee (1984b) *A Strategy for Higher Education into the 1990s*. London: HMSO.

Wagner, L. (1989) 'National Policy and Institutional Development' in Fulton, O. (ed.) *Access and Institutional Change*. Milton Keynes: SRHE and Open University Press.

Wake, C. (1989) 'AS Levels and the Universities', in Hughes, J. (ed.) *AS Levels: Implications for Schools, Examining Boards and Universities*. London: The Falmer Press.

Walkerdine, V. (comp.) (1989) *Counting Girls Out*. Girls and Mathematics Unit, Institute of Education. London: Virago Press.

Weil, S. W. (1989) 'Access: Towards Education or Miseducation? Adults Imagine the Future' in Fulton, O. (ed.) *Access and Institutional Change*. Milton Keynes: SRHE and Open University Press.

Weil, S. W. and McGill, I. (eds.) (1989) *Making Sense of Experiential Learning: Diversity in Theory and Practice*. Milton Keynes: SRHE and Open University Press.

Williams, J. M., Bristow, S. L., Green, P. M., Housee, S., and Willis, P. (1989) *The*

Access Effect. CNAA Development Services Project Report 20. London: CNAA.

Willingham, W. W. (1977) *Principles of Good Practice in Assessing Experiential Learning.* Princeton NJ: Cooperative Assessment of Experiential Learning.

Woodley, A. (1981) 'Age Bias' in Warren Piper, D. (ed.) *Is Higher Education Fair?* Guildford: SRHE.

Woodley, A. (1987) 'Has the Open University been an unqualified success?' *Journal of Access Studies,* **2**, 2.

Woodley, A., Wagner, L., Slowey, M., Hamilton, M. and Fulton, O. (1987) *Choosing to Learn: Adults in Education.* London: Society for Research into Higher Education and Open University Press.

Yelon, S. L. and Duley, J. S. (1978) *Efficient Evaluation of Individual Performance in Field Placement.* Guides for the improvement of instruction in higher education No 14. East Lansing: Michigan State University Instructional Media Center.

Index